ANCIENTS AGAINST MODERNS

ANCIENTS AGAINST MODERNS

*Culture
Wars
and the
Making
of a
Fin
de Siècle*

JOAN DEJEAN

THE UNIVERSITY OF CHICAGO PRESS
Chicago and London

JOAN DEJEAN is Trustee Professor of French at the University of
Pennsylvania. She is the author of *Fictions of Sappho, 1546–1937*
(1989), also published by the University of Chicago Press.

The University of Chicago Press, Chicago 60637
The University of Chicago Press, Ltd., London
© 1997 by The University of Chicago
All rights reserved. Published 1997
Printed in the United States of America

06 05 04 03 02 01 00 99 98 97   1 2 3 4 5

ISBN: 0-226-14137-3 (cloth)
ISBN: 0-226-14138-1 (paper)

Library of Congress Cataloging-in-Publication Data

DeJean, Joan E.
    Ancients against moderns : culture wars and the making of
a fin de siècle / Joan DeJean
        p.   cm.
    Includes bibliographical references (p.   ) and index.
    ISBN 0-226-14137-3 (alk. paper). — ISBN 0-226-14138-1
(paper : alk. paper)
    1. France—Intellectual life—17th century.   2. United
States—Intellectual life—20th century.   3. Ancients and
moderns, Quarrel of.   4. Social change—France—History—
17th century.   5. Social change—United States—History—
20th century.   I. Title.
DC128.D45   1997
303.4—dc20   96-19011
                                                      CIP

    Chapter 1 first appeared as an essay in *Critical Inquiry*, vol.
22, no. 4 (summer 1996). © 1996 by The University of Chicago.
All rights reserved.

Part of chapter 2 first appeared in Elizabeth Goldsmith and
Dena Goodman, eds., *Going Public* (Ithaca, N.Y.: Cornell University Press, 1995). Used by permission of the publisher.

⊖ The paper used in this publication meets the minimum re-
quirements of the American National Standard for Information
Sciences—Permanence of Paper for Printed Library Materials,
ANSI Z39.48-1984.

For

FRANCES BATZER,

JUDITH COLLIGNON,

and

ALAIN ROOK,

with

gratitude

CONTENTS

PREFACE

This is an inherently American attempt to reevaluate a formative moment in the history of French culture. In saying that, I am openly acknowledging what I see as an obvious but too generally unexamined fact: that our view of the past, literally what we are able to see in each particular historical situation, is inevitably shaped by the events and the issues at the heart of our own historical moment. In this particular case, this means that I would never have portrayed the late seventeenth century in France as I do, had I not been writing this book in the thick of what have now become known in this country as Culture Wars.

On occasion, literary change and societal change are closely bound together. At those times, controversy over issues such as which authors should be taught in schools becomes of significant historical importance because it stands for a larger upheaval, as a result of which culture, and even society, come to be redefined in significant ways. On those rare occasions when society goes to war over cultural matters, the importance of literary debate should never be underestimated.

This book is centered on what have been to date the most significant Culture Wars of modern times, the crisis that shattered France in the late seventeenth century, the so-called Quarrel between the Ancients and the Moderns (1687–1715), known in its English incarnation as the Battle of the Books. Each chapter foregrounds a different aspect of the historical importance of this intellectual controversy. I argue that, because the Moderns' claim that France had reached a state of perfection automatically generated an *après nous le déluge* mentality, the literary war served as the catalyst for the first true fin de siècle. Nevertheless, despite the sense of being at the end of the line that permeated this experience, this period of intellectual crisis proved to be a moment of intense cultural creativity, a significant historical turning-point, what Foucault would have termed the signal of a change in episteme. Because of the controversy between Ancients and Moderns, the first public sphere worthy of the designation *public* emerged. At the same time, a new language and theory of the emotions, as well as a major reconception of human psychology—indeed, what could be termed the first true culture of interiority—came into existence. Also as a result of this conflict, our modern understanding of the phenomenon of culture began to be recognized—from the beginning, in opposition to the notion of civilization in its initial modern conception. In short, by the end of the seventeenth-century intellectual crisis, French culture, in the broadest sense of the term, had undergone a significant remapping.

This book has several goals, the most obvious of which is a double project. On the one hand, I reread the Quarrel between the Ancients and the Moderns from the perspective of the Culture Wars that are currently polarizing American intellectual life. By this I mean that I consciously set out to investigate the seventeenth century's end using terminology and questions that have been crucial to today's intellectual conflict. The most obvious example of this practice was the inspiration for my last chapter, in which I try to assess the significance that the buzzwords that have sprung up around the dyad culture/civilization—*multiculturalism* and *Western civilization,* for example—could have had in the late seventeenth century. On the other hand, at the end of the study I review our twentieth-century Culture Wars in the light of issues and concepts that proved crucial in the late seventeenth-century intellectual upheaval that began the revolutionary shift in *mentalité* upon which the Enlightenment was founded. Here I stress the ways in which current calls for pedagogical reform repeat seventeenth-century initiatives.

I cite this example because pedagogical reform is the area in which it is easiest to understand what was a crucial motivating force behind this project: my desire is to show that the history of the seventeenth century's involvement with Culture Wars can serve as a cautionary tale for all those with a stake in the outcome of today's intellectual crisis, by indicating some of the problems we will encounter before we reach the end of this line, and also where we will almost certainly end up, unless we are able to avoid the pitfalls created for each other by our precursor Ancients and Moderns.

In the course of the seventeenth-century struggle between An-

cients and Moderns, a number of developments were initiated, under Modern sponsorship, that proved to be so crucial to the future
of the republic of letters that many have since believed that the Moderns won the war. First, literature became a radically more public
phenomenon, the center of a cultural sphere in which a variety of
previously silent groups began to engage in active participation. Second, this dramatically more public literature played a pivotal role
in the development of new forms of affectivity and interiority, perhaps even in the development of what could be termed modern
subjectivity. Third, the novel—the literary genre intimately linked
to both literature's new publicness and to the new interiority—came
into its first real prominence. Within the seventeenth-century equivalent of today's academy, however, the roles were reversed. The Ancients introduced all the plans for institutional and pedagogical reform that proved successful in the long run, and the Moderns had
virtually no success in initiating change.

Indeed, the outcome of the first Culture Wars serves to alert us
in particular to the risk inherent to any form of conflict in which
political activity is consistently intermingled with literary and cultural affairs. Today's Culture Wars, in which, for example, Ancients
have suggested again and again that new definitions of culture proposed within the university are responsible for a range of problems
facing American society from substance abuse to racism, are a prime
instance of what could be termed the poeticization of the political.
In such cases, the danger is not that such conflict will ultimately
prove so frivolous that it will be viewed as a mere tempest in a
teapot, allegedly political exchange that turns out to be apolitical.
The danger is rather that all our contemporary debate in which the
cultural and the political have become interwoven will ultimately
follow the pattern established by the seventeenth-century Culture
Wars and will in the long run guarantee that all attempts at institutional change are abolished. Unless we take action against the passivity ultimately inherent to all forms of literary politics, all our conflict will have no effect on any of the forces in power—within the
academy, I obviously have in mind the conservative powers that
tend to dominate the university, especially in times of economic
crisis.[1] Considering our Culture Wars from what I think of as a
seventeenth-century viewing angle makes plain the necessity of
countering the drive to resist any type of radical pedagogical and
institutional reform.

From the other perspective, that of the original Quarrel between
the Ancients and the Moderns, my comparative exercise plays a very

different role. It forced me to view the seventeenth century's end
in France in a new light and to foreground the tumultuous and
revolutionary character of the final quarter-century of Louis XIV's
reign. In general, those years—the last of the seventeenth century
and the first of the eighteenth—are simply lost between the lines
of both history and literary history because they belong no longer
to the golden age of classicism, but not yet to the Enlightenment.
If we confront these years head on, however, in order to focus on
their most characteristic aspect, the almost continual climate of intellectual confrontation that then reigned, we come to realize just
how innovative this generally undervalued moment actually was.

Viewing the seventeenth century's cultural conflict in tandem
with that of our century forced me to stress in particular the period's
pivotal role in the history of what we now think of as modernity.
The turmoil that characterized the seventeenth century's end was
immensely productive. It generated a range of ideas and phenomena
that has proved essential to intellectual debate since that time and
that still resonates significantly in our intellectual life today—from
the concept of publicness in its dominant modern meaning to *culture* used for the first time in an aesthetic context. It also generated
new fields of inquiry—ranging from aesthetic philosophy to psychology—at the same time as it provoked established ones, such as
medicine, to undergo radical revisions. The clearest indicator of all
this cultural ferment was linguistic. Perhaps the most significant advantage of the comparative exercise was that it forced me to remain
attentive to the new words that were the creation of some of the
most prominent polemicists in the battle between Ancients and
Moderns. And I do not take the word "creation" lightly here.
Whereas linguistic change and semantic revolutions are in general
accidental, most of the innovations I will be discussing in these pages
are quite evidently the result of conscious attempts to open up the
French language to include new concepts. In the course of examining key documents related to the seventeenth-century Culture Wars,
we will on a number of occasions be able to recreate the process by
which terms still central to the experience of modernity were
brought into existence.

My study of these conflicted years will thus often be about the
relation between words and things. In particular, it will deal with
two zones in which semantic clarity can never be absolute: (1) moments during which words are in the process of changing meanings,
either of suddenly acquiring radically new ones, or of gradually slip-
ping from an established usage to one that, while related, has impor-

tant new connotations; (2) periods during which, even though the
words now used to designate certain concepts do not yet exist, those
concepts are clearly in the process of being formulated. This was the
case with the modern concept of civilization during the seventeenth
century's closing decades: a semantic field was formulated that
makes it clear that what was subsequently conveyed by the word
civilization was already conceptually functional, even though the
term itself would only be created in the mid–eighteenth century.
Indeed, one of the formative impulses for this project occurred a
number of years ago when I was reproached for using anachronisms
in speaking of the seventeenth century, words such as *race* and *gender*, and was told that I couldn't consider the early modern period
in terms of categories for which it had no words. Upon reflection,
that exchange persuaded me of the importance of convincing those
who believe that our current debates are totally foreign to an early
modern context that the relative scarcity, or even the apparent absence of the vocabulary in which those debates are carried out does
not signify that our precursors would not have been able to compre-
hend what we are fighting about. In more ways than one, the following pages are the result of that attempt. They are premised on the
belief that the publicly acknowledged existence of battle lines separating Ancients from Moderns is sufficient to create a powerful kinship between moments at which this distinction proves crucial, a
kinship so powerful that it transcends all the obvious differences
that would seem to render those moments incomparable—in this
case, for example, the obvious distinction between a culture that
was expressed within the constraints imposed by official censorship
and one such as ours in which the lack of censorship might appear
to be the true problem.

My chapters are constructed around a series of what could be
termed, with a phrase coined by Raymond Williams, "key words":
century, public, sensibility, culture, and *civilization.* I came to view
the development of these terms as so crucial to the process of cultural change that I saw these key words as symptomatic of that
change: they testify or bear witness to the truly critical issues of the
day; they point to the period's cultural fault lines. All the while, I
realized that I was enabled to search out these terms in the midst
of the seventeenth century's intellectual conflict by their visibility
in our own cultural modernity. For the most part, these concepts
have recently become important to French studies because of the influence of German thinkers—I have in mind, most notably, the interest in the history of "public" and "public opinion" indissociable

from the fascination exercised by Jürgen Habermas, and also the
concern with the development of the paired concepts, culture-
civilization, that has grown out of recent regard for the work of
Norbert Elias. The histories of the period that concerns me here,
proposed by Habermas and Elias, are both founded on linguistic
case studies—Habermas, for instance, ultimately bases his conviction that what he terms "the bourgeois public sphere" developed
at such and such a time, and not before, on what he presents as the
fact that the semantic cluster that formed around *public* only came
into existence at a precise moment.

Readers are of course aware that our latest *maîtres à penser* have
become influential because of the much delayed transmission of
works written at earlier periods—the 1930s in the case of Elias, the
1960s in that of Habermas. We continue to act, however, as if their
views of history can be taken literally, whereas they are in fact ren-
dered problematic, if not at least partially invalidated, by the very
nature of the evidence on which they were constructed. Working
as they did long before electronic databases came into existence,
and apparently with little sense of the usefulness of early modern
lexicographic tools, these scholars were obliged to rely on late-nineteenth-century French historical dictionaries that, unlike the *OED*,
base their findings for the most part on a relatively limited corpus.
As far as the early modern period is concerned, that corpus is almost
exclusively composed of the works considered the classics of French
literature at the end of the nineteenth century.[2] So eager have specialists of French history and literature been to embrace these new
"intellectual masters" that we have been willing to overlook the fact
that these Germans rely on outdated evidence for the history of the
French language that they are proposing.

Yet it is crucial to pinpoint with as much precision as possible
the moment at which key words are coming into existence. That
origin has a great deal to teach us first about the terms themselves,
about their initial semantic charge, about their earliest connotations.
It has even more important lessons for us about the society and the
period that felt the need to create these symptomatic terms—from
information about those who invented the usage to facts about the
context in which it first became essential. As long as we accept a
dubious history of these terms, we will be accepting at the same
time a false history of the phenomenon to which they bear witness,
the story of the development of modernity.

In the case of the expression *le public*, for example, the fact that
it was being used in French decades before Habermas (following

the example of Auerbach) contends, suggests a very different image of the closing decades of the seventeenth century from that which has most often been promoted. It suggests, most notably, that the most glorious years of Versailles knew far less social rigidity and far more social ferment than is generally imagined. Our modern usage of *public* was born of a desire to explore what were evidently burning cultural issues, a desire so powerful that, faced with it, traditional class divisions ceased to function in an airtight way.

That *public* originated in cultural controversy rather than, as Habermas contends, in more traditional forms of political dissent, should not lead us to conclude that the terminology's connotations for its early practitioners would have been more frivolous than, following Habermas's lead, we have been imagining. The period that gave birth to the modern vocabulary of public—from *the public* to *public opinion*—sensed that the cultural matters around which conflict raged would have long-term consequences so momentous that they would reveal the full force of the cultural realm's political implications. Debate over such apparently purely cultural matters as the legitimacy of modern authors led to debate over issues such as women's right to participate in the public sphere, issues whose long-term social and political implications far transcended their initial cultural valence.

These reflections bring me to a second justification of the importance of pinpointing the precise context in which words come into existence, the fact that this context imparts connotations to these terms to which their initial users are sensitive. In the case of *le public,* for instance, for those who first had access to it the terminology was not, as the Habermasian view would have it, primarily evocative of a "medium of political confrontation" constructed "against the public authorities themselves" for the purpose of generating "debate over . . . the sphere of commodity exchange and social labor" (Habermas 27). Instead, the modern vocabulary of public exchange was initially most remarkable for its connotations of a sphere in which a socially and sexually diverse audience debated for the first time the meaning and the function of public culture.

Acceptance of the German vision of early modern France has led to implicit acceptance of a view of the history of the French language that situates its most active period in its progression toward modernity in the second half of the eighteenth century. The most telling evidence for my claim that we should look instead to the closing decades of the seventeenth century is provided by the fact that the first three great dictionaries of the French language were all produced at that time. This embarrassment of lexicographic riches testifies eloquently to the intensity with which linguistic usage was being debated at the same time as Ancients and Moderns were at war. Throughout the following pages, I rely heavily on the three monuments to the lexicographic ferment of the late seventeenth century: Pierre Richelet's in 1680, Antoine Furetière's in 1690, and the first edition of the Académie Française's in 1694. These volumes—especially because of the phrasing of their definitions and the range of examples they include—provide unusually detailed insight into the state of the French language at a crucial moment in its evolution, as it was gathering its forces to become accepted as the universal intellectual and political medium of exchange.

The second linguistic tool on which I rely throughout the following pages is a kind of research aid only possible because of recent technological advances. Nearly three centuries later, we can finally supplement the intuitions of those who were arguably the most perspicacious French lexicographers of all time, thanks to the database originally assembled to prepare a new French historical dictionary. With the vastly expanded resources put at our disposal by the ARTFL database,[3] it is finally possible to outstrip the limits to our knowledge fixed by both the seventeenth-century dictionaries and the late-nineteenth-century historical dictionaries on which the currently influential German scholars relied. It is now possible, for example, to prove that the key words on which the presently fashionable vision of the Enlightenment is premised—from *public* to *culture*—far from being eighteenth-century creations, came into existence some fifty years before it is generally thought and were thus the product of the needs and the desires of a very different period and of very different individuals.

This chronological shift has many consequences. Most obviously, it turns this study into an attempted rehabilitation—a rehabilitation first of all of those aristocrats of the late seventeenth century whose thinking was so free that it led them to collaborate with bourgeois intellectuals in the creation of structures that in the long term would help bring down the entire class system; an attempted rehabilitation of a period as well. For, at the same time that I will be arguing that the seventeenth-century conflict between Ancients and Moderns was responsible for the invention of concepts that in turn generated the first fin de siècle, I will be attempting to defend this period and those individuals who shared the sense of being at the end of the line, and to suggest that their example is in some ways one we might wish to emulate. For them, the fin de siècle experience was among the most creative moments in ancien régime culture, a time when intellectual collisions were taken so seriously that they became creative—generating new concepts, new social structures, new literary forms, and a new collective sexual imagination.[4]

I close with a suggestion for reading. Throughout this study, I present a great deal of the documentation that supports my claims in the endnotes. I wanted to save the body of the text for the big story of the seventeenth century's end and hoped to make that story as accessible as possible to those readers who would not necessarily be interested in specific details about the business of literary life or the limits of contemporary scientific knowledge. However, I make those details available to specialists in the notes, which I consider almost a separate reading experience, simply because there are at times so many of them and because certain notes are so extensive. Readers interested in a particular section of the text or a particular subject should turn to the notes for a wider range of examples and approaches. In the case of chapter 2, for instance, readers seeking additional information on such topics as the history of newspapers, the history of the novel's rise to prominence, and circulation figures for the new reading matter will find relevant facts and statistics in the notes to the sections in which I make claims about the importance of these cultural phenomena. In the same way, readers of chapter 3 interested in the history of the new affective vocabulary should turn to the notes for additional findings available in databases and in seventeenth-century dictionaries. This is not to say that the notes are purely factual: I tell a story in them, too, but it can be kept separate from the main history.

ACKNOWLEDGMENTS

I am grateful for the generosity of numerous friends and colleagues. It is convenient that Herbert Blau's name comes first in alphabetical order, for his careful reading of each part of my manuscript did more than anything else to keep me going on this project. Frank Bowman and Margreta de Grazia provided stimulating critiques of the manuscript at an early stage. English Showalter gave me a necessary last push with his careful reading of the next-to-final version. With their timely encouragement, Michel Jeanneret, Christian Jouhaud, Michael Malone, Maureen Quilligan, and Kathleen Woodward prodded me at times when I was ready to give it all up. To Ann Jones, François and Doranne Lecercle, and Peter Stallybrass I am grateful for many discussions that caused my thinking to shift in important ways. Héloïse and Jacques Neefs loaned countless books and dictionaries. Lance Donaldson-Evans went beyond the call of duty to make sure that I had the time to complete the project. Vassilis Lambropoulos and Gregory Jusdanis shared work and ideas with me. Juliette Cherbuliez, Claire Goldstein, Nicholas Paige, and Roland Racevskis provided superb research assistance.

To all of them, and to the readers for the University of Chicago Press, I owe a great deal.

1

Did the Seventeenth Century Create Our Fin de Siècle? or, The Making of the Enlightenment That We May at Last Be Leaving Behind

Man as a force must be measured by motion from a fixed point. Psychology helped here by suggesting a unit—the point of history when man held the highest idea of himself as a unit in a unified universe. Eight or ten years of study had led Adams to think he might use the century 1150–1250, expressed in Amiens Cathedral and the Works of Thomas Aquinas, as the unit from which he might measure motion down to his own time, without assuming anything as true or untrue, except relation. . . . Setting himself to the task, he began a volume which he mentally knew as "Mont Saint-Michel and Chartres: A Study of Thirteenth-Century Unity." From that point he proposed to fix a position for himself, which he could label: "The Education of Henry Adams: A Study of Twentieth-Century Multiplicity." With the help of these two points of relation, he hoped to project his lines forward and backward indefinitely, subject to correction from any one who should know better.

—Henry Adams, *The Education of Henry Adams*

Figure 1. *La Danse de la vie humaine* (c. 1639–40), by Nicolas Poussin. Wallace Collection, London. Photo: Bridgeman/Art Resource, New York.

Siècle: Period of one hundred years.
  —Littré Dictionary, first edition (1873), no. 1

A period famous for a renowned prince, for a great man.
  —Littré Dictionary, no. 4

The four ages of the world, as the poets saw them: the golden
age [*le siècle d'or*] . . .
  —Littré Dictionary, no. 10

During the last years of the seventeenth century, the music of time to which the French were dancing suddenly received a new orchestration. Roughly prior to the 1670s, the nation was still on classical time, literally the time of ages (fig. 1).[1] By this, I mean not only that the overall pace of life was slower, though that, of course, seems to have been true. A prodigious acceleration in the speed of communication—both possible and desired—is eloquently testified to from the late 1660s on, nowhere more vividly than in Sévigné's correspondence, though also by such authors as Molière and Lafayette. In a significant way, this acceleration in the gathering and the perception of information began the process by which the human clock came to be set on modern time—or "modern times," as Chaplin eventually renamed it—the ever-accelerating march to the rhythm of progress.

Simultaneous with this acceleration and essential to its development was the growing acceptance of a new temporal demarcation, one initially introduced in an attempt to find closure for the turbulent period I am about to describe. *Siècle* (century) came no longer to be used exclusively in the traditional, temporally vague sense of "an age" (Littré no. 10) but acquired two new meanings. One of them (Littré no. 4) was linked to monarchs, their reigns, and a personified view of history. The other (Littré no. 1) initially slipped in, as it were, on the coattails of the first new meaning. What has become the term's most common meaning today, "century," in the sense of precisely one hundred years, was originally called into being as a means of putting an end—to an age and its turmoil, to a period we would characterize, in a terminology not yet available to those who brought *siècle* into modern time, as a fin de siècle.[2] We will return in due course to *century*'s semantic drift, but first a closer look at some of the issues that caused the French to jolt from classical time to modern time (fig. 2).[3]

In the 1690s, Culture Wars were a necessary prelude to the first fin de siècle; they were thus at the origin of the phenomenon of seeing particular significance in a century's end, a phenomenon that would only be named two centuries later.[4] Indeed, the initial fin de siècle, in seventeenth-century France, was bound up with a period of intense intellectual controversy with striking resemblances to the conflict that is currently dividing American society—the Culture Wars that are a sure sign that our fin de siècle is following the earlier French model, rather than what is commonly considered the only pattern for a fin de siècle, the nineteenth-century fall into decadence. In fact, the end of the seventeenth century in France may well be the only prior fin de siècle with any clear relation to the phenomenon Americans are experiencing today.

The term *Culture Wars* has become increasingly visible in recent years to designate the conflicts dividing contemporary American society. It has been used in a variety of ways, at times to refer to contention exclusively cultural in its origin, such as the Mapplethorpe controversy, at others to designate the upheaval generated by issues as unrelated to culture as the battle over abortion rights.[5] My defini-

tion of Culture Wars falls in the middle, largely because it skirts the question of origin. Whether anxiety over societal change preceded or even gave birth to anxiety over intellectual change, or whether the opposite is true, is less important than the fact that, during Culture Wars, these two anxieties become grafted onto each other—to such an extent that it is in general impossible to define the point where one type of anxiety ends and another begins.

Culture is as appropriate and as essential as *war* to designate the controversies that can be included in this category. The conflict is

Figure 2. *L'Enseigne de Gersaint* (1720), by Antoine Watteau. Charlottenburg Castle, Staatliche Schloesser und Gaerten, Berlin. Photo: Foto Marburg/Art Resource, New York.

far more bitterly divisive and is waged on a far broader scale than is otherwise the case with controversies over cultural matters. However, in times of Culture Wars—in France at the seventeenth century's end as much as in America today—intellectual matters acquire a momentousness unheard of in less anxious periods. In these instances, traditionalists and progressives square off as Ancients and Moderns and do battle over such issues as the appropriate subject matter for great literature and the literary curriculum best suited to the needs of contemporary students. The resulting conflict becomes swept up in contemporary controversy over societal problems, from the rights and the status of women to the threat of addictive behavior (whether produced by today's drugs or, in the seventeenth century, tobacco and chocolate).

Presumably with some degree of good faith—the status of such allegations can never be precisely defined—blame for threatening societal change is placed on the literary modifications that were the initial basis for the distinction between Ancients and Moderns: it is because there are new great books that women have become unruly, or even simply because the Moderns have begun to challenge the authority of the Ancients that addictive behavior is on the rise.[6] That these allegations may seem hopelessly wild only makes the fact that they are widely circulated, and presumably believed, more significant. At these moments, as at no other time, controversies over literary matters help generate the momentum toward an end-of-century atmosphere. Both in the seventeenth century and today, Culture Wars mark a highly divisive period in which a society comes to believe first that civilization as it knows it is coming to an end, and then that literary factors are both symptomatic of this decline and responsible for it.

The end of the century that gave France both neoclassicism and Versailles was a period of increasingly widespread and deep-seated turmoil. This unrest has traditionally been presented proleptically, as a mere anticipation of the truly significant unrest to come, that of the Enlightenment. This is to repeat a traditional gesture of French literary history, whereby the periods that can be called turns of centuries (in this case, roughly 1685–1715, though the exact dates vary from century to century) are always left virtually unaccounted for.[7] If, however, the decades at the end of the seventeenth century and the beginning of the eighteenth are dealt with head on, rather than as the tail end of a more significant period or the prelude to another more important epoch, they can be shown to constitute a moment during which numerous structures essential to intellectual modernity were invented.[8] This moment of crisis became intellectually fertile as a result of a phenomenon baptized long after the fact by literary history as the *Querelle des Anciens et des Modernes.*

For centuries, the French have been officially shielded from the impact of certain major societal upheavals by a series of characteristic euphemisms. The most successful of these is now the most familiar: *affaire,* more commonly used in a range of handy and somewhat vague expressions to mean "business," "question," or "annoyance," but which can also appear in a political or judicial context. The quickly accepted practice of referring to the phenomenon that was tearing fin de (nineteenth) siècle French society apart as "the Dreyfus affair," or simply *l'affaire,* is the best-known example of a practice that seems to have caught on some fifty years after the turn of the century that interests me here, when Voltaire defended a number of highly controversial figures, whose cases were known as *affaires* (the Calas affair, the Sirven affair, and so forth).[9] Granted, *affaire* can signify in legal terms a trial or a dispute; in military terms, it can also designate a struggle. However, as it is used in the instances I have in mind, *affaire* really means something closer to a "scandal" or "scandalous business," either an unpleasantness that just might go away if only it does not receive too much attention, or an impropriety that one would prefer not to see. In semantic weight, the term seems woefully inadequate to convey the true significance of all these "affairs"—a crisis that tears a society apart and from which it emerges in a profoundly different shape.

The phenomenon now referred to as the Querelle des Anciens et des Modernes was, in this last, officially unrecognized sense of the term, an *affaire.* It was in fact the first true *affaire,* even though literary history, ever blind to its innovativeness, refers to it as the last of the *querelles.* In this usage, *querelle* is the similarly euphemistic precursor of *affaire:* this relatively lightweight term is used to designate intellectual controversies as sustained and as momentous as the centuries-long conflict over women's rights and status known as the *Querelle des Femmes.*[10] From the late Middle Ages through the seventeenth century, these so-called quarrels are a recurrent phenomenon in French literary life—the Quarrel of the *Roman de la Rose,* the Quarrel of *Le Cid,* and so forth.[11]

It is undoubtedly because this type of quarrel is such a familiar early modern event that French literary historians have always assimilated the controversy between Ancients and Moderns to this model and failed thereby to appreciate the phenomenon's distinctiveness. Their conviction that they were dealing with just one more in the long line of literary quarrels would have been reinforced by the stance of certain participants who, true to the spirit of the euphemism, mocked the phenomenon even as they helped create it. There is no better example than François de Callières's *Histoire poétique de la guerre nouvellement declarée entre les Anciens et les Modernes* (1688), published in the first year of the controversy's unfolding. Callières—whose volume was the model for Jonathan Swift's more

celebrated *The Battle of the Books* (1704), the work that performed
the parallel deprecatory function during the English continuation
of the French dispute—literalizes the bellicose connotations of *querelle:* he describes authors ancient and modern lining up their troops
and doing battle in defense of their reputations. He does so, however, only to prove that it would be foolish to take seriously a mere
war of words, a battle over nothing more important than books.

Such mockery inevitably punctuates the most serious literary disputes—in general, the more serious the dispute, the more strident
the laughter dismissing it as a trivial pursuit. Contemporary commentators who dismiss today's Culture Wars as the insular squab-
bles of tenured radicals out of touch with mainstream society are
thus following in the footsteps of Callières and Swift. To argue that
the only fitting response to such inconsequential controversies is
laughter may well be the one effective means of eliminating the
threat posed by all true confrontations between Ancients and Moderns. The late-seventeenth-century conflict became more than a
"querelle" precisely because, just as has happened in recent years,
it transcended the insularity of previous literary disputes and became the first literary controversy to reach a broad audience not
otherwise concerned with academic affairs. And it was that very
fact—the dispute's ability to touch a public nerve—that transformed this quarrel into an *affaire,* into Culture Wars, and, in turn,
led those who would have preferred that the issues thus publicly
aired be negotiated solely behind closed doors to attempt to mock
the phenomenon out of existence.

Previous literary controversies never rose above the status of a
so-called quarrel because they had remained exclusively ivory-tower
disputes. They were played out strictly within the confines of some
academy (the university, the Académie Française, any community
of scholars with institutional definition). These controversies never
succeeded in capturing the attention of the public at large, the community of more or less informed readers outside the academy—
what we would call a general audience.[12] What went on between the
seventeenth-century incarnations of the Ancients and the Moderns,
however, quickly touched a public nerve. A far broader spectrum
of readers than ever before became involved in this controversy—
many of whom eventually even decided that they had a right to
express their opinions on the issues being debated. Indeed, just as
has happened in our Culture Wars, the public right to judge became
a highly controversial issue when the Ancients protested that only
professional scholars had the right to pronounce on literary issues

and the Moderns countered with the argument that nonprofessional readers might even possess superior judgment.[13]

It is undoubtedly significant that, even though the term would have been the obvious choice, the participants in this controversy did not refer to it as a *querelle*. They turned instead to more forceful terminology to characterize their dispute, preferring to think of it as a "war"— or even, in what seems to have been the earliest occurrence of this usage, as an "affaire."[14] Subsequent literary historians downgraded it to the status of a "quarrel," undoubtedly in an effort to minimize the importance of its long-term consequences—something that could well happen in decades to come with today's Culture Wars.[15]

The participants' instinct, however, was sound. This controversy was no mere quarrel: it reached the status of an *affaire*. For, at the same time as it shaped the nationwide crisis I am calling a fin de siècle, it brought to the surface tensions—in particular those related to the categories we term today gender, class, and race—tensions that had been building in French society in the decades prior to the controversy. Somehow—and the same unlikely convergence has taken place again today—a literary war becomes the context in which questions are debated that seem, just as much now as then, on the surface totally unrelated to what is allegedly the fundamental issue, the worthiness of modern authors to be compared to their ancient predecessors. These questions, which took on such proportions that they often overshadowed the premises on which the war had been launched, included whether women had the right to social and intellectual equality, whether education could function as a tool for cultural assimilation, and whether the nation's social fabric could remain intact at a time when voices from outside the traditional intellectual elite were making themselves heard.

This incongruent convergence took place because, in the course of this first *affaire,* the new literary public that had become involved in the issues initially raised within the academy became worthy of that name, became a true public greater than the sum of its isolated readers. Upon encouragement (which I will describe in chapter 2), these readers joined forces to form the earliest public literary communities in France: in other words, the controversy brought them together and caused them to influence each other until they worked as a collective. The seventeenth-century Culture Wars thus created that popular force for change that we now refer to as "public opinion."[16]

It was this conjuncture between a mood of national crisis and an increasingly widespread perception that public opinion could help shape the outcome of this crisis that provoked the precursor to our fin de siècle. Admittedly, this scenario is a far cry from the generally accepted model for a fin de siècle. It is commonly believed that the climactic sense of a century's end can exist only in the aftermath of war, as though the fin de siècle were inseparable from the experience of rebuilding from the rubble. From this perspective, the French Revolution and the period in its wake constitute the prototype: a nation torn apart by military catastrophe traverses a period of social and artistic dissoluteness, the kind of dissoluteness that would later be termed decadence. In his life as in his works, the marquis de Sade is an emblematic figure for this type of century's end with its aura of catastrophic limits: the *homme noir* who systematically sought to destroy all conventions—even, according to Foucault, who sees him as a sort of "last man," the "convention" of man himself.

The fin de siècle during which both *fin de siècle* and *decadence* were named, a century later in France, though hardly as dramatic in its catastrophic dimensions, nevertheless is cut from the same mold: it took shape in the shadow of the Franco-Prussian War, the siege of Paris, the Commune and the massacres that accompanied its suppression. In that shadow, the conventional social fabric unraveled, and literature also came apart at the seams. In a manner (appropriately) less violent than that devised by Sade, violence was nonetheless done to traditional literary values: an excessively ornate stylistic surface was privileged, largely at the expense of psychological development and interiority. Around and during the first fin de siècle to be called by that name, the literary characteristics that are now associated with the movements known as modernism and postmodernism underwent their initial formulation.

Is it because the last century's end succeeded in imposing a name on the phenomenon that it is now generally assumed that any true fin de siècle will follow its lead? Or is it the repetition, in France at least, of essentially the same structure at the close of the last two centuries that has convinced us that the only century's end worthy of consideration originates in catastrophe, preferably of apocalyptic proportions?[17] Witness the example of the most detailed commentary on the phenomenon to date, that of Hillel Schwartz. Despite numerous attempts to make this view nuanced, Schwartz really recognizes only the type of fin de siècle seemingly brought on by wars and devastation: "There seems to be a rhythm to the modern centuries, with some unavoidable revolution at the end of each" (134). Furthermore, in the aftermath of this recurrent revolution, Schwartz

claims, decadence is always equally recurrent—"To be fin de siècle
. . . is to languish with one's century, to decay along with it" (159)—
especially the ultimate decadence, literary decadence. Schwartz considers the phenomenon over ten centuries, beginning with the 990s,
yet nowhere does he admit that only in the eighteenth century does
a truly cataclysmic war coincide with a century's end and that only
in the nineteenth century is true literary decadence present at a century's close.

Schwartz should have more difficulty accounting for all other
instances he examines. Each time, however, he simply sweeps away
any evidence that stands in the way of the perfect conjuncture he
seeks. His two most difficult cases, in fact, are those that interest
me here, the 1690s and the 1990s. To deal with them, he develops
reasoning that is simultaneously his most contorted and in some
way his most suggestive. Thus, for the example of the seventeenth
century, Schwartz argues: "This was . . . proof of the awareness of
standard centuries and centuries' end at the end of a century whose
true apocalypses of ruin and of revelation had taken place forty,
fifty, sixty years before" (114). For him, the century "climaxes near
the midcentury with the traumas of the Thirty Years' War that dev-
astated Germany, the Fronde or French insurrection that would not
quit (1648–53–58), the English Civil War and the Cromwellian Pro-
tectorate (1642–60). . . . The 1690s had been practically eviscerated
of dramatic potential by events earlier in the century" (114). The
only other fin de siècle to resist Schwartz's classification as defiantly
as the 1690s is our present one: "Were it not for the grandeur of
the year 2000, this fin de siècle must seem about as hollow as that
of . . . the 1690s. The Holocaust, Hiroshima, H-Bombs. . . . Our
Nineties could only be aftermath" (200).

Indeed, rather than deny the seventeenth century a fin de siècle,
Schwartz very nearly contends that this absence of cataclysmic content is the ultimate proof that the phenomenon was indeed alive
and well: "Notwithstanding the relative plainness of the 1690s, a
decade neither spectacular nor tragic nor frightening nor mysteri-
ous, the years 1699, 1700, and 1701 were still tantalizing" (121).
Schwartz is forced into this theoretical corner because he will not
admit the existence of any other model for the fin de siècle. It is
true, as he sees, that the change from the seventeenth to the eighteenth century was remarked upon at that time and was widely considered to be significant. What he does not see is the likelihood that
this was the first time the turn of a century had taken on such prominence, in France at least. This was the case because, at the end of

the seventeenth century, literature took on a role not allowed for in the apocalyptic model, in which fin de siècle production can only be decadent. In the alternate, Culture Wars model for a century's end, however, literary affairs play a far more significant role: literature becomes, in fact, a central fin de siècle phenomenon, a moving force behind public opinion.

In the 1990s in America, a pattern is taking shape that repeats significant structures first produced in the 1690s in France: debate about literary issues provides the forum in which the anxieties that fuel Culture Wars are aired—above all, anxieties about the redisposition of control over the transmission of culture and about the contamination of bloodlines that would result from the phenomena we now term gender trouble (the seventeenth century's major preoccupation) and *métissage* (our dominant concern today).[18] Then as now, these debates brought new readers into the republic of letters. Then as now, Ancients reacted to this influx by lamenting the resulting decline in civilization, while Moderns responded by defending the democratization of culture and of the object of study—defending some form of what we call popular culture, even though in the seventeenth century this meant now-canonical genres, in particular, the novel and opera. Then as now, these new readers moved from issues of culture to issues of judgment. Thus, by producing communities of readers who feel empowered to judge together, Culture Wars in effect generate a public sphere. In late-seventeenth-century France, this process was centered around early periodicals such as *Le Mercure galant*. In America today, we seem to be witnessing a proliferation of self-proclaimed public spheres, corresponding to the new publics for literature whose right to judge has been defended by recent Moderns—a gay public sphere, a black public sphere, and so forth—once again centered around journals in which new views can be aired. A Habermasian might argue that none of these public spheres is truly public, but this would be to obscure the role played by Culture Wars in producing the desire to participate in a public sphere, as well as the no longer negligible resonance of once marginal voices.

In France at the end of the seventeenth century, Culture Wars were followed by a literary revolution—a revolution we may well be starting to repeat in America today. As part of the fin de siècle upheaval, literature radically changed face, much as it did in the wake of the subsequent, cataclysmic type of century's end. In this case, however, even though the new style thus produced was denounced by its opponents (the Ancients) as decadent because of what was alleged to be its potential to erode the nation's moral fiber, it was a far cry from the phenomena subsequently accepted as decadent.

Indeed, the primary characteristics of the new literary style were the heightened importance it placed on character psychology, as well as its general emphasis on interiority, in particular on increasingly intense emotionality. It is to the 1690s that we can trace the origins of the phenomenon that, more than any other, signals the radical difference between seventeenth- and eighteenth-century literature in France, *sensibilité*, the concentration on the depiction of ever more heightened and intense emotional states.[19] The literary sentimentalism that authors began to create in the 1690s was the first sustained attempt in the French tradition to define literature by its ability to depict the interior rather than the exterior, reaction rather than action. Perhaps the most significant contribution made by the creators of *sensibilité* was linguistic: they sparked the invention of a new language with which to designate emotional states. In French, the words still used today to describe the emotions originated at the seventeenth century's end, along with the sentimental style in literature.

It might seem merely ironic that sentimentalism was a creation of the first true fin de siècle, since literary interiority was the principal target of the forms of literary decadence that were produced in the aftermath of the next two ends of centuries. The forms of decadence developed in the 1790s and the 1890s were attempts to eviscerate, as it were, sentimentalism, to hollow out the appearance of psychological depth, or an inside, behind the literary surface, an appearance that the late-seventeenth-century proponents of *sensibilité* had tried to develop with greater precision than any of their precursors. I would argue, however, that the attacks against the sentimental style involved far more than a simple reversal of literary values. The crafting of *sensibilité* in the 1690s in France signaled the beginning of a long intellectual trajectory that others have tried to short-circuit before (notably in prior fins de siècle), and from which we appear finally to be exiting only in the 1990s—and the signs of the completion of that development are clearest, not in France, but in this country, the site of the current Culture Wars.

Hence my insistence on the existence of an alternate model for the fin de siècle. For if we assume, as do Schwartz and other commentators, that the phenomenon always takes the same shape, we are of necessity blind to the implications of this broader intellectual trajectory, delimited by the two fins de siècle sparked by Culture

Wars.[20] This is to ignore the historical precedent for the conflict
dividing American society today. And this in turn is to lose sight
of the long-term (in the French cultural historians' sense of *longue
durée*) historical context in which the current, widely proclaimed
end of the Enlightenment can be situated.

Recent studies trumpeting the Enlightenment's demise abound.
Witness Iain Chambers's analysis, from a cultural-studies perspective, of what is proclaimed to be the relation between such contemporary issues as homelessness and migration and "the last of the
dim haze of the Enlightenment." Or the French new philosopher-
historian of science, Bruno Latour's, call for a reversal of the Coper-
nican Revolution and of all the scientific values on which the Enlightenment was founded, in favor of a return to what he calls a
state of premodernism, in order to eliminate the errors and ruptures
in history introduced by the desire to be Modern.

Perhaps the most nuanced of these proclamations was formulated by a (in our current terms) less radically innovative figure, the
historian Philippe Ariès. In an article intended as an introduction
to *l'histoire des mentalités,* Ariès explains recent changes in this historical methodology in whose creation he played such a pivotal role:
"We are witnessing today, in the last third of the twentieth century,
the end of the Enlightenment, or at least the end of the belief in the
irreversibility and the absolute beneficence of scientific and technical
progress. Certainly not the end of progress, but the end of the religion of progress" (411). Once again according to Ariès, the rever-
ence for the Enlightenment so widespread in recent decades can be
explained principally as the result of the desire to establish a beginning for modernity. Modernity was considered inseparable from scientific progress, and the Enlightenment became the focus of wide
attention because it was seen in turn as the origin of the belief in
scientific progress (411). Once, therefore, scientific progress came
no longer to be viewed, in Ariès's term, as "beneficent," then interest
in the Enlightenment became in a sense irrelevant, even something
to be condemned.[21]

Hence (even if the premises on which they are based often differ
widely from those motivating the proclamations Ariès has in mind)
the increasingly frequent recent attacks not only on modernity, but
more precisely on those who call themselves "the Moderns." Witness Latour's battle cry in the title of his work, *We Have Never Been
Modern.* Hence also a renewed interest in the notion of a quarrel
between Ancients and Moderns and in particular in the idea that
such a quarrel is a recurrent phenomenon, in many different indi-

vidual domains—and even a global intellectual phenomenon. Hence finally the notion, advanced in recent years with a level of vehemence not mustered since the time of the original quarrel, that the Ancients defended the superior position and that the principal intellectual problems of the past two centuries can be seen as a result of the Moderns' victories.[22]

These various proclamations, counterproclamations, and attacks establish the following design for the intellectual trajectory between the two concluding decades that interest me here, the 1690s and the 1990s: the "religion" of scientific progress generated the Enlightenment; the Enlightenment was the first precursor of modernity; modernity was subsequently fully generated by the turmoil of what is known as the first true fin de siècle. Because this design has won such wide acceptance in the past thirty years, the Enlightenment became first the object of intense and admiring scrutiny insofar as it could be shown to be modern, and then a prime target for criticism precisely because of its dual association with scientific progress and with modernity.

Both the making and the unmaking of the Enlightenment are founded first on a need to establish *the* origin of modernity, which is founded in turn on an unavowed need for periodization—a need that can only seem ironic in an age in which critics widely proclaim that periodization is hopelessly *dépassé*.[23] By giving into these related needs, however, critics have inadvertently given shelter to other insufficiently examined premises as well. Most notably, they have consistently taken the Enlightenment out of context and isolated it as an origin, rather than seeing it as a sort of central marker from which can be studied both the warning quakes and the repercussions first generated in the process of creation and then in the wake of a revolutionary set of ideas.

They have thus promoted in particular a deformed vision of the relation that, more than any other, explains the exceptional force of attraction that the Enlightenment has exerted ever since, the relation between science, progress, and modernity. It was only while trying to understand the two fins de siècle that refused to fit the accepted mold that I realized that today's neo-Ancients are wrong to blame the creation of the myth of scientific progress, and therefore of science as universal panacea, on the Moderns of the 1690s. In fact, the seventeenth-century French controversy indicates that the emphasis on the causal role of science is misleading—that progress, rather than science, was the determining factor for the first Moderns.

True, at the seventeenth century's end, scientific progress was loudly proclaimed—with ample reason, since the recent examples of the discoveries of Newton, Harvey, and others could be evoked. Significantly, however, science's role was always promoted by literary figures, in particular by the individual who became the chief spokesperson for the Moderns, Charles Perrault.[24] In addition, whenever men of letters made this gesture of including science, scientific progress was put at the service of literary progress: as is true in today's Culture Wars, literary progress (that is, the allegation that modern literature was at least the equivalent of, if not superior to, ancient literature) was the principal bone of contention; scientific progress was introduced only to provide a secure base from which progress in artistic domains could be argued for.[25] By making science alone responsible for the modern success of the notion of progress, recent critics of the Enlightenment have placed on science a weight that the first theoreticians of progress never intended for it to bear. And this at the same time has served to distract attention from the pivotal role played by literature in provoking Culture Wars, those critical periods from which a society emerges in a profoundly different guise.

When the original Ancients and Moderns went to war, they debated the issue of human perfectibility exclusively on literary grounds: if modern authors were superior to their ancient precursors, then it followed logically, or so the public was informed again and again by Perrault and all his followers in the Modern camp, that modern men were likewise superior to their counterparts in previous ages. Their Ancient opponents were equally insistent in maintaining the opposing stance. And so it came to pass that the first true fin de siècle was still another logical result of the Moderns' founding argument for the superiority of modern authors. If modern authors were superior to ancient authors, then modern men were also a superior race. If, however, the greatest modern authors and men were those who were fortunate enough to have been born under the rule of the greatest monarch of all time, Louis XIV, as the Moderns were always careful to argue, then the Moderns thereby automatically raised the question of the fate of those who would come after them. How would it be possible to outdo the accomplishments achieved during the reign of "Louis, the most perfect model of all kings / On whose creation the Heavens exhausted their treasures" (Perrault, Siècle, 22)? Once Perrault had constructed his call to arms for Moderns on the foundation of Louis XIV's incomparability, he willed into existence the crucial element for a fin de siècle, the belief that civilization has begun to decline.[26]

Not even Perrault, normally such an astute tactician, understood this repercussion of his argument immediately. *Le Siècle de Louis le Grand,* the poem that launched the Culture Wars in 1687, reveals no preoccupation with the aftermath of perfection.[27] By the time the initial volume of his most detailed contribution to the controversy, *Parallèle des Anciens et des Modernes, en ce qui regarde les arts et les sciences,* appeared the following year, however, Perrault had clearly grasped the consequences that his claims for modern superiority implied for generations to come. In the very volume in which Perrault explains for the first time in detailed fashion the doctrine of progress on which the Moderns' case rested, he simultaneously warns that the slow unfolding of progress has already come to an end.

In the *Parallèle,* each time that the doctrine of progress is explained, the explanation is accompanied by a pronouncement that the momentum of progress is already slowing down: "Our century has reached the summit of progress. And for the past few years [*depuis quelques années*] progress moves at a much slower pace, and now appears almost imperceptible" (99).[28] On occasion, the anxiety before the decline of civilization implicit in Perrault's argument infiltrates his rhetoric. Witness his version of a stock image of the Moderns' rhetoric, the ages or the seasons of the world: "The duration of the world is usually thought of as that of the life of a man. Childhood, youth, and the prime of life are over, and it is presently in its old age. If we reason in the same fashion that human nature is like an individual man, it is certain that that man was a child in the childhood of the world, an adolescent in its adolescence, fully a man in the prime of its life, and that at present both the world and that man are in their old age" (49–50).[29]

It was as if, the original Culture Wars once launched, the optimism and the cultural superiority that constituted their raison d'être immediately and somehow inevitably unleashed the ominous sense of decline that is the principal mark of the phenomenon we now know as a fin de siècle. For the first Moderns, progress was literally always/already over.[30] Indeed, even their own modernity was tainted by their self-positioning at the end of the line.

In France, the seventeenth century may well have been the first age to know the obsession with being modern. Already in 1623, Théophile de Viau was proclaiming that "il faut écrire à la moderne" (you have to write as a modern) (14). Inevitably, it was also the first age to understand the terror of finding oneself an Ancient. "C'est nous qui sommes les Anciens" (We ourselves are the Ancients) (50), another voice announced in 1688, immediately after the Culture

Wars' outbreak. And that line comes, not from one of the numerous tracts touting the superiority of classical authors and their classical ways, but from the definitive declaration of the Modern position, Perrault's *Parallèle,* in which one of Perrault's characters quickly comes to this understanding of the wages of Modernism.

The first lesson of the seventeenth-century conflict between Ancients and Moderns was that any proclamation of modernity automatically forces those who do not agree with it to define themselves defiantly as Ancients, thereby provoking a cycle of Culture Wars, i.e., struggles for authority and for the right to speak for classical authors and to determine who they are. And this lesson leads in turn to a second one, which, once again, no one seems to have grasped as clearly as Perrault. A proclamation of modernity—"we are the Moderns"—inevitably provokes a kind of intellectual fatigue, even among those in the Modern camp. The Moderns are Moderns precisely because they come so long after the original ancients, the ancients in antiquity, those against whom all Ancients and Moderns ultimately measure others and themselves. They are, therefore, quite literally older than their precursors in antiquity, coming as they do at the end of what Perrault's Moderns clearly present as a long development leading straight from antiquity to the late seventeenth century. The claim to Modern status is at the same time a recognition of the burden of tradition and an admission of a sense of belatedness, of decadence.[31] Inseparable from the rallying cry "we are the Moderns" is "we are the Ancients," a clear sign of a fin de siècle mentality.

The Pandora's box that released progress contained other notions that, while less evidently destructive, have nonetheless recently been increasingly perceived as mixed blessings. Most notable is the concept first displayed prominently in its modern formulation once again by Perrault, that of a century. Still somewhat dimly in the work whose title would for decades be evoked along with the new concept, *Le Siècle de Louis le Grand,* and then with clarity in the *Parallèle,* Perrault gradually developed the sense of *siècle* that overwhelmingly dominates its modern usage. Schwartz retraces in detail the process by which, in the course of the fifteenth and the sixteenth centuries, *century* lost its earlier meaning of a collection of one hundred similar things (poems, stories, and so forth) and became a new way of dividing history into precise periods (93). For Schwartz, this semantic drift had been completed by the end of the seventeenth century (121).[32]

In French, however, *siècle* was never used as *century* originally was, to refer to a collection of one hundred objects.[33] In French, the parallel evolution is strictly temporal: from a vaguely delimited state, that of an "age" or a "generation" (from the Latin *saeculum*), the term moved into its modern temporal precision. This transition had been completed by the time the Culture Wars were over. Moreover, the key texts that initiated the Culture Wars reveal clearly that *siècle*'s passage from the vaguer sense of "an age" to a more or less precise sense of "one hundred years" was intimately bound up with the simultaneous making and unmaking of the doctrine of progress— and therefore with the impetus that led the Culture Wars to generate a fin de siècle. In Perrault's Modernist manifestos, we can both trace the term's evolution and understand how the structure of the Culture Wars forced *siècle* out of classical time, the time of ages.

In Perrault's *Le Siècle de Louis le Grand*, the term acquires an intermediate meaning. No longer really "an age," not yet precisely "a century," it designates quite plainly "a period famous for a renowned prince, for a great man" (Littré no. 4). Here, the term's implications are more overtly regnal than temporal. *Siècle* means the age of Louis XIV, a period whose length was to be determined by that monarch's years, rather than by the fixed span of a hundred years. In the process of defining this more limited type of "age," however, Perrault, as though driven by the fin de siècle forces he was helping to unleash, had clearly begun to grasp the role *siècle*'s new implications could play in his Modernist project.

In the *Parallèle*, perhaps for the first time clearly in French, *siècle*'s limits are temporal more than regnal: the term acquires a function in the culture of decline that Perrault was constructing. In the *Parallèle*, the monarch's life no longer determines the duration of the *siècle* that had attained the summit of progress thanks to the perfection of his reign. Under the joint pressure of progress and decline, Perrault had by then understood that a century had its own beginning, its own end, and its own character, that it was, therefore, independent from the monarch who reigned over it—even a monarch whose reign had been as long as that of the Sun King. In a crucial passage, he first establishes the distinction between an age and a century: "In the overall unfolding of time from the creation of the world until today, different ages [*âges*] can be distinguished; [different ages] can also be noted within each individual century [*siècle*]" (54). He illustrates his point with a dissection of "the century [*siècle*] in which we live": "The time that elapsed between the end of the wars of the League and the beginning of Cardinal Richelieu's ministry was its childhood; its adolescence came next and saw the birth of the Académie Française; virility followed; we are now perhaps entering old age" (54). Perrault goes on to explain that he means by this that each form of artistic expression has been gradually perfected in the course of the century and by now "has already been taken as far as possible" (55).

The passage is centered on Perrault's awareness that the "siècle de Louis XIV" had to have temporal confines rather than regnal ones, and that its beginning had therefore to be fixed, by hook or by crook, as close as possible to the year 1600. Perrault is naturally enough still somewhat threatened by *century*'s recent arbitrariness. He therefore feels obliged to make 1600 coincide as nearly as possible with a major historical marker. The end of the sixteenth-century wars of religion ("the wars of the League") provides the ideal solution to this problem.[34] More striking still is the fact that, even though the monarch's end surely seemed nowhere in sight at the time (Louis XIV actually died in 1715), in 1688 Perrault already foresaw an end to his century and explicitly linked the century's end with a sense of cultural and physical decay: "We are now perhaps entering old age."[35]

In other words, just as with the concept of progress, the notion of a century was no sooner given its modern definition, than the idea became caught up in the mood of decline and fall. It was as if the recognition of the new concept of a century led immediately and inevitably to the recognition of the concept of a century's close. *Le siècle* was no sooner created than it was given a *fin*.[36]

Century's redefinition also had its role to play in a kind of domino effect, whereby a series of concepts forced each other into existence. The last such concept I will evoke is one whose relation to the century's end was more arbitrary, except to the extent their simultaneity provides additional confirmation of the literary origins of the fin de siècle phenomenon. Perrault's redefinition of century had among its side effects the creation of the notion of literary periodization. When he named "the century of Louis the Great," Perrault demarcated an epoch, consistently and primarily defined in artistic, and especially in literary, terms. In France, the period during which the Culture Wars were waged was the first age to be confronted with the obligation of understanding itself as an era, an entity stylistically distinct from those that had preceded it. The gesture with which Perrault created the seventeenth century as a cultural entity, an image, of necessity simultaneously invented other epochs, those from which Louis's century had distinguished itself. In this sense, the original battle between Ancients and Moderns was the major watershed in French literary history, the period marker that created the / need for other period markers.

Prior to the Culture Wars, literary history was in its infancy. Even in the *Parallèle*, periodization remains timid: the sixteenth century is called into existence as a foil for the greatness to follow, a century and a literary era that remained rather primitive, even though progress was made to prepare the way for the seventeenth century and the golden age of French arts and letters. From this simple beginning, however, Perrault had created a new need for literary commentary. It gradually became standard practice to ask periodizing questions: for instance, what makes one century or period different from those around it? More importantly, commentators gradually came to decide that the end of a century was the best marker to separate one literary age from another.

In Perrault's wake, literary history, founded on this nascent belief in the succession of *literary* centuries, each with its distinct character, came in the course of the next century slowly into its own. Initially, it was the province of literary Moderns, such as Bernard Le Bovier de Fontenelle and Marie-Catherine d'Aulnoy, who produced the five-volume *Recueil des plus belles pièces des poètes français depuis Villon jusqu'à M. de Benserade* in 1692.[37] What is already implicit in the idea of a collection like the *Recueil des plus belles pièces* becomes evident in the immediate aftermath of the Culture Wars, when literary history, for reasons that will become evident, was taken over by Ancients such as Abbé Claude-Pierre Goujet, who produced an eighteen-volume *Histoire de la littérature française* in 1740. With the success of periodization, commentators like Goujet began to consider the sum total of the different literary centuries. Thus, out of the nationalism on which Perrault founded his rallying cry for literary Moderns, the sense of a French national literary tradition was created.

That sense of a literary tradition was equally important to all of the radically different schools of commentary that took shape during and after the Culture Wars, but it was exploited by each of them to very different ends. In the early 1960s, Roland Barthes helped launch our current Culture Wars when he implied that a division between Ancients and Moderns was already in effect in the French cultural world and proposed terms to characterize what he saw as the two opposing critical tendencies that were engaged in then silent warfare. Those terms are equally appropriate designations for the opposing camps in the seventeenth century: interpretive criticism (which Barthes defined as ideological) and academic (*universitaire*) criticism (which Barthes characterized as positivistic and anti-ideological [246]).[38]

For the seventeenth-century Ancients and Moderns, the meaning of the distinction between ideological and anti-ideological literary commentary is evident. Ancients such as Goujet (almost all of whom had pedagogical connections) considered literature a means of preserving the status quo, of guaranteeing that the composition of the traditional French intellectual elite would not be modified even as educational practices began increasingly to be considered a prerogative of the French state and, therefore, could potentially be opened up to democratizing tendencies.[39] Moderns such as Perrault and Fontenelle (none of whom were professional pedagogues) conceived of literature in the opposite way, as the principal means by which culture could be made ever more public and by which a new public—increasingly diverse in terms of gender as well as class—could be brought into the cultural mainstream and be encouraged to participate in the development of public opinion.

Perhaps more than any other factor, the social functions assigned literature as a result of its deployment during the Culture Wars explain the formation of the ideological channel that links the Culture Wars to the Enlightenment project. Thus, to cite but one example at this point, in 1738 Voltaire revived Perrault's rallying cry in the title of one of his most influential historical works, *Le Siècle de Louis XIV*. First in a prefatory "letter to M. l'Abbé Du Bos" and again in his opening chapter, Voltaire stresses that he is using the key term, *siècle*, no longer in the older sense of an age dominated by a great ruler, but both with increased chronological precision and with the goal of presenting the seventeenth century as a golden age: "It is not only the life of Louis XIV that I [*on*] am aspiring to write. . . . I [*on*] want to try to paint for posterity, not the actions of an individual man, but the mentality of the men in the most enlightened century that ever was" (616). In the immediate aftermath of the Culture Wars, progress had become synonymous with enlightenment, and the new cultural flexibility promoted by the Moderns was seen as having taken their century to unprecedented heights of philosophical broad-mindedness—to a level of openness undoubtedly far beyond anything the Moderns had actually dared aspire to. This was true to such an extent that that quintessential Enlightenment figure, Voltaire, portrayed the seventeenth-century Moderns as having perfected the process of enlightenment.

Well before the Culture Wars were over, other essential elements of the set of revolutionary new ideas called into being by the controversy had already become part of the popular imaginary, in particular the notion that the turning point from one century to the next possessed, naturally, a momentous significance. No set of documents reveals this more clearly than the relevant issues of *Le Mercure galant,* the most popular French periodical of the period. Thus, after the obligatory praise of the king, the December 1699 issue opens with an extended article (pp. 10–82) entitled "feelings on the question of the century to come." The paper's editor, longtime Modern supporter Jean Donneau de Visé, enters into a detailed discussion of the differences between a series of temporal markers (*age, epoch, century,* and so forth) of the significance of those differences, and of the importance of such terms. The discussion functions to showcase the term that had recently been transformed: "We are reaching the year 1700 and the question of the new century has not yet been decided. Some claim that it is about to begin, others contend that it will only begin in 1701" (10). Donneau de Visé casts his vote for 1701; consequently, there are only scattered references to the question in the January 1700 issue. However, the January 1701 paper opens with: "I cannot think of a more appropriate beginning for my letter in this new year, the first of the eighteenth century" (1). The fin de siècle had had perhaps no more important result than to instill this belief in an absolute divide between centuries, and along with it the belief that everything belonging to the new century would be somehow inherently different.[40]

In the immediate aftermath of both the Culture Wars and the death of Louis XIV, in 1719, Abbé Jean-Baptiste Du Bos, the first of the Enlightenment's great aesthetic theoreticians, demonstrates that *siècle*'s evolution had been completed.[41] The term was by then absolutely fixed in its modern sense and had been made completely independent of the notion of regnal duration: "The word century signifies precisely a period of one hundred years." In addition, Du Bos sees that this meaning has been particularly useful to (literary) history: "It was decided that each century would be one hundred years long just to facilitate chronological calculations and citations" (135). In what was surely the first critique of the new concept of periodization that had only begun to function a few decades before, Du Bos longs for a return to the time of ages and the older, more fluid notion of *siècle*.[42] Du Bos's justifications teach us how quickly *siècle,* once it had served its function of putting an end to a period of decadence and decline, became enshrined most actively as an absolute divide upon which the stable classification of cultural production could be founded. They serve as further proof of the extent to which the blame for the upheaval of the first French fin de siècle could be laid at literature's feet.[43]

My goal here is not to argue the most radical position, that the only unrest that played a role in either the generation or the aftermath of the Culture Wars—in the seventeenth century or in the twentieth century—was solely literary in nature. How could it be claimed, to cite but the most extreme example, that the French student revolts of May 1968 were completely overshadowed by the literary war that divided Ancients and Moderns? My point is rather that, during fins de siècle dominated by Culture Wars, the political arena is constantly infiltrated by the literary, in the broadest definition of the term. At these times as at no other, literature becomes the stuff of history rather than of literary history, not only activity or event but *political* event.

The next two chapters will try to measure the consequences of literature's involvement in the seventeenth-century Culture Wars. On the most obvious level, this means an attempt to account for the radical difference between literature on either side of the fin de siècle divide. In addition, this means an attempt to understand the consequences of literature's involvement in the political arena, to understand the altered ways in which literature functioned in the republic of letters and in the business of literature during and after the fin de siècle. Finally, because of my belief that literature became event and even political event at this time, this means that I will try to account for the enormous difference between France, or at least its *mentalité*, before and after the Culture Wars, on each side of the Enlightenment's divide.

The next two chapters will be organized to highlight the two problems or breaks in the chronology of the seventeenth-century Culture Wars. The two chronological breaks are moments when it is hard to understand why the conflict evolved as it did. Thus, chapter 2 will be devoted in particular to the period 1670–87, the years that hold the key to understanding why the hostilities between Ancients and Moderns were finally openly declared only in 1687, even though the conflict had been simmering at least since the early 1670s. Chapter 3 will concentrate on the period 1694–1714, on questions related to the controversy's abrupt end in 1694, and on the very different nature of all subsequent manifestations of the Culture Wars. The answers to these chronological mysteries hold clues important to an understanding of any fin de siècle that unfolds in tandem with Culture Wars. They can help us, for instance, to see how certain seemingly unrelated issues such as demographic diversity and canonic diversity become intertwined at these times. They can also shed light on the outcome of Culture Wars, explaining the formation of unexpected alliances and especially their long-term consequences.

Each of the next two chapters will also be organized around a group of key words that testifies in a particularly telling manner to the period's crucial concerns. Chapter 2, devoted to the seventeenth century and to its fin de siècle, will be centered on the ramifications of the process by which *public* acquired its modern sense. The chapter is first and foremost a reconstruction of the Culture Wars, an attempt to situate the original Quarrel between Ancients and Moderns as a phenomenon enmeshed in the anxieties of a century's end. For this reason, I will foreground the forging of a new bond between public and culture—from the techniques devised for attracting the attention of a more diverse public, to the changes in both literature and literary criticism that can be attributed to the new public's growing influence, finally to the sharply repressive reaction against the newly public culture mounted by those who had previously enjoyed uncontested rule over the republic of letters. It is that reaction that most clearly reveals the profound similarities between that age and ours: the anxieties born from the fear of public culture are the telltale mark of a fin de siècle generated by Culture Wars.

Chapter 3, centered on the ramifications of the invention of "emotion" in its modern usage, is devoted to the final phase of the Culture Wars and in particular to the vastly altered literary landscape that then became increasingly apparent. I will try to convey here a sense both of the importance of *sensibilité* and of the exceptional *place* it occupies in French (literary) history. I intend that spatial term literally: perhaps the most vexed question to be answered in order to understand sentimentalism's reign in France is that of its relation to the two periods that surround it, during which the heart not only did not reign supreme in literature, but was always completely under the control of what are known as the interests of the head. This situation is of particular interest to us in our century's end, when it seems increasingly that we are entering a new age of sentimentalism: the results of the seventeenth century's Culture Wars may even allow us to see where we may be heading when we emerge from our own fin de siècle.

In the seventeenth century, the process by which literature became a public phenomenon was accompanied by early signs of the type of reappraisal of accepted systems on which the Enlightenment project was based. The reliability of received ideas about literary value and of interpretive tradition, for instance, came increasingly to be doubted. The reign of sentimentalism—the initial signs of which are evident in the early 1690s, just as the first phase of the Culture Wars was coming to an end, and which begins to reach its full expression in the teens and twenties of the eighteenth century—thus seems to merit explanation as a result of this doubting of accepted systems and traditional values. Subsequently, this process is reversed, when the age of sentimentalism leads into the period during which the Enlightenment project comes fully into its own.

The only gesture I will offer in explanation for this cycle, from reassessment to emotive outpouring to more intensive doubt, involves Lucien Febvre as interpreted by Georges Duby. In a long essay intended as an introduction to *l'histoire des mentalités,* Duby stresses that the emotions have their history. He offers a series of speculations that tentatively, oh so tentatively, suggest the broad lines of that history. Thus, via a reference to Febvre's pathbreaking study of Rabelais, Duby wonders "if the more intense emotivity of certain periods does not stem from an anxiety, a disequilibrium, from the insecurity that results from a questioning of accepted . . . traditions, if it does not correspond to a passage, from the collapse of an outdated world view to the laborious reconstruction of a new one" (965). By referring again to Febvre, this time quoting an article in *Combats pour l'histoire,* Duby hints at a theory for the reverse movement: "periods during which intellectual life predominates follow periods during which affective life is particularly developed" (951).

Without taking any more risks than Febvre and Duby in the direction of causal precision—in order to claim, for example, that *sensibilité* was a necessary prelude to the Enlightenment, or that the Enlightenment was an inevitable and logical result of the age of sentimentalism—it is nonetheless possible to move from Duby's and Febvre's suggestions to a revised view of the Enlightenment's place in modern intellectual history. It thus becomes possible to imagine, if even more tentatively still, the long-term effects of our current fin de siècle.

These are the goals of my final chapter, in which I will review the origins of "culture" in the late seventeenth century before considering the history of our current Culture Wars. By that time, the unfolding of the seventeenth century's end should be familiar to readers. Even though I will not continue to remind them of recent events, I hope that they will keep today's controversy in mind during my account of the original conflict between Ancients and Moderns. It is only when this parallelism is maintained that the concept of a fin de siècle generated by Culture Wars becomes clear—and thus that the nature of the current fin de siècle in America acquires a historical context. For this century's end may well prove to be the crucial American encounter with this phenomenon: it appears to be at the same time the first true fin de siècle in America and the fin de siècle that serves as confirmation of a crucial shift in cultural power from the old world to the new.

The notion of a fin de siècle has proved consistently problematic as far as America is concerned. Schwartz, for example, has trouble identifying any signs of activity that can be related to his cataclysmic model for the phenomenon, beginning in late-eighteenth-century America (152–53), then in late-nineteenth-century America (160–61), and finally in recent years (200).[44] Indeed, most studies of the phenomenon, while they consider fin de siècle anxieties on a broad scale, indicate that the fin de siècle could be considered, if not an inherently French development, at least a phenomenon that origi-nates in France and, from there, infiltrates other nations. The end of this century, at least as it has taken shape so far, would seem to imply, however, that the French monopoly has ended: for the first time, it seems as if America will dominate a fin de siècle—hence the importance of foregrounding the anxieties that are generated by perceived shifts in the balance of cultural power.

As far as our Culture Wars are concerned, the developments now portrayed as the origin of the controversy date from the late 1960s and the early 1970s. True to the pattern established in seventeenth-century France, the intermingling of anxiety over societal change and anxiety over intellectual change has been so thorough that the conflict's origins by now seem hopelessly obscured. Among the most convincing theories—and certainly the most useful for my purposes here—is that developed by Herbert Blau, who contends that Ameri-can counterculture, with its blend of political and intellectual dis-sent, infiltrated Europe, where it helped spark a similar blend of political and cultural unrest, and then came back to the New World, both in the concrete form of further student revolt, and, sublimated, in the guise of literary theory. (Thus, in Blau's vision, the ideology that Barthes portrays as the hallmark of the theory produced by Moderns was of American inspiration.)[45]

This analysis highlights what are for me the two distinctive fea-tures of our current fin de siècle: its fidelity to a Culture Wars model and the originating role played for the first time by America in the sense of ending. In this context, it is important to note that even those gloom-and-doom forecasters such as Allan Bloom and Alvin

Kernan, who assign exclusively French origins to what they portray as the harbingers of civilization's decline—from student unrest to critical theory—now see the U.S. as the home of all threatening discourses and forms of social unrest. The U.S. has now assumed control over the anxiety before the decline of civilization, without which there is no fin de siècle.

The cultural baggage that comes with this type of intellectual prominence has already proven to be a heavy burden indeed. Throughout the 1970s, the rallying cries continued on both sides of the Atlantic, pitting Ancients against Moderns in increasingly acrimonious terms. In the course of the 1980s, the conflict gradually disappeared as a factor in French cultural life—so much so that, in recent years, the only coverage of the Culture Wars in the French press is devoted to the situation in America. At the same time, in America Ancients and Moderns went to war: the accusations flung about have become ever wilder and ever more violent. More importantly, when developments championed by the Moderns began to be blamed for the decline in civilization, time and again literary and theoretical issues were assigned an originating role. Literature and literary criticism have consistently served as the apparently necessary prelude to any discussion of the issues that explain why the controversy has raged for so long and with such vehemence: race, gender, and class. Note the recent example of Gertrude Himmelfarb's paired volumes. In the first, *On Looking into the Abyss,* Himmelfarb lumps together a variety of theoretical discourses—from deconstruction to cultural history—to blame them for what she presents as history's current paralysis.[46] In the second, *The De-Moralization of Society,* she moves from "purely" intellectual issues to the terrain of what are now known as family values in order to lay the blame for the degeneration of contemporary society at the Moderns' feet.

A fin de siècle generated by Culture Wars is a moment during which many Moderns promote what is hardly otherwise a commonplace desire, the pull toward a fundamental state of confusion, an attraction to the idea of making raids across traditionally impermeable boundaries. They glorify the confusion that could result from such transgressions by transforming it into a positive myth, centered for today's Moderns in the state of being beyond—beyond gender, beyond race, and so forth.[47] During these fins de siècle, Moderns revel in theoretical dreams of blending that most epochs would consider dangerously savage—as do the Ancients, for whom the very idea of cultural *métissage* is barbaric, a position beyond civilization. On the practical level, any proclamation of the potential of blending results in a backlash: the suggested ideal of a position beyond gender, for example, will cause those who promote it to be blamed for everything from the spread of bad taste and bad writing to the most basic of civilization's ills.

All the anxieties fundamental to the fin de siècle that unfolds in the shadow of Culture Wars—from the fear of social promiscuity, to the fear of public culture, to the fear that those not previously part of the intellectual elite would dare to interfere in cultural matters—define the particular sense of ending that such centuries have in common. Civilization as "we" know it is coming to an end because culture is becoming too public, because there are those who seek to cross and to shatter traditional boundaries and time-honored structures, rather than to police and to enforce them, because these self-proclaimed barbarians have moved into positions of influence. In a Culture Wars fin de siècle, the sense of ending radiates from the cultural sphere until it becomes generalized—not just the republic of letters, but the republic itself is presented as on the verge of collapse. The twentieth century in America has acquired its sense of ending as the seventeenth century did in France.

Now we are moving through the 1990s, and as the Culture Wars sometimes show signs of abating, I often remember that the first and most serious phase of the seventeenth-century conflict came to an official close in 1694. From that point on, the fin de siècle anxieties that had been unleashed settled down until the literary/critical scene became unnaturally calm. When literary energies did resurface, they were redeployed on the completely new terrain of an ever-widening search for new forms of emotionality.

In the mid-1990s in America, forms of expression traditionally considered part of the domain of popular culture—from mass-audience cinema to advertisements—may be the most accurate barometer of the national mood. In part as a result of the Culture Wars' success, the line between high and popular culture has been blurred as at no other time since the beginning of the early modern period: no sooner are they created than our latest "popular" trends are brought into the university by our neo-Moderns. Consequently, media shifts in focus may even function as indicators of the future of American intellectual life. Currently, popular culture is filled with signs pointing to a longing for interiority after the long domination—in high culture, but with a spillover effect into popular culture as well—of postmodernism's hall of mirrors. Witness the recent appearance of icons of emotivity as diverse as Francis Ford Coppola's Dracula with a heart and the paired Swatches dedicated to the yearning for romance.[48] Philippe Starck, among the most influential designers of the facade of our postmodern minimalism (who formerly worked exclusively in France, but who is currently developing the look of the future in this country), recently summed up the "fundamental shift in cultural values" he believes is taking place in these terms: "Less to see, more to feel" (*International Herald Tribune*, 9 August 1994).[49] According to these signs, an age of sentimentalism, a counterpart to the one that first took form in France in the 1690s, but this time one of American inspiration, is moving onto our cultural horizon. In keeping with the spirit of the age, the new sentimentalism will almost certainly be less primal and more techno than its precursor: America could well succeed in creating virtual sentimentalism.[50]

This speculation inevitably leads me to further speculation. Is a second fin de siècle generated by Culture Wars somehow necessary to provide closure to the forces for change unleashed by its precursor fin de siècle? Does the parallel between our unruly fin de siècle and its equally unruly precursor in seventeenth-century France indicate that we have at long last reached the end of three centuries of development initiated by the first century's end to be dominated by Culture Wars? Are we now poised on the threshold of what Foucault terms an epistemological break—to be followed by a future we can in no way predict?

Or, on the other hand, does the parallel between two fins de siècle point to a cyclical parallel as well? Would a new culture of emotionality indicate that we should begin to prepare ourselves for what, if Duby and Febvre are correct, will inevitably follow: a second Enlightenment, but this time an Enlightenment made in the U.S.A.?

2

The Invention
of a Public for
Literature

PUBLIC MATTERS

Public (n.): L'intérêt public, la chose publique (vieilli).
—Littré Dictionary, first edition (1873), no. 14

Le peuple pris en général.
—Littré Dictionary, no. 12

Nombre de personnes réunies pour un spectacle.
—Littré Dictionary, no. 13

In the course of the seventeenth century in France, the expression *le public* gradually evolved from a centuries-old position of semantic stability to the threshold of the new position it has occupied throughout the modern period. This evolution was a complex process with at least two components. The first was a standard case of semantic drift, as a result of which the definition that had long been accepted as primary—*the public* in the sense of "the body politic" or "the state" (*la chose publique*)[1]—yielded ground in favor of a modern meaning, the usage to which Littré, in the first edition of his historical dictionary, assigned the number 12 (the initial definition of *public* as a noun): "the people in general."

Alongside this semantic drift, however, is also visible a process of what might be termed semantic slippage. A still more modern usage, *the public* in the sense of "an audience," comes to be increasingly widespread as the century progresses: in this final usage, however, *le public* makes its inroads into the language via the meaning "the people in general." As a result, in French the notion of an audience was from its origins inextricably bound up with the kind of anxieties—from the fear of social promiscuity, to the fear of public culture, to the fear that those not previously part of the social elite would dare to interfere in cultural matters—that are fundamental to any fin de siècle that unfolds in the shadow of Culture Wars. In French, the notion of an audience was from the outset tied to the belief in cultural decline, in the end of civilization as "we" know it.

I am not the first to attempt to decipher *the public*'s early life in French. Erich Auerbach opens a well-known 1951 essay, "La Cour et la Ville" (reprinted in English translation in *Scenes from the Drama of European Literature*), with a meditation on the development in the seventeenth century of this new terminology to designate the audience for literature. Auerbach's commentary, however, is marked by a double limitation. The first is technical: the fact that, despite his awareness of its inadequacies, Auerbach's reflections were guided by Littré's dictionary; he appears to have had access only to scattered seventeenth-century works to help him flesh out the history presented by Littré, a history Auerbach recognized as defective.

The second limitation is theoretical: the result of Auerbach's refusal to see in the French classical age any hint of even social diversity, much less of social conflict, any suggestion that the age did not present him with what he vehemently criticized it for being, "a self-contained, homogeneous society" (179)—the type of society, in short, that would never allow true social contamination to threaten its perfect homogeneity. For Auerbach, "the public" came into being in seventeenth-century France without strife and without diversity, as "a unified whole" (161). Auerbach's essay is an extended denunciation of what, in his vision, is in essence an ironic situation: the formula *the public* first acquired a primary modern meaning at a time when that newly defined audience for literature was anything but public in its values and in its composition—though even Auerbach, the sternest critic of the "siècle de Louis XIV" conceivable, is willing to admit the existence of a segment of the population "which may already be termed a 'public' in the modern sense" (179). Closed and closed-minded, the public as Auerbach presents it turned its back on all the harsh realities of the day—from the plight of the peasantry and the common people (167) to economic affairs in general (174).

Now, not even a commentator annoyed by Auerbach's oversimplifications could claim that, in its seventeenth-century incarnation, "le public" functioned in any way as a truly popular phenomenon.

By reopening the dossier of the creation of the first modern literary public, however, and by examining evidence to which Auerbach may not have had access, it becomes apparent just how public—in the sense of open to new interest groups and to new centers of public opinion—"le public" became. I also hope to show how those involved in the new public's creation, in a complicated simultaneous give-and-take movement, both responded to the claims of these fledgling interest groups and helped to foster their proliferation. For the critic not intent on castigating the classical age because of its avoidance of certain types of "reality," the context in which *the public* came into its now dominant meaning reveals a society that was far from "self-contained." In fact, it is precisely around the emergence of this new public for literature that the French classical age displays itself as a society in the process of shaking off its homogeneity and moving toward the intellectual turmoil of the Enlightenment. Finally, in addition to the testimony to real social and cultural change that this process provides, it also offers evidence of the role played by this making public of the literary process, if not exactly in the popular imaginary, at least in the imaginary of those members of the formally stable cultural elite who saw the changes as proof that the world as they knew it—not just the republic of letters, but the republic itself, *la chose publique*—was on the verge of collapse.

Before the process, however, a return to the expression itself and, therefore, to the dictionaries and their evidence. The first type of evidence that allows us to correct the view promoted by the standard authority, Littré, is found in seventeenth-century dictionaries, three superb sources of information: the Genevan Pierre Richelet's 1680 dictionary; the *Dictionnaire universel des arts et des sciences* (1690), compiled by the renegade Academician, Antoine Furetière; and the first edition (1694) of the Académie Française's officially sponsored dictionary. Given the very different sources from which they came, it is hardly surprising that these three compilations are seldom in complete agreement in their presentation of key words. The complicated case of *le public* is, however, one of those rare instances. All three dictionaries first introduce the larger category: "citizens or men in general" (Furetière). Then, in the examples given to illustrate this usage, each dictionary includes a sentence containing the phrase "in public" or "for the public" ("to appear in public" [Richelet and Furetière], "to work for the public" [Académie Française]). Along with this subset of "the people," which means in effect "to go public," Furetière sounds a clearly cautionary note: "One has to be very bold in order to appear in public."

In this context ever so slightly tinged with danger, the notion of the public as an audience receives its first official introduction into French lexicography. It is obvious that the innovative usage is not yet firmly in place, for not one of the dictionaries grants it the status of a separate definition. Instead, each slips it in—almost as if the lexicographers were not fully aware of the significance of what they were proposing—slips it in via the new meaning, "the people," and therefore via "to go public."

In each case, the initial example presenting the phrase "to the public" is followed by a second example also using the phrase, but this time in a literary sense: "an author gives his works to the public when he has them printed" (Furetière). Richelet even adds—in an uncanny foreshadowing of the Culture Wars that broke out shortly after his dictionary's publication, during which Ancient and Modern forces would be led by Nicolas Boileau and Charles Perrault— "Apollo inspires Despréaux [Boileau], Perraux [*sic*] and Racine to give their poetry to the public." Almost as an afterthought, and with a tinge of anxiety, at the time when Ancients and Moderns went to war over which set of authors deserved the public's primary attention, the notion of a *public* audience for literature was gaining a toehold on a lexicographical existence.

Such timidity—or incomprehension of the phenomenon whose creation they were helping to record—on the part of these remarkable lexicographers is difficult to understand, for *the public* used unmistakably in this sense had clearly become more and more standard usage as the century advanced. Littré's dictionary situates the appearance of meaning number 12 ("the people in general") in 1668 and meaning number 13 ("an audience") only in 1684. However— pace Littré—the semantic drift I have been describing is already evident in the 1668 example, a letter from the marquise de Sévigné to her notorious cousin, the comte de Bussy (known as Bussy-Rabutin). This letter is a bitter complaint about his betrayal in having published her portrait in his scandalous roman à clef, *Histoire amoureuse des Gaules* (1665): "When I saw myself given to the public and spread throughout the provinces, I was in despair" (28 August 1668; 1:101).[2] Already at its long-accepted official origin, *the public* was a troubled term, colored with the threat of wholesale and indiscriminate exposure.

At the time of its actual initial appearance, the term is equally, though very differently, dangerous. Littré—in unwitting homage to Perrault's credo—took it for granted that the first great writers in the French tradition were those active during the height of Louis

XIV's reign. He very rarely, therefore, looks to earlier writers for his evidence. Had he done so in the case of *the public*, he would have found that it could be noted, clearly used in the sense of an audience, as early as 1637.[3] At that time, *the public* occurs in texts by a variety of authors during what is known as "the Quarrel over *Le Cid*," the most public literary controversy before the Ancients and the Moderns went to war, in which the alleged defects of Pierre Corneille's play were extensively aired under the fairly close supervision of the Académie Française. Several anonymous pamphlets addressed to one or another of the warring parties feature the phrases "the voice of the public" (la voix publique) and just plain "le public": one is even entitled "The Voice of the Public to M. de Scudéry concerning His Observations on *Le Cid*."[4]

As far as this innovative linguistic usage is concerned, pay dirt is hit in the most significant of all documents related to the controversy, Jean Chapelain's *Sentiments de l'Académie Française sur la tragi-comédie du "Cid,"* which features the term twice in its initial sentence alone: "Those who, desiring glory, give their works to the public should not find it strange that the public becomes their judge" (Gasté 355). The simple fact that the expression is given such prominence in the official response—and that response was among the Académie's first open displays of its power—of the body newly founded (1634) by Cardinal Richelieu to oversee the republic of letters clearly indicates that "the public" already had an official, a highly public existence in 1637—even if histories of the French language have yet to recognize it. From that beginning in an atmosphere of literary crisis, the newly acknowledged public is evoked with caution, if not with outright suspicion: the public will judge; it will condemn; it will attempt to impose silence. The public, in short, was a force perceived to be uncontrollable, even by the body granted authority by the Crown to impose order on the literary house.

As we have seen, that air of suspicion remains stubbornly attached to the nascent term, even when, as was the case with Sévigné, it is employed in a context free of literary conflict. Given this negative semantic charge, it is hardly surprising that, during the years when "the public" was gradually acquiring complete official recognition, the term was never given more prominence than during the fin de siècle Culture Wars. At that time, the most prominent Moderns became the first to recognize the potential of the previously unharnessed constituency portrayed by the new phrase. In their hands, "the public" was represented, no longer as a harshly

judgmental power, but as a potentially beneficent force to be ap-
pealed to and well worth winning over. Thus, in the preface to the
initial volume of his *Parallèle,* to cite but one example, Perrault recalls the outbreak of the controversy between Ancients and Moderns
and his expectations that a critic would soon come forward "to set
the public straight" about what was at stake.

In fact, Perrault's usage is a consecration in high culture of a
situation already plain a decade earlier in a more popular literary
context. It takes no more than a cursory reading of any of the issues
of *Le Mercure galant* during 1677 and 1678 that played a role in
setting the stage for the Culture Wars, the issues that I will evoke
in the following pages, to make it obvious that, after such extensive
exposure, this expression was destined to achieve general acceptance. Just as we see happening today, when new words move into
the public domain after having been bandied about in the media,
sure enough, in the October 1678 issue, a reader writes to the editor,
Jean Donneau de Visé, to thank him for his coverage of the literary
scene: "The Public is infinitely obliged to you, Sir. Without you, it
would have a hard time knowing itself [*se connaître*]." Thanks to
Donneau de Visé's efforts on behalf of the Moderns, "the public,"
by the admission of one of its own members, was no longer anonymous. Its members had learned to "recognize" themselves and each
other as participants in a common enterprise.

Thus, *the public* acquired its meaning of "an audience" in the
context of two successive moments of conflict over literary matters.
Because of these particular circumstances, in fact, it could be argued
that the expression's initial meaning was less that of "an audience
for literature" than that of "an audience for criticism," in the sense
of a group assembled both to assess the conflicting opinions of professional literary critics and to formulate its own critical judgments.
From this perspective, the seventeenth-century Culture Wars can
be seen as the final step in the process by which was created a truly
public audience for literary affairs.

Finally, one additional confusion about *the public*'s initial meaning must be stressed. Littré defines it as "the audience assembled for
a performance," and, in his reflections on the new usage, Auerbach
follows Littré's lead and assumes that seventeenth-century evidence
always refers to the theatrical public. All seventeenth-century dictionaries, as well as all the other documents I have cited, make it
clear, however, that they have in mind an audience of *readers.* Furetière's example sums it up: "An author gives his works to the public
when he has them printed." The public's emergence in the seven-

teenth century is intimately bound up with the development of publishing, of print culture. As we will see, the term's early history in
French makes plain the mutual dependency of print in its different
manifestations (in particular, the newspaper, the novel, and literary
criticism) and of a growing public for print culture. The opening
up with which the new public was associated was a democratization,
not of spectatorship, but of readership—"when he has them
printed." The importance of the new term was recognized at the
moment when it was first evident that print culture was rapidly becoming vastly more public. And, whereas any potential broadening
of the audience for the theater could only be limited, the making
public associated with new readerships and the new genres to which
the new readers might be attracted theoretically had no limits.
Hence the crucial role played by "the public" in the creation of fin
de siècle cultural anxieties.

In recent years, under the influence of Jürgen Habermas, the the-
sis has become generally accepted that the establishment of a public
sphere was an Enlightenment project and that the public sphere then
established was a bourgeois phenomenon.[5] In Habermas's view, a
new sphere of judgment was constituted when private individuals
began to make public use of their faculty of reason in the literary
realm. According to the chronology Habermas has succeeded in imposing, this new public reasoning originated in England in the late
seventeenth century and spread to France beginning in the 1730s.
Subsequently, still according to Habermas's theory, in the course of
the eighteenth century the literary public sphere was at the origin
of a newly democratic political public sphere, in which all authority—that of Church as much as that of state—was subjected to critical examination at the hands of what began to be referred to as
"public opinion."[6]

I have retraced *the public*'s early history in French in order to lay
the foundation for a revision of Habermas's view. My quarrel with
Habermas is far more than chronological, as would be the case if I
agreed with his characterization of the phenomena with which we
are both concerned but were simply proposing that they originate
roughly a half-century earlier than he believes. I want to show first
that the development of a publicly critical culture was largely in
place before the Enlightenment was launched. In addition, I want
to demonstrate that the public literary sphere was, just as much as
the public political sphere, at its origin a French phenomenon. Finally, I hope to show that the first public sphere was far from a
totally bourgeois phenomenon. On the contrary, the situation

during the post-Fronde years, the second half of the seventeenth century, was much like that at the end of the Enlightenment, when politically liberal aristocrats initially supported and helped spark off the Revolution.[7] In the case of the seventeenth-century example, intellectually (and often politically as well) liberal aristocrats helped initiate the process of the democratization of taste and judgment that was a founding principle of the Culture Wars.

In other words, I am suggesting a radically different image of the origin and the consequences of the first public literary and political spheres. The republic of letters was opened up to public debate for the first time in France and as a result of a fin de siècle momentum. From this geographic and temporal origin, the new concern for literary publicity spread, along with the Culture Wars with which it initially shared a relation of mutual dependence, to other European nations. In every case, the existence of a sphere in which literary and cultural matters could be publicly debated played a crucial role in launching the only period ever to be primarily distinguished by the cultivation of public contentiousness, the Enlightenment. This tempers the view of the Enlightenment's class politics that the general acceptance of Habermas's theory has promoted: to continue to refer to the first public sphere as bourgeois is vastly to underestimate the range of its social implications.

My portrayal of the first public cultural sphere differs from Habermas's in another, equally significant manner. When the birth of the phenomenon is situated in late-seventeenth-century France, it becomes evident that the sexual politics that surrounded its creation were just as complex as the class politics. In particular, women played an active, at times the most active, role in the democratization of culture. This exceptional situation may partly be explained by the fact that the coffeehouse, an institution elsewhere inseparable from the first stirrings of public culture and one in which women played no role, only began to function as an important center for critical debate in France in the early eighteenth century—or the fact that the coffeehouse excluded women may explain its delayed rise to prominence in France. My revision of Habermas, by filling in the first half-century of *public*'s existence, suggests that gender, rather than class, may have been the determining factor in the creation of a public sphere.[8]

For this reason, it would be difficult to argue that class, above all the potential for the embourgeoisement of French taste, was the unique or even the most acute source of anxiety during the first fin de siècle. As we shall see, the most widely perceived menace was that of the potential for the feminization of French taste. Gender, rather than class, was the primary factor fueling the wave of cultural anxiety that swept over France at the seventeenth century's end. In order to understand the conjunction of forces that I have in mind, it will be necessary to evoke the ways in which two histories became intertwined during the closing decades of the seventeenth century: the history of the original conflict between Ancients and Moderns and that of the emergence of a new public for literature.

Historians and literary historians have often been attracted to the problem of the radical transformation in *mentalités* that took place suddenly and virtually without evident, brutal provocation during the closing decades of the seventeenth century, by the end of which the French had massively evolved from a position of relative acceptance of orthodox views to one in which is already evident the questioning of all accepted systems on which the Enlightenment project was founded. How, in other words, could the Enlightenment have taken place when it did? How could the French, who were apparently so uncritical during the century of Louis XIV—this is the foundation of Auerbach's critique—have come to behave so differently in the space of a few decades?[9] To date, however, in their search for explanations for this dramatic epistemological shift, historians have always privileged a quite traditional definition of historical phenomena. Paul Hazard's 1935 classic, *La Crise de la conscience européenne, 1680–1715,* is a textbook example of this tendency. In his search for Enlightenment doubt, Hazard explores such factors as the spread of religious heterodoxy and the vast increase in foreign travel at the seventeenth century's end. All the factors he studies are part of the domain of traditional intellectual history.

Yet a radically different version of the epistemological shift to which Hazard first drew systematic attention is possible. It would obviously be foolish to disclaim the importance of the historical factors (political, economic, and social) traditionally considered worthy of attention. In the process of transformation that made the eighteenth century so different from its precursor, however, such events were certainly not the only, and perhaps not even the primary, forces for change. Instead, it is possible, as recent cultural historians have proposed, to give literature—in the broad sense of all the factors that surround the production and the reception of literary works—a central role in the transformation in *mentalités.* This transformation can be explained as much by what individuals read and how they read as by the events of the turn of the eighteenth century that correspond to a more conventional view of the historical. Literary works and a new way of reading them made it possible for individuals to think in new ways and in particular to begin to experience the kind of propensity to doubt on which the project of the Enlightenment was founded.

To argue for this redefined view of the period during which the Enlightenment took shape is to take stock of how radically literary history has been reconceived in the sixty years since Hazard's *La Crise de la conscience européenne*. Far less historical and far more literary, literary history is now far more likely to find its raison d'être in the business of literature itself. The most influential recent models for literary history have been proposed by cultural historians, who argue for the centrality of literary texts and the literary enterprise, and who have given these literary "events" the kind of prominence previously accorded only to the events of political, economic, or social history. The new literary history now being written is the history of the book in the broadest sense of the term—from the work of booksellers, to the legal context in which books were published, to the influence of readers and their responses both on the shape of literature to come and on the shaping of *mentalités*.[10]

To date, the influence of the book on French history has been explored almost exclusively within the confines of the eighteenth century. This eighteenth-century history was prepared, however, by a crucial evolution at the seventeenth century's end. Nowhere is the role played by literary event in setting the stage for the eighteenth century more evident or more crucial than during the thirty-year span of the most famous literary controversy of all time, the Querelle des Anciens et des Modernes or, as it was known in its subsequent incarnation in England, the Battle of the Books. Historians of the Quarrel have rehearsed the facts of its unfolding—who wrote what when and in response to whom.[11] They then offer two sorts of explanations for the course taken by the controversy, either political events or what the French call *petite histoire*. These theories are used to explain why the controversy broke out when it did, and so forth. Blame for the continued and often violent discord in the republic of letters is placed most prominently on the kind of historical event traditionally considered most significant, events such as wars and the death of Louis XIV. It is also placed on a second type of explanation, from the realm of *petite histoire*—one individual attacked another out of personal animosity, and so forth. To date, however, the history of the Quarrel that I prefer to think of as the ancestor of our Culture Wars has only been scripted with a conventional definition of historical material in mind. Never has the most recently privileged type of historical fact, the events of the history of the book, been taken into account.

I began my involvement with the literary war by rewriting, once again, the facts of its internal history. However, I decided that those alleged facts did little to help answer the central questions of why the Culture Wars exploded when they did and why they unfolded as they did. In addition, as long as a traditional view of the historical was maintained, external historical events were no more useful in providing convincing answers to these quandaries. Far more central to an understanding of the controversy's mechanisms, I found, was another history, one simultaneously external to the events of the Culture Wars and also enmeshed in the life of the republic of letters. This history, which I will retrace in tandem with that of the controversy, is a tale bound up with the commerce of literature. It is the story of how the public for literature was suddenly broadened, as well as that of the effects of that perceived broadening on both the producers and the consumers of literature.

As I go through the controversy's history, the basic outline of which will be familiar to readers who already know the standard surveys, I will draw attention to key questions about the conflict's chronology that have never received satisfactory answers. These are precisely the questions that are crucial both to any understanding of the link between these Culture Wars and the phenomenon of Culture Wars in general and to any understanding of the relation between Culture Wars and a fin de siècle. I will also weave into the controversy's official story a parallel tale, that of the single most important generic evolution in the history of French literature, an evolution whose unfolding is simultaneous with that of the Culture Wars.

Prior to the time of the *affaire,* all the official literary dreams of the French classical age were theatrical. The triumvirate on which the traditional image of French literature's golden age is founded— Corneille, Molière, Racine—reigned over the century with such un- questioned supremacy that fledgling writers almost invariably as- pired to the theater, and preferably to the noblest theatrical genre, tragedy. The age was also possessed by an unofficial literary dream, one that was never to be realized, that of producing a great French epic. Both the official and the unofficial dream had this much in common: they were founded on the belief that all great French liter- ature was written in verse.

During the period in which France was divided by Culture Wars, the center of literary energy began quite clearly to shift—from poetry to prose, from the genres traditionally considered noblest (tragedy and the epic) to more humble ones (various manifestations of what we would think of as the novel, but that were often known by a variety of names at the time of their development). This evolution is generally thought of as a result of the Culture Wars: prose, and the novel in particular, dominated French literature of the eighteenth century (in reality, that of subsequent centuries as well) because the Moderns won the war. However, I see this evolution not as a result, but as a cause, a view that the following history of the seventeenth-century Culture Wars is designed to explain. The Ancients went to war because they understood that this crucial evolution had begun, because they feared that the literary world was changing too fast and too completely, and because they hoped that, if they could humiliate the Moderns, they could reverse the shifting tide of literary values.

THE WORLD AT WAR

On peut soutenir qu'Homère n'était pas un bon poète, et
que même il n'a jamais été, sans se rendre suspect d'être mal
affectionné à la couronne, ni de mal penser de la religion.
—Abbé François Hédelin d'Aubignac

On January 22, 1687, all hell broke out in the Académie Française. When the academicians arrived for the session, most of them must have been expecting an ordinary day: the program was to consist of the usual mix of reports, occasional poetry, and assorted texts on literary subjects.[12] By the end, however, serious accusations and vicious insults had been widely hurled about, even by such normally decorous men as Pierre-Daniel Huet, bishop of Avranches and noted classical scholar. One key player (royal historiographer and literary arbiter Nicolas Boileau) had screamed so loudly that, shortly thereafter, he lost his voice. The storm unleashed that January day roared on unabated for decades in the French republic of letters. By the time its energy was spent, the literary-scholarly world had been transformed.

According to the story promoted by literary historians, this literary cataclysm was provoked by the reading of a fairly lengthy (twenty-six-page) narrative poem, Charles Perrault's *Le Siècle de Louis le Grand,* structured around a complex interweaving of state and literary politics.[13] Perrault turns, on the one hand, to an overtly nationalistic discourse to justify his claims for modern literature: a great king and a great nation are providing the necessary foundation for great literary achievements. At the same time, he suggests that, without the particular contributions of literary modernity, his century would be less great.

Perrault begins his argument for modern superiority by establishing a powerfully monarchist and nationalistic rhetoric. To this end, he initiates his claims not in any of the areas with which the Culture Wars are traditionally associated, but from the point of view of military capabilities. No other monarch has led his people to more spectacular victories; the century of Louis XIV is, therefore, worthy of comparison to that of Augustus (1). His foundation thus neatly laid, Perrault pairs off representative figures from antiquity with individuals he presents as their modern counterparts to illustrate ways in which the moderns have the advantage over their precursors: Why, he concludes, should we be surprised at the inadequacies of Aristotle's physics? We need only remember that he was working in an "obscure darkness," without the benefit of modern inventions such as the telescope (6). After a first safe start with the example of the martial arts, Perrault thus chose a second safe start, for what became known as the doctrine of scientific progress was among the rare Modernist tenets that always met with ready acceptance— it is undoubtedly for this reason that it is generally considered the only basis from which the Moderns argued for the doctrine of progress.

From there, however, Perrault moved onto the less stable terrain of literature. He develops a tripartite strategy to account for the superiority of literary Moderns over their Ancient precursors. First, Perrault singles out Homer as the dominant literary figure from antiquity. He then proceeds to enumerate Homer's "defects" (using too many digressions, creating heroes who are too brutal, and so forth), which Perrault dismisses as only natural, since Homer, like all the ancients, must be viewed as a product of his age. Had he been fortunate enough to have been born in Louis's century, Homer would never have made these mistakes. With this attack, Perrault gives the initial formulation of the war's central controversy, between personal and transcendent values. To take on Homer was the simplest way possible of announcing that the Moderns put their trust in the individual's right to interpret without being influenced by traditional views—not even by three thousand years of unquestioned veneration. Second, Perrault questions the notion of a stable classical canon. He wonders if the "rare authors" from antiquity "whom we venerate today" (he mentions Virgil and Ovid) "were venerated during their lifetime" (10). He cites ancient critics to prove that this was not the case and indeed that authors considered inferior by Perrault's contemporaries were preferred in antiquity to the current idols. Third, the conclusion to this second argument thus established—that canons change and that we are unable to judge which authors from our age will be appreciated by ages to come (10)—Perrault proposes a canon of contemporary authors he felt would be remembered by the "siècles à venir."

War broke out even before the reading of Perrault's poem was completed. The text produced widespread and violent reaction, especially on the part of the man who with his histrionics immediately sought to establish himself as Perrault's archrival in the enemy camp, Boileau. The numerous accounts left of that fateful day all agree that Boileau could not sit still during the reading of *Le Siècle de Louis le Grand*. Despite the fact that the king had chosen him to be his historiographer a decade before, Boileau seems to have been strangely insensitive to Perrault's glorification of Louis XIV and to his overwhelmingly nationalistic rhetoric and to have heard only the criticism of ancient authors.

All accounts confirm that the session produced wear and tear on Boileau's voice in various ways. According to reports from opposing camps, he kept muttering to himself throughout the reading. In Perrault's version of the events, Boileau interrupted the reading by leaping up and crying out that "it was scandalous to read this work that criticized the great men of antiquity" (*Mémoires* 137). According to the version coproduced by the Moderns Regnault de Segrais and Antoine Furetière, Boileau "could not listen to this reading without protesting to everyone about its false premises. He promised loudly to attack it in writing as soon as he could take time from his work [as royal historiographer]" (*Furetiriana* 26). Huet apparently told Boileau to sit still and be quiet and added that "if anyone were to defend the Ancients, he [Huet] should be the one to do so rather than Boileau because he knew so much more about antiquity, but that they were only there to listen" (Perrault, *Mémoires* 136).

The phenomenon said to have been generated by the reading of Perrault's poem is the *affaire* baptized by literary history as the Querelle des Anciens et des Modernes. Perrault's poem actually contains in a nutshell all the arguments to which the Ancients responded most vehemently throughout the literary war, including the essence of his own subsequent amplification of the Modernist position, *Parallèle des Anciens et des Modernes, en ce qui regarde les arts et les sciences* (1688–97). He even foregrounds the critique of

Homer, destined to become the unique subject of the controversy's ultimate phase (1711–16). Indeed, it is as if Perrault had sensed that *Le Siècle* could prove the catalyst that it did in fact become: he openly inscribes the names under which the warring factions became known and refers at the very beginning of his poem, as if in provocation, to "les anciens."[14]

With the level of animosity Perrault's poem was able to provoke among many major players present that January day, it is no wonder that the reading forced such a long suspension in the order that had governed the French literary house. It is clear that Perrault's poem served as the lightning rod that allowed passions that had been simmering for decades finally to be openly expressed. However, whenever literary history has gone on from there to characterize *Le Siècle* as the origin of the literary war, the principal explanations offered to explain why it was able to play this role come from the domain of *petite histoire.* According to this view, the Culture Wars that turned the seventeenth century's end into a fin de siècle were really at their origin merely an affair of personal animosity. (Commentators who favor this *petite histoire* explanation for their genesis inevitably stress, for instance, that Boileau hated Perrault above all because he thought that the malpractice of his brother Claude, a doctor, had caused several deaths in the Déspreaux clan.)[15] To accept these views is vastly to underestimate the controversy's significance, to present it as (at most) merely the sum total of its participants, rather than as one of the truly original and truly profound intellectual movements in the early modern period.

Yet for those who refuse to accept *petite histoire* theories, it is hard not only to understand why this intellectual conflict that was to prove so central for so long broke out over the reading of Perrault's poem, but also why it finally erupted at this point. Hostilities had been simmering for about fifteen years, and most academicians had long since declared their allegiance to one of the two camps. Most striking, all the opinions that the Ancients apparently found so threatening when Perrault put them forward had, without exception, been expressed before, most notably by one of the founders of the Académie Française itself, Jean Desmarets de Saint-Sorlin, in a series of highly polemical works published in the 1670s. Indeed, Desmarets's rhetoric is so violent in works such as *La Comparaison de la langue et de la poésie française avec la grecque et la latine, et des poètes grecs, latins, et français* (1670), his poem *Le Triomphe de Louis et de son siècle* (1674), and *La Défense de la poésie et de la langue française,* a 1675 work Perrault can hardly have failed to read, since it was addressed, as its subtitle indicates, to him—his tone is so polemical in these works and others that it is hard to imagine why they, rather than Perrault's far milder poem, did not set the Ancients off.

Indeed, Perrault knew just where to turn for the ideas and the rhetoric that guaranteed that *Le Siècle* would become an incendiary manifesto. His opening salvo—

> Antiquity was always venerable,
> But I never believed it was worthy of adoration (1)

—merely gives a minimally poetic turn to a sentence from Desmarets's initial Modernist tract: "Antiquity is venerable, but it is not worthy of slavish imitation."[16] The three parts of Perrault's strategy, down to the list of modern authors he suggests will be the object of future "veneration," can all be found in the same work by Desmarets. Perrault does add a brief comparison of ancient and modern accomplishments in the realms of painting, sculpture, music, and architecture to the argument Desmarets sets forth on the basis of literature alone, but surely this was not all it took to detonate the bomb? If, therefore, the essential argument had not changed, then the climate and the moment surely must no longer have been the same.

And thus the nagging question refuses to go away. Why was Perrault able to set off the war in 1687 when Desmarets, despite his extraordinary persistence in the early 1670s, had been extraordinarily unsuccessful in provoking hostility? What had changed to make it possible that the program of the Moderns at long last began to touch nerves?

On the rare occasions when those literary historians with no interest in *petite histoire* theories address the question of why it was that a literary war could have begun not only with the reading of *Le Siècle*, but also in 1687, they search for explanations completely outside the history of literature and turn to the domains in which historical explanations are traditionally found, the military and economic history of France. From this perspective, it is true that France's situation had become dramatically more pessimistic between 1670 and 1687. In 1670, when Desmarets began to goad the Ancients, Louis XIV, whose reign was only nine years old, was completely the glorious Sun King, the monarch who guaranteed his subjects prosperity and pleasure. But by 1687, when Perrault succeeded in provoking a response from the Moderns' enemies, the national

mood, like the image of Louis's reign, had darkened. The recent
revocation of the Edict of Nantes, for instance, had severely impov-
erished the country intellectually, financially, and in terms of man-
power. The country was weakened in similar ways by the endless
wars on which its by then aging monarch had continued to squander
its resources.[17]

All such talk of a darkened political context, however, seems in
contradiction with the fact that both a cross section of Academicians
and a wide public outside the Académie alike responded in 1687 to
a discourse of nationalism that had left them all cold in 1670, when
the nation and the king were both more overtly grand. In addition,
history thus conventionally defined offers no help in explaining the
particular issues that were addressed with greatest urgency when the
Culture Wars exploded. If we look closely at their initial development, however, we may begin to understand the changes that had
taken place between 1670 and 1687, changes that were responsible
for Le Siècle's succès de scandale. So, before a search for explanations
in the history that runs parallel to that of the Culture Wars, the
history of the business of literature, here is an overview of the initial
contributions by Ancients and Moderns.

Perrault's contemporaries were evidently ready for serious, all-
out conflict. Before the end of 1687, perhaps the most intelligent
formulation of the Ancient position ever conceived, the baron de
Longepierre's Discours sur les Anciens, was already in print. Also that
year, La Fontaine contributed an "Epître à Huet," his personal view
of the Ancient credo. In the course of the following year, Perrault
published the first volume of his most extensive contribution, what
stands as the definitive and most broadly formulated declaration of
the Modern stance, Parallèle des Anciens et des Modernes, en ce qui
regarde les arts et les sciences (subsequent volumes appeared in 1690,
1692, and 1697). And, nine months before Perrault got his amplification of Le Siècle de Louis le Grand into print, Fontenelle brought
out Digression sur les Anciens et les Modernes, a more moderate Modern contribution. Finally, that same year and before the controversy
was two years old, it had generated sufficient material to inspire a
book-length parody, François de Callières's Histoire poétique de la
guerre nouvellement déclarée entre anciens et modernes. Perrault's
poem had launched two years of frenzied debate. During this period,
all the key issues that would provoke controversy for the duration
of the Culture Wars were promptly put forward. Indeed, in all the
excessively intense textual production of those angry decades, no

more comprehensive articulations of the beliefs that divided Ancients and Moderns can be found than those Longepierre and Perrault published at the war's inception in 1687 and 1688.

Longepierre's *Discours* is the thoughtful, detailed response to Perrault's provocations that a number of those present for that tumultuous January 1687 session (and Boileau in particular) had
promised to compose. The central motivation that had prompted
Longepierre to jump into the fray so quickly becomes clear in the
detailed comparison he develops between what he sees as the two
opposing types of critical vision. On the one hand, Longepierre criticizes what might be termed a personal criticism (obviously the Modern stance) on the grounds that this type of critic sees in a work
only those elements that can be shown to have a direct relation to
contemporary issues: "What a strange stubbornness . . . to want to
bring everything back to one's own century [and] never to be able
to convince oneself to let it out of one's sight for an instant!" (96).
Longepierre contrasts this myopic vision with a sort of panoptic
critical viewing angle (clearly that of the Ancients): "A broad mind
[*un esprit vaste*] belongs . . . to all centuries. It takes them all in at
once, as if in a single glance" (100). He presents the Moderns' attempts to find fault with classical authors as determined by the narrowness of their perceptions. According to Longepierre, the Moderns are trying to hold classical authors responsible for the ideology
of the age in which they lived (what he calls "the customs of those
times") and for not having respected modern standards of behavior
and modern systems of belief (93–94).

For Longepierre, the Moderns' greatest critical sin was their defense—in the name of this personal criticism, this personal judgment, and their new interest in issues of contemporary concern—
of their right to depart from interpretive tradition in order to investigate areas previously considered unimportant. At the core of his
Discours is a warning to authors and to critics not to stray from
well-worn paths. He advises modern writers that, since the ancients
long since "perfected" all genres, the only sure way to mastery is to
follow exactly in their footsteps (43–44). He admonishes would-be
critics that, since modern "eyes" are not "good" enough to measure
beauty, they should bask instead in the intellectual security that can
only come from remaining faithful to interpretive tradition: "All
people with good taste from all preceding ages have always felt the
way we do. . . . The Romans of the Augustan Age admired the
Greeks; later Romans admired both their ancestors and the Greeks,
just as our fathers admired all of them, and just as we admire them

ourselves" (25–26).[18] In the entire history of the Culture Wars, there is no clearer formulation than this of the doctrine on which the entire Ancient credo reposed. Good taste and correct literary values never vary: they are timeless *because* they are shared within the confines of a centuries-old tradition of the intellectual elite. "All people with good taste from all preceding ages have always felt the way we do."

To this formulation of the might and the right of a united and a unified "we," Perrault responds, in the initial 1688 volume of his *Parallèle des Anciens et des Modernes, en ce qui regarde les arts et les sciences*, with a far more developed formulation of the positions that, even in their embryonic development in *Le Siècle*, had brought down the wrath of the Ancients upon him. In its final form, the *Parallèle* is a prophetic creation: a miniature *Encyclopédie*, it is the first work to treat literary, artistic, and scientific accomplishments at the same time and as equally worthy of consideration. With the comparative method he developed in the *Parallèle*, Perrault pointed the way to the most characteristic Enlightenment production.

The *Parallèle* takes the form of a series of five dialogues among three friends, one Ancient, one Modern, and one divided in his opinions. The Modern is defined as an ideal participant in their exchanges because he is "richer in his own thoughts than in those of others." Because he is constantly "judging each thing on its own merits," all his ideas are "original" (3–4). The undecided interlocutor shares both the knowledge of the past ("science") that is the Ancient's principal contribution to their dialogue and the Modern's intellectual independence (4). All the theories central to the four imposing volumes of the *Parallèle*—the superiority of the Moderns over the Ancients; the existence of progress, artistic as well as scientific, which explains this superiority; and so forth—are clearly set forth in the initial volume. All in fact are a logical development of one central idea, the doctrine on which the entire Modern credo reposed: a nuanced and aggressive formulation of the doctrine of personal judgment. To the transcendental values of a timeless "we," Perrault opposes the right to individual choices and the infinitely varied and contemporary values of an "I" determined to maintain its critical independence.

In the opening lines of *Le Siècle*, Perrault had already coined a term for this personal judgment, a term with a prodigious future in France: that Louis's century is worthy of comparison to that of Augustus should be evident, he contends, to anyone with faith in his "propres lumières" (1).[19] In the *Parallèle*, Perrault uses another term to characterize this personal judgment and refers to what he had called in the *Siècle* an individual's "propres lumières" as "genius." To call attention to this new terminology, he closes the *Parallèle*'s initial volume by reprinting a previously published poem entitled "Le Génie."[20] In these lines, Perrault takes "genius" far beyond the sense of faith in one's personal abilities in which it initially functions in the *Parallèle*. "Le Génie" makes clear just how far the turning away from tradition could lead, just how dangerous—and how at odds with the neoclassical aesthetic doctrine then reigning in France—the defense of personal judgment could become. For Perrault, genius is not only personal and original; it is also an uncontrolled and an uncontrollable force:

> It is that [sacred] fire that shaped thunder and lightning
>
> . . . .
>
> Which . . . produces . . .
> All those men over whom one sees the sway
> Of a wonderful knowledge [*science*] that cannot be taught
>
> . . . .
>
> And all the other gifts that are part of genius. (1:30–31)

"Le Génie" conceals a remarkable intellectual document within its dreadful poetry. At a time when Perrault's contemporaries (notably Boileau in his notes to his translation of the pseudo-Longinus) were attempting to tame the uncontrolled aspects of the sublime and were preaching instead a more impersonal sublime dominated by the values of imitation rather than those of invention, Perrault advanced the terms of the debate radically. Perrault's "Le Génie" is an early indication that the defense of originality—we have a right to our personal taste (*Parallèle* 1:3–4, 36–37)—leads inevitably to the cult of originality, the notion that original, personal genius was the only value, that, beside it, (mere) imitation was virtually worthless. Indeed, in "Le Génie" and the *Parallèle* together, the entire trajectory of *genius* for more than a century to come can in fact be glimpsed—from its origins in the Moderns' affirmation of the right to personal judgment and taste, which they valued as signs of originality; to the eighteenth century's emphasis on *lumières*, genius as personal enlightenment or self-acquired knowledge uncontaminated by superstition; to the early nineteenth century's image of the inspired, visionary seer. It is hard to imagine a document more at odds with the Ancient credo that imitation and repetition, the foundation of the elite "we," were the only values. To conclude the initial volume of the *Parallèle* with "Le Génie" was a gesture of overt provocation.

Thus, the first two years of the literary war produced major texts and defined the issues that would remain controversial until the end. Despite so much clarity, however, this initial phase remains amazingly elusive. First, no matter how much intense passion they provoked within the Académie, the major issues then raised do not seem to have attracted the attention of a wide public. In contrast to subsequent stages, which became what we would call media events and received, once again in today's terminology, extensive press coverage, the war's initial salvos, from the *Siècle* to the *Parallèle*, were ignored by contemporary periodicals.[21] In addition, it is never exactly clear who is responding to what—in particular, if the Ancients were responding to the texts that make up the official history that I have just been describing or to documents in the parallel history I am about to describe. For example, at the time when Longepierre and other Ancient spokesmen were composing their initial attacks, they had access to the Modern doctrine only as it was represented in *Le Siècle*—and *Le Siècle*, it must be remembered, contains only a fraction of Perrault's arguments and none of them in their most developed state. Of course, controversial ideas (then as much as today) were surely in the air, even if in the seventeenth century they could not be bandied about with the speed we have acquired with our virtually instantaneous communication. It nevertheless seems likely that the Ancients were responding to other sources of provocation as well. Finally, whereas the Moderns were represented by their most vigorous spokesman, Perrault's self-delegated counterpart in the Ancient camp, Boileau, failed to come forward with the major response he had publicly promised the day the hostilities were declared. He maintained his silence in the face of renewed provocation. And that official silence on the part of the head Ancient is the surest indication that the controversy's initial development is more complicated than it seems—that the center of the Culture Wars was somehow hidden—although perhaps hidden in plain sight.

BEHIND THE SCENES

Je ne veux jamais entrer dans ce qui peut avoir quelque apparence de nouveauté que pour en empêcher le progrès.
—Louis XIV, speaking of Fénelon

After the fight in the Académie, Boileau mysteriously lost his voice. He left to take the waters; he returned a few months later in full voice, although the principal twentieth-century historian of French classical literature, Antoine Adam, implies that his loss of voice had been hysterical when he contends that "the waters played no role in curing him of his illness" (Boileau, *O.c.* xxxviii)—and Adam is hardly given to insidious insinuations of this kind. Commentators have never understood why, after all his threats and promises of retaliation, Boileau published nothing more impressive than a few occasional poems in defense of the Ancients (*O.c.* 257–58, 262–65). True, he claimed that the first nine of his *Réflexions critiques sur quelques passages de Longin* were his refutation of Perrault's positions in *Le Siècle de Louis le Grand* and the *Parallèle,* but this would hardly seem the most direct and forceful way of taking on an adversary who had driven him to public fury and literally out of his own voice. Besides, the first *Réflexions critiques* were not composed until five to seven years later (1692–94), when the war was well into its second phase and already centered on a totally new set of issues, so this was not the prompt response worthy of the man who would be head Ancient.[22]

Boileau did not, however, return from his "cure" empty-handed. What may have rid him of his symptom was the forthcoming appearance of the first edition, published in Holland, of the *Dialogue des héros de roman* (in 1688—that's the kind of speed the major players in the controversy always maintained). Boileau consistently denounced this edition and claimed it had been published without his consent, but its appearance in this context was, to say the least, convenient.[23] In this edition the dialogue bore a different title, *Dialogue des morts,* intended to identify it as a contribution to the literary war by evoking the already copious production by Moderns of so-called dialogues of the dead.[24] Unlike true dialogues of the dead, however, Boileau's text does not pair famous dead men, one ancient and one modern, for debate on a particular question. Boileau evokes a cast of mythological figures, notably Minos, who sit in judgment and condemn one modern literary form, the novel. They also condemn the authors of these works, in particular one author still very much alive in 1688, the foremost novelist of the first half of the seventeenth century, Madeleine de Scudéry. Boileau's *Dialogues des morts,* later *Dialogue des héros de roman,* is a violent attack on the novel genre, the first sign of what was to become a critical commonplace throughout the eighteenth century: the novel as an agent of corruption, as a dangerously subversive form of literature and a threat to the nation's moral fiber. To take on the novel during the first full year of the Culture Wars was also a perfect, albeit an indirect, attack on the Modern doctrine that originality was to be prized over tradition: the novel was the only genre to be developed in an important way in the seventeenth century that was *not* in any way an imitation of a genre known since antiquity.

If the *Dialogue*, rather than the occasional poetry he openly identified as contributions to the literary controversy, really was the detailed response to Perrault that he had vowed to produce ("as soon as he had the time") in January 1687, then this would not have been the first time that Boileau had crafted a highly circuitous rejoinder to the provocations of the literary Moderns. According to Desmarets de Saint-Sorlin, who for years waged war against the Ancients virtually single-handedly, the work considered Boileau's masterpiece and the foundation of his unsurpassed critical authority over the French tradition, *L'Art poétique* (1674), was composed in an attempt to discredit the "poèmes héroïques" of the Moderns.[25]

In the early 1670s, when Boileau was composing *L'Art poétique* and Desmarets was relentlessly provoking the Ancients, the expression *poème héroïque* had two referents. It designated in the first place the attempts to produce a great French epic, of which Desmarets's own *Clovis, ou la France chrétienne, poème héroïque* (1657) was perhaps the most prominent, as well as the most prominently disastrous, example. For *Clovis*'s third edition in 1673 (the year when Boileau was putting the finishing touches to *L'Art poétique*), Desmarets reprinted along with it the 1670 manifesto with which he had begun his career as proto-Modern polemicist, *Traité pour juger des poètes grecs, latins, et français*. In the *Traité*, Desmarets pleads the cause of the Moderns above all on grounds that already predict Perrault's credo: he praises their "inventiveness," their originality, which he defines as their ability to revitalize canonical literary genres and to imagine new ones. Among the rejuvenated genres, epic poetry leads Desmarets's list. Among those invented, he singles out "their excellent and delicious novels" (52). And this was the second possible referent of the term *poème héroïque* in the early 1670s: the novel, or rather the type of multivolume roman-fleuve that we refer to in English as a romance but which was known in French as a *roman* or a *poème héroïque*. Among the authors associated with this, the Modern genre par excellence according to Desmarets, none was more prominent than Madeleine de Scudéry, known above all for two ten-volume best-sellers, *Artamène, ou le Grand Cyrus* (1649–53) and *Clélie, histoire romaine* (1654–60).

By 1670, this link between epic and novel, the two forms of *poèmes héroïques*, was already a critical commonplace. The authors of the multivolume novels, and Scudéry in particular, had for some time proclaimed their right to be known as Homer's modern heirs.[26] In 1670, that theory received its most comprehensive and erudite formulation in Pierre-Daniel Huet's "Traité de l'origine des romans," which establishes an elaborate genealogy designed to present the *romans héroïques*, and in particular those of Madeleine de Scudéry, as the direct descendants of the classical epic.

Thus, when Desmarets suggested that Boileau wrote *L'Art poétique* in order to eradicate the Moderns' "poèmes héroïques," he clearly had the novel of epic proportions in mind. Boileau's masterpiece contains ample material to support this theory. In particular, in canto 3 Boileau devotes an extensive and particularly vituperative attack to Scudéry's best-known works, *Artamène* and *Clélie*. He attacks Scudéry above all on the grounds that she has degraded the standards for heroism set by the epic poetry of Greece and Rome. She has taken ancient heroes—Cyrus, Cato, Brutus—and made them "small," "weak," "sweet." Worst of all, she has feminized them, "portray[ing] Cato as gallant and Brutus as effeminate [*dameret*]" (Boileau 1969, 2:100–101).

By the early 1670s, the French "heroic novel" was thus widely perceived as having occupied the literary preserve traditionally reserved for classical epic poetry. By 1687–88 and the outbreak of the Culture Wars, to anyone who, like Boileau, considered the novel's new prominence a form of sacrilege, the situation would have appeared far darker still. In the intervening decades, the genre had continued to gain ground: more and more novels were being published, and a new generation of novelists—in particular, the comtesse de Lafayette and Marie-Catherine Desjardins, known as Madame de Villedieu—had begun to invent shorter, more modern, variants of the novel. By the time Boileau's *Dialogue des héros de roman* appeared in 1688, Scudéry was far from the only, or even the principal, threat: new women writers were demonstrating that the novel really had conquered epic's territory—Huet's treatise on the origin of novels was, in fact, published as a preface to Lafayette's first major novel, *Zayde*. By 1687, as the history of the novel's rise during the preceding two decades makes clear, the new generation of novelists had provided ample evidence of the more modern novel's ability both to obtain an even wider audience for prose fiction than the already broad readership won by Scudéry's heroic fiction and to promote what Boileau portrayed as social corruption, in particular what he thought of as the weakening and feminization of heroic values.[27]

In addition, in the years between 1670 and 1688, the stakes had become far higher. Boileau would perhaps have predicted this development, for, almost as an aside in his attack on the novel because of its desecration of epic's terrain, he slipped in a swipe at the theater for having, like the novel, lowered its standards for heroism and for having portrayed its heroes as governed by love's power: "Soon love . . . / Took over the theater, and the novel as well" (Boileau 1969, 2:100). (Boileau names no names here, but the obvious target was Racine, who was widely cited by his contemporaries for having made love the motivating passion for his heroes.) By 1688, what Boileau had perhaps guessed in the early 1670s was becoming clear: the novel was adding new territory to that it had already taken over from the epic. The novel's rise to prominence was simultaneous with the initial decline of tragedy, the genre whose modern development always received highest praise from Ancient critics. In 1637, a theatrical work, Le Cid, generated the controversy from which "the public" first emerged in its modern literary sense. The next time a literary work became the subject of such public debate in France, it was no longer a play, but a novel, Lafayette's La Princesse de Clèves (1678).

Indeed, the last French classical tragedy to provoke any significant level of public dissent was Racine's Phèdre (1677). However, the debate it generated, just the year before Lafayette's novel became the center of a storm so public (in all the new senses of the term) that it revolutionized the history of reading and the reception of literary works, proved that tragedy was no longer on the cutting edge of public literary concern. In 1677, the Parisian literary scene was divided over the relative merits of two plays based on the story of Phèdre that had been staged simultaneously: Racine's on 1 January 1677 and Nicolas Pradon's on 3 January. The conflict—and throughout my description I will be implicitly contrasting it with the very different controversy over Lafayette's novel that I will describe shortly—was almost entirely oral. It was acted out in the salons, at that time the most traditional setting for the expression of public literary opinion, but a forum that, as would soon be demonstrated, was in fact public only in a restricted sense.

The debate over the two Phèdres received no more than minimal coverage in the contemporary press. Le Mercure galant takes note of it on two occasions. The January 1677 issue contains a six-page letter comparing the plays and proclaiming the superiority of

Racine's (26–32). The April issue, which appeared after the plays had been published, contains an eight-page rehash of these questions, and also comes down on Racine's side (73–81). On that note, the paper's editor, Donneau de Visé, drops the issue for good.[28] The fact that this debate had nothing like the impact, in terms of both social and geographic scope, of the controversy that was generated by *La Princesse de Clèves* just one year later surely indicates that tragedy was losing public ground to the novel.

By the time the Culture Wars broke out a decade later, it must have been evident to all concerned that the novel—whose practitioners had continued to develop the analysis of love, the area that Racine had put at the center of his tragedies—that the novel, after having taken over the audience for epic, was now acquiring the territory traditionally reserved for tragedy, too.[29] Ancients such as Boileau must surely have been concerned that the theater—the seventeenth century's officially sanctioned art form and its official literary dream—seemed increasingly less able to inspire the progressively larger and more diverse public for literature that, as debate about *La Princesse de Clèves* had proved, was eager to respond to at least one other literary genre.[30] Before the story of that newly public debate, however, a last word on Boileau's voice and the relation between its disappearance and the outbreak of the Culture Wars in 1687.

When I hypothesize that Boileau allowed the publication of his attack on the novel as part of his effort to recover his voice, I want to suggest that he understood two factors that I will describe shortly: the genre's potential as a catalyst for public opinion as well as its role in creating a new public for literature. For Boileau the critic, the most essential task was to wipe out a new form that, by threatening to make literature dangerously Modern and promiscuously public, menaced the very foundation of the republic of letters as he wished to define it.

It would appear that the hostilities between Ancients and Moderns were finally openly declared in 1687 because the modifications in the business of literature associated with the new novel were by then becoming widely recognized. War broke out at that time, and the Ancients finally responded to the Moderns' provocations, because all involved sensed that something fundamental about the nature of literature was in the process of changing—and, furthermore, that the new changes were advancing the novel's takeover of territory previously reserved for nobler (Ancient) genres. Henceforth, as a result of this realignment, the stakes in making and evaluating literature were about to go up. This new context for literature is more to the point than any analysis of altered political or economic circumstances or any tale of personal animosity between key Ancients and Moderns. None of the types of history traditionally put at the service of literary history, *grande* no more than *petite*, can help account for the Culture Wars' chronology in the way that the history of readership can. In 1687, the Ancients responded to the Moderns' latest attempt to provoke them because they sensed that this polemic had a big future outside the academy. They sensed that by making it public, by appealing to a public audience to sit in judgment on these issues, they could make in the long run important territorial gains.

The Ancients were able to have these intuitions because, between 1670 and 1687, a major change had taken place in the literary world. A new public had been created for literature, invented by the gesture that made readers of literature literary critics. Readers, not scholarly or specialist readers, but average readers—a true literary public— had begun to decide in important numbers that they had a stake in the production of literature—that they were competent to decide what types of works should be produced and how these works should be interpreted.[31] This fundamental change in the operation of the French republic of letters had been instigated by literary Moderns. It was in fact a putting into practice of the key Modern credo— that nonspecialist readers, all those willing, as Perrault says, to be confident in "their personal understanding," their personal judgment, were able to think for themselves rather than blindly follow the dictates of scholars and scholarly tradition. The process and its potential consequences were so revolutionary that it is easy to see why the Ancients would have felt compelled to act.

The process I have in mind here, what may be the most revolutionary development on the French literary scene between 1670 and 1687, was orchestrated almost single-handedly by a rather unlikely player on that scene, Jean Donneau de Visé, best known for his role as the longtime editor (1672 to 1710) of *Le Mercure galant,* the most influential and most widely circulated early French public paper, the periodical that was in many ways the first true newspaper in France.[32] Donneau de Visé seems to have known instinctively what in fact became the case first in the pages of his paper, and subsequently during the fin de siècle Culture Wars, that literature had the potential to become news, even hot news. And, more than anyone else, he knew how to shape literature, how to stage it, so that the new public he reached out to came to view it as news. Moreover, he positioned himself resolutely on the Modern side throughout the period during which he was bringing about this revolution on the literary scene. Because of Donneau de Visé's efforts, literature went public and won a newly broad audience as a strictly Modern phenomenon.

There is ample evidence to suggest that the most influential Ancients understood the nature of the energy unharnessed by Donneau de Visé and realized that this phenomenon of literary news was coming under Modern control. For instance, in one of the occasional poems that were his overt response to the declaration of hostilities, "A Mr P***" (Perrault), Boileau announces that all the gods have resolved to avenge Homer, warns Perrault that he should be "afraid" of what lies ahead for him, and mocks the fact that he has no divine help on his side, only a "Mercure Galant."[33] In his *Caractères,* La Bruyère scornfully dismisses "Le H* G*"—*Le Hermès galant;* in other words, *Le Mercure galant*—as "just higher than nothing" (83, "Des Ouvrages de l'esprit," no. 46). He includes lengthy and repeated attacks on the "nouvelliste," that is, on the image of the journalist incarnated for his age by Donneau de Visé. He chastises him in particular for having made literary criticism a subject for public debate. According to La Bruyère, the "nouvelliste" should limit himself to reporting the simple facts of literary publishing and leave the business of interpretation to professional critics: "The responsibility of a journalist is to say: 'Such and such a book is being circulated, which was published by Cramoisy [a popular contemporary publisher] in this typeface, it is handsomely bound on fine paper, it is selling for this price'; he must know even the sign of the bookseller who is selling it: his madness leads him to want to talk about it as a critic would" ("Des Ouvrages de l'esprit," no. 33, 1689 ed.). La Bruyère was right: in the pages of *Le Mercure galant,* coverage of the literary scene was hardly limited to the facts. Donneau de Visé went to great lengths to involve his readers in noteworthy literary matters.[34] He went far beyond the simple business of informing them of the facts of the republic of letters in order to encourage them to become active participants in the business of literature.

Beginning with his preface to the paper's first issue in 1672, Donneau de Visé took pains to declare his intention of redefining the content of news. To the mixture of military and court news that was the standard fare in contemporary periodicals, *Le Mercure galant* added a particular focus—on novels and all types of publications that did not deal with arts and sciences (8). In addition to marking his paper's difference from its principal competitor, *Le Journal des savants*, Donneau de Visé's chosen content sent a message that those who believed that literary matters would continue to be negotiated only among scholars were wrong: Donneau de Visé clearly sensed that a new public was waiting to be constituted; he intended to target it specifically.

This chosen direction becomes even clearer when the paper was relaunched in 1678. The January issue features a short story, "La Vertu malheureuse," which is clearly a fiction but which Donneau de Visé, despite readers' objections, persisted in discussing in subsequent issues exactly as if it were just as real as the report of a battle, indicating thereby that the still developing new novel could be treated as news. Also that January, he began the practice of publishing supplements (*extraordinaires*). The inaugural one opens with an "éloge des femmes," in which Donneau de Visé formulates what will become, under Perrault's plume, a quintessential Modern argument—that women are at the origin of the best contemporary taste and judgment—and then targets female readers by promising that the new supplements "will be full, either with your own production, or with that which you have inspired others to produce" (1).[35]

A new content thus defined and a new audience thus targeted, Donneau de Visé immediately set about trying to commit the two principal crimes of which Longepierre would later find the Moderns guilty: he sought to identify issues of contemporary concern, and he encouraged his readers to believe in their right to personal judgment. From the outset, Donneau de Visé included various society games—enigmas and so forth—to encourage reader participation; he published responses in subsequent issues. By the time of the first supplement in January 1678, reader response was evidently flourishing: in a preface, Donneau de Visé reports that he has been receiving some five hundred to six hundred letters a month!

In order to guarantee the success of the revitalized *Mercure galant*, which was resuming publication at this time, Donneau de Visé capitalized on his ability to involve his readers. He made his campaign for the newspaper virtually synonymous with a campaign for what was destined to be known as the best of the new novels, *La Princesse de Clèves*. The centerpiece of both campaigns was a new type of letter to the editor: Donneau de Visé managed to provoke his readers to read in groups and to elect a secretary who sent in the reading collective's opinion on the issues about the novel that Donneau de Visé had raised. He was so successful that he received letters, almost always collective, from all over France and from a wide variety of milieus. Donneau de Visé's commercial strategy, in other words, resulted in the creation of by far the most public literary audience to date.[36]

Donneau de Visé's revitalization of *Le Mercure galant* was based on the spread of literary debate into groups and areas where it had undoubtedly been previously unknown. The quintessential *Mercure galant* scene, recreated in every issue at the time of the relaunching, stages a literary discussion, a debate, or, more exactly, a quarrel over literary issues. In early versions of it, Donneau de Visé describes a group of friends who meet to consider the merits of a work and end up fighting over literary issues. Once his idea took off, and vast numbers of readers began to do just what Donneau de Visé had encouraged them to do from the start—write in to give their opinions on questions raised in these staged scenes—he was able to take *Le Mercure galant*'s signature scene to a higher level and quote letters from his readers in which they describe actually engaging in just the kind of debate that Donneau de Visé had first envisioned in print. According to the testimony provided by these letters, he was actually able to use his newspaper to generate miniature literary quarrels all over France, especially in milieus in which such debate had undoubtedly not previously been conceivable. The literary-critical debates staged by Donneau de Visé in the pages of the first truly public French newspaper define the business of the nascent genre in the following manner: the news that a newspaper should report was the proliferation of new publics for literature, the process by which ordinary readers with no literary training were, according to the terms of La Bruyère's critique of the "nouvelliste," being encouraged to become "crazy" enough to think they were qualified to "faire de la critique," "to talk about [books] as a critic would."

To illustrate the process I have in mind, let us examine the most significant example of the invention of a new public for literature in the pages of *Le Mercure galant*. In the months just preceding the publication of the seventeenth century's best-known novel, *La Princesse de Clèves*, in March 1678, and for just over a year after the novel's appearance, Donneau de Visé (who had close political ties to Lafayette and her circle) staged an impressive publicity campaign for the new work.[37] This campaign functioned both to create public interest for a new work (what we would think of as a standard journalistic endeavor) and to do so by convincing nonprofessional readers that they could judge a literary work (that is, by encouraging the practice of criticism in the way that provoked La Bruyère's fury). In addition, the campaign demonstrates that, from the beginning of the novel's existence (*La Princesse de Clèves* is generally accepted as the first modern French novel), a special bond was forged between the newspaper and the novel. When Boileau subsequently attacked the novel, therefore, he was taking on at the same time the democratization of literary criticism that public papers were bringing about.

Initially, Donneau de Visé published some opinions composed by professional critics, most famously, an early interpretation of *La Princesse de Clèves* known as the "letter by a geometrician from Guienne," alias future Modern activist Fontenelle. Fontenelle provides a model for the untrained responses to follow. His commentary on *La Princesse de Clèves* blends critical judgment ("nothing could be more artistically crafted than the birth and the development of [Madame de Clèves's] passion for the duc de Nemours") with moral judgment ("She makes a crime out of her inclination [for Nemours]"). Throughout, Fontenelle reduces the novel to a series of issues on which virtually any reader would have an opinion (a wife's conduct after her husband's death, and so forth). Throughout, he frames his commentary in resolutely personal terms: "All this seems exactly right *to me*" (May 1678, 58, my emphasis). This was literary criticism formulated expressly to encourage nonprofessional readers to have faith in their personal judgment and to offer their opinions on the questions raised.

Then, immediately after the novel's publication, Donneau de Visé printed the first of a series of "gallant questions" phrased as an invitation to his readers to do just that. The questions were designed both to render the novel controversial (to make it newsworthy) and to incite his readers to discourse on the novel (to empower them to sit in literary judgment): "I ask if a virtuous woman, who has all the esteem possible for her husband . . . , but who is also torn by a wildly strong passion for a lover, [a passion] that she tries to suppress in every way; I ask . . . if this woman . . . would do better to confide in her husband about this passion or to keep quiet about it, knowing that she will be constantly obliged to do battle with herself when she is forced to see this lover, from whom she has no other way of distancing herself than by confiding [in her husband]" (April 1678).[38]

Donneau de Visé's leading question was printed in the April issue (the month immediately following the novel's publication), Fontenelle's model reply in the May paper. By October, the traditional month of the *rentrée* for all Parisian entertainment seasons, Donneau de Visé was able to report that readers had been responding in droves—so much so that, for an entire year, each issue of *Le Mercure galant* contained a selection of letters to the editor written in response to the invitation to sit in judgment on Lafayette's novel. The second stage in Donneau de Visé's invention of a new audience for literature involved the reproduction in the pages of *Le Mercure galant* of the process by which the interpretive communities he had fostered had come to formulate literary judgments.

By far the most striking aspect of this process is the fact that each letter, as Donneau de Visé points out when he publishes the first selection, goes beyond reporting the views of a solitary reader and records literary debate and dissent among a group of readers, representing thereby the judgment "of a society that had gathered together to debate such a delicate question" (October 1678, 317). Donneau de Visé had succeeded in provoking his readers to help found the genre of personal criticism, and he had also succeeded in making the process a collective effort. Furthermore, as the letters' signatures prove, these new publics had been constituted all over France and among readers who, as far as can be told, were seldom members of the traditional cultural elite. For the first time in France, a literary controversy was both being formulated and being played out largely outside what had always been the unique center of cultural power, the almost exclusively aristocratic Parisian audience. *Le Mercure galant*'s campaign for the new novel had created a truly public audience for literature.[39]

In fact, the letters Donneau de Visé publishes record a process of coming to authority that was triply participatory, triply public. There was, in the first place, an experience of collective reading. One correspondent notes, for example, how excited people are to see you if you have *Le Mercure galant* in your hand so that they can read it with you (July 1678, 39–40). The most complex missive in the August 1678 issue recounts the story of a provincial family gathered together for the signing of a marriage contract. One member arrives with a copy of the April issue with its "gallant question" regarding "a virtuous woman's" marital conduct: the question is read aloud to the assembled guests, and they proceed to argue among themselves about the proper behavior (320).

Thus, collective reading seems to lead inevitably to the second phase, collective dispute. And that process leads in turn to a third phase, a process of writing that, while it obviously could not have been truly collective, was designed to take the collective's views into account. Each interpretive community chose a member to serve as its secretary; the secretary usually remained anonymous and used a signature that designated the collectivity: "the Academy of Great Minds [*Beaux-Esprits*] of the rue de la Monnoye" (a street in Troyes; April 1678, supplement, 177), for example, or simply "the city of Beauvais" for a group from that town (April 1678, supplement, 211). By the end of the *Princesse de Clèves* affair, even as unlikely a group as the "Bakers from Gonnesse" sends in its joint opinion (January 1679, supplement, 125).[40]

In their answers to Donneau de Visé's questions, these reading collectives recorded their debates about the novel's merits (they sat as literary judges). They also related its actions to their own lives (they sat as moral judges). These fledgling critics, in other words, responded to the work in the manner of literary Moderns by relying on what Perrault later termed their "personal judgment" to see literature in its relation to modern life, rather than as a vehicle for timeless values, as Ancients such as Longepierre believed was necessary. Their responses are marked above all by a sense of the work's novelty, its newness. One reader, for example, contrasts "husbands of today" with their precursors (July 1678, 40). Other readers are taken aback by what they consider an excess of honesty. One after another they insist that undue sincerity is bound to be misinterpreted. For example, the princess's husband may think that she wants to remain in the country because her "retreat" would shelter her rendezvous with her lover (July 1678, 334). A reader from Grenoble expresses this collective bewilderment best: "We have to admit that marriage has its laws, and that it is dangerous for those embarked on it not to follow them" (July 1678, 306). In the opinion of this man, named Bouchet, the princess broke the law with her honesty and with her desire for a life in "retirement."

The responses are also marked by a sense of irresolution. Within each collective there is dissent, and the secretary gives a sense of the different views represented. Nowhere is this more evident than in the case of a provincial couple from Bassigny who meet in the company of family and friends to sign their marriage contract. In the midst of the ensuing free-for-all over the princess's behavior, the couple quickly discover their opposing views. Their quarrel becomes so heated that only through mediation are they persuaded to go ahead with their union (August 1678, 317–21).

Thus, the scenario played out by Donneau de Visé in his newspaper and fed back to him by his obviously eager readers served as a repeated *mise en abyme* of the critical act, an open call to other readers to enter into debate about literary issues. In the pages of *Le Mercure galant* in 1678, what we now call literary criticism was for the first time staged in public.[41] Donneau de Visé's decision to use his newspaper to invest readers with the authority to judge literary texts signaled a major turning point for criticism: from an ivory tower discourse the classical age had inherited from humanism and the pronouncements of scholars speaking for and to an audience of their colleagues, criticism began moving into the public sphere and becoming something closer to a form of collective judgment. Donneau de Visé was promoting the democratization of criticism, and, lest anyone miss the point, he continued for years to stage what I call critical scenes like the one just described—and to stage them in the most public print forum available at the time.

A major consequence of this opening up of literary criticism was obviously the democratization of taste. The traditional intellectual elite's claim to cultural leadership in France was seriously threatened by this appeal to the taste of the century's equivalent of a mass audience. By arguing that any reader could pass judgment on literary works, Donneau de Visé was in effect contending that all readers were created equal, and implying that the reign of one class's—and one sex's—cultural superiority was over.[42] Indeed, in 1719, just after the Culture Wars had ended, Abbé Jean-Baptiste Du Bos, in what came to be known as the first major expression of Enlightenment aesthetic theory, *Réflexions critiques sur la peinture et sur la poésie*, provides a definition of *le public* that proves just how influential Donneau de Visé and the Moderns had been and just how far a leading aesthetic philosopher was prepared to take the notion of a democratization of taste: "The word *public* is used here to mean those persons who have acquired enlightenment, either through reading or through life in society [*le commerce du monde*]. They are the only ones who can determine the value of poems or paintings" (2:351). For Du Bos, the right to judge is acquired solely as a result of exposure to a number of works sufficient to develop a comparative sense, and print culture can provide this exposure just as effectively as salons and other then traditional forms of social commerce. Du Bos is even prepared to make *le public* a truly popular concept— "outstanding works contain beauty that can be felt by those in the lowest ranks" (2:351)—except for the fact that this audience does not have sufficient occasion for comparison to allow it to determine a work's relative value.

With the help of coconspirators, many of whom were aristocrats (Lafayette, for instance, was certainly active in shaping the campaign around her novel), Donneau de Visé was creating a new, far more public space for criticism and for literature. With the developments in *Le Mercure galant,* we can retrace the creation of a place for public opinion. In this case, however, a place was made for public opinion not on matters political, as had previously been the case in France, but for public literary opinion. In *Le Mercure galant* in 1678, literature had become news.

This complicated process could never have taken place had criticism not forged a union in the 1670s with the public papers, or at least with *Le Mercure galant.* Also in the 1670s criticism and periodicals made a parallel union with a new literary form, which we now call the novel but was then called either *histoire* or *nouvelle.* Those contemporary names indicate just where the literary form fit into the new scheme of things. The novel was a genre with which readers could identify, in whose actions, as *Le Mercure galant's* readers prove to us, they could recognize themselves. It was the genre that could shape their lives—could make them decide, for instance, if they wanted to be more like "husbands of today" or "husbands of yesterday"—at least in the image of those categories proposed by the literary circle from Grenoble in July 1678. Donneau de Visé, ever the clever promoter, sensed that the novel was the only contemporary literary form for which he could work up such widespread interest. This explains why he devised a radically new format for dealing with the debate over *La Princesse de Clèves,* whereas only the year before he had reported the controversy over the two *Phèdres* in a perfectly traditional manner.[43]

In the course of the controversy he created over Lafayette's novel, Donneau de Visé played still another pedagogical role. He was teaching his readers a new way of reading: to read a newspaper like a novel and to read a novel like a newspaper. Hence his insistence in January 1678 that "La Vertu malheureuse," a short story that miniaturizes the plot of *La Princesse de Clèves* and whose publication therefore announced the upcoming campaign, was a true story, as though he were reporting a news flash and not a fiction. In his critique, La Bruyère revealed his understanding of this aspect of the *nouvelliste's* project: "If he reports news [*conte une nouvelle*], it's less in order to reveal it to his public than to have the merit of telling it and telling it well; in his hands, news becomes a novel" (33).[44]

By choosing *La Princesse de Clèves* as the centerpiece for the first literary controversy in the new mode, Donneau de Visé in effect established the novel as the literary form to be associated with the Moderns.[45] It was fitting both that the controversy be staged around Lafayette's novel and that *La Princesse de Clèves* become the exemplary Modern literary work. Composed in Paris by an aristocrat, with the collaboration of a group of aristocrats and bourgeois who lived as though they were aristocrats, then served up to a wide audience of provincial readers of mixed social background so that they could recognize themselves in its plot—Lafayette's novel pinpoints the complex class origins of the first true literary public in France.

THE REMAINS OF THE DAY

Sous Louis XIV, la France a appris à se connaître.
—Bossuet, *Oraison funèbre de Marie-Thérèse d'Autriche*

Together the newspaper, the novel, and literary criticism had made literature newly public, had opened a public space for literature, a space in which it was appreciated, evaluated, even lived out. The new space for public opinion coinhabited by the newspaper and the novel proved at the same time immensely appealing to Moderns and immensely threatening to Ancients. The structure on which Donneau de Visé had founded it, the public quarrel over literary issues, also proved immensely influential. I am suggesting that the Culture Wars finally broke out when they did because their principal players understood that there was a newly invented public for literary debate.[46] They staged a literary controversy designed to capitalize on this new public interest; in so doing, they were reproducing on a large scale scenarios initially tried out in the pages of *Le Mercure galant.* In addition, the first seven years of the literary war's activity were dominated by concerns brought obsessively to public attention by *Le Mercure galant.*

In particular, *Le Mercure galant* first made its diverse readership aware of an issue that is at the origin of the Culture Wars: the role of women as producers and as consumers of literature. From this perspective, the fact that Donneau de Visé staged his most elaborate attempt to inspire the desire for interpretive communities around a novel written by a woman is not only a logical extension of the paper's pro-female bias that Donneau de Visé had made explicit from the beginning—it also appears an act of provocation worthy of a Perrault. For, even if the new public for literature generated in the 1670s was not as radically diverse in class terms as the literary public would become in the eighteenth century, its diversity was radical in another way: in terms of gender. In "the public"'s initial incarnation as an audience for literature, the new audience was designed to be gender blind.

If Boileau's attack on the novel, his *Dialogue des héros de roman,* is indeed his principal response to Perrault's *Le Siècle de Louis le Grand*, then it could be argued that for the man the Ancients referred to as "the lawmaker of Parnassus," women's role as producers and judges of literature was a, perhaps even the, central motivation behind his decision to lead his cohorts into battle. Indeed, in all Perrault's writing during the time of controversy, he did everything he could to provoke his adversary on this question. He rarely misses an opportunity to introduce the related issues of women as consumers of literature, and even as arbiters of literary taste. Time after time, he links the new, independent critical thinking that was at the center of the Moderns' position to what he terms "women's judgment" (1:31). According to Perrault's fictive Modern, the abbé, women are gifted with an inherent "discernment," a "sensitivity . . . to all that is clear, lively, natural, and sensible."

Perrault then moves from this essentialist view to present perhaps the most interesting construction of gender in the early modern age. In the *Parallèle*, women's judgment serves as the model for the Modern vision of authority, taste, and genius (see, in particular, 1: 3–4, 36–37). The Moderns would be victorious if they could learn to imitate "women's judgment," in particular "the accuracy of their discernment" (1:30). In the *Parallèle*, personal judgment, the right to individual taste and to personal criticism that was the Moderns' rallying cry, becomes synonymous with women's judgment. To be a Modern, according to the movement's most vocal proponent, it was not necessary to be a woman, but it was necessary to think, to judge, and to reason as a Woman.

The question of women's role in the republic of letters—and even in the republic in general—was apparently the subject that finally raised the level of animosity between Ancients and Moderns to the breaking point. Boileau attacked Perrault's Modernist stance with his most violent contribution to date, not on Perrault's own grounds of gender, a construction of the female, but on far more literal terms of essentialism by claiming that women were ruining contemporary family life as a result of their new participation in the republic of letters. In March 1694, Boileau published his tenth satire, referred to by contemporaries such as Racine as the "Satire on Women." In it, he combines an attack on women writers (Scudéry's *Clélie* is denounced as a work dangerous enough to inspire its female readers to "a début in crime" [*O.c.* 110]) with an attack on women as consumers of literature (for them, "any poetry is good, as long as it is new" [*O.c.* 113]) with an attack on women as literary arbiters (they are responsible for the success of all bad modern authors and for contemporary "bad taste" in general [113]). These attacks, as well as Boileau's contemptuous references to modern authors and to women's role in promoting them in the struggle over ancient and modern authors (O.c. 113), prove that he was responding in the satire to the link established by Perrault between Modern judgment and women's judgment.[47]

Throughout the satire, Boileau's attacks against women become ever wilder. They all culminate in an accusation that women have become the principal agents of corruption in an ever-more-corrupt society. In its concluding lines, the satire degenerates into a fantastic vision of women infiltrating good families in order to bring them down. Boileau warns young men that one scenario has become increasingly pervasive: you marry an angel; she turns out to be a devil; you think you can part ways amicably; she takes you to court and cleans you out. The triumph of literary modernity, in other words, would inevitably signify the ruin of the families that were the foundation of the French state.[48] Boileau's "Satire on Women" is perhaps the clearest illustration of the evolution from the anxiety over a loss of control over the process by which cultural judgments were passed, the anxiety that had led to the outbreak of the Culture Wars, to a fin de siècle mentality. By the satire's conclusion, women are blamed, no longer simply for the spread of bad literary taste and the promotion of inferior authors, but for the end of civilization as the French knew it. By 1694, the fin de siècle mentality, the foundations of which had been laid in 1688, had fully set in.

Within months, Perrault had taken up this latest challenge from the Ancient camp. When he published a work entitled *Apologie des femmes,* he made it clear that the alleged *literary* war was in fact a struggle between conflicting visions of French society. In a preface, Perrault complains that his adversary has no right to "follow the example of ancients such as Horace and Juvenal" in their "scandalous" and "shameless" attacks on women; contemporary mores, like contemporary women, are "completely different." In the "apology" itself, Perrault imagines a dialogue between a father and his unmarried son, in which the father contends that talk of women's pernicious influence is highly exaggerated. If the son looks closely, he will discover that women are most often virtuous. The man who had first given rise to fin de siècle anxieties by announcing the end of progress, when faced with the way that blame for the end of civilization was being laid at the Moderns' feet, turned to a new, anxiety-free discourse.

As soon as rumors of the impending publication of these two

works began to circulate, the most respected authorities evidently decided that things had gone far enough, that the Culture Wars had gotten so out of control that they had to be brought to an official close. After all, the "Satire on Women" and the *Apology for Women* indicate clearly that the head Ancient (and perhaps his followers as well) was more anxious about the rising influence of women and novels than about issues such as Homer's existence. Eight years of the most frenzied debate of the entire classical age—during which issues as fundamental to literary life as the importance of the author, the status of imitation, and the right to critical judgment received their first extensive airing in early modern times—had culminated in petty charges and countercharges about women's marital virtue.

Antoine Arnauld, the spokesman for Jansenism known as "the great Arnauld," a name synonymous with intellectual integrity, was selected to stage a public reconciliation. An elaborately casual scenario was approved by both sides. Appropriately, the setting chosen was the Académie Française, the place where all the trouble had begun in January 1687. Accordingly, on 30 August 1694, in front of their fellow Academicians, Boileau and Perrault formally embraced. After years of increasingly public and increasingly acrimonious conflict, the matter seemed finally to have been brought under a precarious control—although, since the ink was hardly dry on the wildest accusations made by the two Academicians acting out that public embrace, many of those present can hardly have failed to wonder just how authentic the reconciliation between Ancients and Moderns would prove to be.

Amazingly, however, it was to last for more than fifteen years, despite the fact that, during that time, the influence of novels, of newspapers, and of women writers all continued to develop, most often together, so that anyone of Boileau's ilk could have believed that the Modern style was sweeping the nation. And, when the conflict finally did break out again, its second stage was so different from what had preceded that it most often seems as if one were dealing with a new development. Indeed, it is possible to argue that this was in fact the case. True, Ancients and Moderns began attacking each other all over again. True, many familiar issues were at the heart of their disputes: whether one should prefer ancient authors or the modern counterparts; whether personal judgment or faith in tradition should be the basis for cultural values, and so forth. However, the new Culture Wars were no longer truly Culture Wars, for they were no longer a fin de siècle phenomenon. As I will try to show when I return to the controversy's history in the following chapter, they were no longer bound up in the anxieties of a century's end. They were no longer driven principally by a belief in the imminent dissolution of civilization, but by forces that were seeking ways of rebuilding after the questioning of long-accepted values that the first controversy had unleashed.

In the midst, however, of the unfamiliar terrain of the new Culture Wars that were not, a familiar presence can be noted—*Le Mercure galant* structuring its coverage of the controversy around techniques first developed for the promotion of *La Princesse de Clèves.* During the dispute's final, most active phase, the paper was under the direction of a new editor, Hardouin Le Fèvre de Fontenay (editor from 1714 to 1716). If we are to believe the running account of the controversy's last years printed by Le Fèvre, it is clear that, by 1715, the public first reached out to by Donneau de Visé had truly become a power to be reckoned with in the republic of letters. In a lengthy article in the February 1715 issue, Le Fèvre stresses the immense power it now enjoyed: "The affair [the literary war] became serious; poets and literary judges, in league with *le peuple commentateur,* swept the masses along—who dared oppose this torrent?" (February 1715, 186–87). It was a scenario out of Boileau's worst dreams. By 1715, the new audience that initially recognized itself via debate on issues such as a virtuous woman's conduct was described as a vast audience and one so clearly confident of its powers of judgment that, in its new guise as "le peuple commentateur," it had become a true eighteenth-century force, capable of decisive influence, a force with the revolutionary potential of "swe[eping] the masses along." It a major way, the events of this particular history of the book were clearly setting the stage for the Enlightenment.

In the following issues, Le Fèvre addresses himself directly to this interpretive community, which he defines, just as Du Bos would four years later, in what was evidently the term's newly accepted meaning, as all those who are neither professional scholars nor the masses. To this end, he adopts the techniques developed by his precursor to foster the development of its original incarnation. Once again, therefore, literary quarrels are provoked and recreated in the pages of the newspaper. This time, however, "le public commentateur" is asked to involve itself, no longer in any way with literary texts, but solely with literary commentary. Thus, in April 1715—in the manner of Donneau de Visé's tale of the betrothed couple at war over *La Princesse de Clèves*—Le Fèvre recounts a quarrel overheard in the Tuilleries between two women at war over a recently published Ancient manifesto, Anne Dacier's *Des Causes de la cor-*

ruption du goût: the brunette takes the side of the Moderns, while her blond companion defends the Ancient position on Homer (162–78). The May issue contains word games (*bouts-rimés*) about Homer; its follow-up prints readers' solutions (250–51).

And in the July issue, the space reserved for the interpretive community is opened further still when, like his precursor posing "questions galantes" about the conduct of Lafayette's heroine, Le Fèvre asks readers, "Who is right, Mme Dacier, who has given us her translation of Homer as though it were perfectly faithful to the original, or M. de La Motte, who chose to give an imitation of the same author?" (257). He continues this tactic in the October issue, when he asks "if anyone can tell us at last if there really was a Homer, and if this time we can get a definitive yes or no" (238–41).

The familiar presence of *Le Mercure galant* during the final phase of the Culture Wars proves how complete the victory of Donneau de Visé and the Moderns had been in this area at least. They had successfully promoted the belief that an informed public had a right to its opinions about subjects in which it took an interest. They had created a new public, a public willing to question and doubt, trusting in its own judgment and taste. The process initiated by Donneau de Visé in the name of the Moderns is a major piece in the puzzle that, when assembled, can explain the radical shift in *mentalité* that was taking place at the time of the Culture Wars. The questioning and doubting of established systems that is so fundamental to Enlightenment thought first became a widespread and an accepted practice on the relatively unthreatening terrain of the novel and of literary criticism. French readers tried out their personal judgment debating the conduct of husbands, literary and real, or the question of Homer's existence. Through this process of coming to doubt the validity of received ideas and interpretive tradition, they became a public prepared to tackle the far more sweeping questioning of accepted systems and values on which the Enlightenment project was constructed. Perhaps at no other time have the history of readers and reading and literary opinion's role in the public sphere exercised such a powerful influence, first within the republic of letters and eventually outside it as well, both as forces for intellectual change and even as forces for political change.

In addition, *Le Mercure galant*'s rapid success in creating a new public, in conjunction with the propensity for intellectual dispute that was the trademark of the Culture Wars, had a decisive impact on the history of the press. *Le Mercure galant* was the first French paper to predict the functioning of our modern newspapers. It was the earliest paper to include true articles, rather than mere listings, articles that presented detailed coverage of incidents. It was also the first paper never to have served as an official court organ. Thus, just as the novel eventually found an audience far broader and more diverse than that reached by the genre previously dominant in France, classical theater, so Donneau de Visé's newly redesigned *Mercure galant* marked the beginning of a new age for the newspaper. It was the first sign of what a paper should be in order to find a modern audience. Indeed, just at the end of the Culture Wars, in 1716, the first two ancestors of our daily press were created: Du Bois de Saint-Gelais's *Histoire journalière de Paris* and Jean Dugonne's *Affiches de Paris, des provinces, et des pays étrangers*. With the controversy staged in *Le Mercure galant*'s pages over the novel and questions essential to the Moderns' program for change, the conflict between Ancients and Moderns became bound up, therefore, with the most significant opening up in the circulation of information in early modern France.

Furthermore, Jean Sgard has called the 1680s, the decade just after *Le Mercure galant* had invented its new public, the moment when "the press in French took off economically" (Martin and Chartier 199). Note that he says "the press in French," rather than the French press: just as the Moderns encouraged French readers to broaden their horizons to include modern authors and even— in a gesture that made of them perhaps the earliest proponents of what is now know as comparative literature—other European literary traditions, so, under the influence of such expansiveness, in the 1680s newspapers printed in French began to be published in other European capitals. This new press became increasingly wide-ranging and more truly critical. In 1683, Pierre Bayle began editing *Nouvelles de la République des Lettres*, featuring a great diversity of literary and scientific subjects. In 1686, Jean Le Clerc initiated *Bibliothèque universelle et historique*, and the following year Basnage de Beauval started *Histoire des ouvrages des savants*, both of which included analysis of books published in many languages. All three were published outside of France and widely distributed; all three were more judgmental than their precursors. Their example was quickly and widely imitated.[49]

Indeed, this expansion was so remarkably efficient that, in the issue in which Le Fèvre defines "le public commentateur," he cites newspapers published in French in several European cities and refers to them as "tribunals constituted to sit in judgment on works" (February 1715, 188). Not only had the public become more open and more diverse within France—by the end of the Culture Wars, there was a pan-European, French-speaking audience for literature. The brand of nationalism practiced by the Moderns had had perhaps no more significant victory than this: it had played a crucial role in setting off the most impressive flowering that the French language would ever know. Had not French been transformed into the so-called universal language by the time the Enlightenment became an intellectual movement, had there not existed a public large, diverse, critical, *and* French-speaking, even if not necessarily French, as well, French thinkers could never have achieved such universally recognized control over the entire project.

In other ways, however, the victory of the Moderns seems less glowing. For instance, whereas the rapid expansion of the literary public was in general a phenomenon with remarkably positive consequences, it had at least one important negative effect on the future of French intellectual life: it created a rift between the two audiences for literature that has never been successfully bridged. In this case, it is clear that the Moderns not only saw what could happen, but encouraged the split between the traditional audience of scholars and the new general audience. In the preface to the *Parallèle*, Perrault unleashes his most inflammatory rhetoric on what he terms the "nation of scholars" who will never "be able to accept my reasoning . . . because they have too much to lose." In the redefined intellectual world that Perrault hopes to make a reality, all intellectual "riches" on which such scholars have traditionally lived would become worthless, and all their "merits" would be "abolished," while at the same time "every man with intelligence and good sense" would obtain "a distinguished rank" (11–12). Perrault's description seems to have been designed to provoke as much antagonism as possible. The victory of the Moderns, according to their chief spokesperson, was to signify both financial ruin and social humiliation for the traditional intellectual elite.

Such a stance makes it clear why, even though the Moderns won the battle for the general audience, they lost the war, in the sense that they permanently alienated those with power over the major institutions of the republic of letters, above all over what we would term today simply the university.[50] This alienation, furthermore, could not have taken place at a more influential moment: the Culture Wars mark the beginning of the transition from literature's existence primarily within the confines of the court and related, largely aristocratic structures, to literature's existence within systems, such as the university, dominated by pedagogues, critics, and journalists. Thus, in a development whose consequences are so far-reaching that they are often still visible today, the Moderns virtually lost control over sectors in which the choice between the opposing programs of Ancients and Moderns would have made a crucial difference: above all, the writing of literary history and the establishment of a pedagogical canon. And they created an antagonism at the core of the republic of letters the likes of which has never existed in any other country and that remains persistent in France: witness the example of Barthes as neo-Modern once again and still lashing out against the French university system and *la critique universitaire* in the late 1960s, hoping to get a new general audience involved in the latest round of internecine critical warfare.

The Moderns also created anxieties that were truly repressed only decades later, when the Enlightenment had gathered considerable force, of which the anxiety about the class of the scholar, which Perrault made agonizingly evident, is but one example. These manifestations of fin de siècle anguish were, therefore, woven into the very fabric of Enlightenment thought.

Furthermore, the initial rise of the French language on its way to enjoying hegemony over all modern languages was also involved with these complicated and ambivalent developments. The language's first wave of prominence was simultaneous with the recognition of the attraction of what we would now term *métissage*—in the sense of cultural creolization—the fantasy of somehow having two cultures at the same time. Indeed, this recurrence of what is hardly a commonplace culture desire, the pull toward a fundamental state of confusion, may well be the most striking similarity between the two fins de siècle born in the shadow of Culture Wars. How many periods generate an attraction to the idea of raiding across traditionally impermeable boundaries—of gender, of class, and so forth? How many periods glorify the confusion that would result from such transgressions by transforming it into a positive myth?

Our age, of course, in which, under Modern inspiration, we have gone far beyond simple attraction to revel in theoretical dreams of blending that most epochs would consider pure barbarism. Witness the currently fashionable theoretical dream of finding a state, as the saying goes, beyond gender, beyond race, and so forth. And similar theoretical dreams are evident at the seventeenth century's end, though naturally in a more timid way. Then, under Modern inspiration, men fantasized about being women, in their heads at least. Aristocrats entertained the notion that individual merit rather than class distinctions might decide who was fit to determine cultural values.

There were even hints, perhaps the first ever, that racial purity was not a necessary foundation for cultural hegemony. Witness, for example, Fontenelle, in his *Digression sur les Anciens et les Modernes*, published during that explosive opening year 1688, already arguing *against* the soon to be widely held theory that the effects of climate on a race's intellectual development were absolute: just because there have been no examples so far, this does not mean that we cannot "hope to see one day great authors who are Lapp or Negro" (213). In fact, the striking receptiveness to what we would now term diversity on the part of Moderns such as Fontenelle and Perrault may be among the only factors that could help account for the nearly contemporaneous counterproclamation that racial purity was a necessary precondition for cultural superiority, perhaps the most impressive such proclamation ever formulated by any European nation: the *code noir,* the first systematic legal code for the regulation of relationships between the races, was promulgated at Versailles in 1685, on the eve of the Culture Wars' explosion.[51]

As all these closely related conflicts make clear, any publication of the attraction to a new status beyond commonly accepted boundaries, even if it remains purely theoretical, is double-edged—as certain to provoke at least as much anxiety and, therefore, a backlash of -isms (sexism, and so forth) as it inspires enthusiasm. It may even be, I would further suggest, that such intense conflict from within a culture about the extent to which that culture should be open to otherness is an ironic, necessary prelude to that culture's rise to a position of absolute dominance. It is as if an inherently conflicted origin formed an essential backdrop to national greatness.

Of all the concepts associated with the desire for cultural *métissage,* none was more productive than Perrault's suggestion that, to be a true Modern, it was necessary to reason as a Woman. Thus, one of the creators of the Enlightenment, Montesquieu—in many ways, the perfect moderate, whose thinking was divided between Ancient and Modern positions—records in his *Pensées* an observation that proves how powerfully Perrault's suggestion continued to resonate a half-century later. He concludes a passage in which he reflects, obviously under the influence of issues raised during the Culture Wars, on changing taste in reading by declaring that "there is only one sex, and we are all women in our thinking" (389).[52]

To this point, Montesquieu's reflection could be mistaken for a renewed expression of Perrault's enthusiasm at the prospect of men thinking as women. However, the sentence continues: "If, one night, we were to change faces, no one would even notice that there was a difference." Furthermore, elsewhere in the passage this anxiety at the prospect of complete sexual indifference gives way to open misogyny: "All we know anymore are vaguely defined objects [*les objets généraux*], and, in practice, this comes down to nothing. The commerce of women has brought us to this: because it's not in their nature to remain attached to anything stable" (389).

Thus, in Montesquieu's conflicted musings, the complex heritage of even the Moderns' victories is evident. The Moderns' fascination with the possibility of thinking as a Woman reverberated in the *mentalité* produced by the Culture Wars in a double fashion—just as is happening today with the violently opposing reactions to new proposals for cultural *métissage* or creolization. On the one hand, certain writers exalted in the possibility of being confused and confusing, in the prospect of uncanny double-voicing—Marivaux is the prime example—and experimented with the creation of a literary style that, from the early eighteenth century to our day, has been simultaneously acclaimed and reviled because it is seen as inherently feminine. On the other hand, writers such as Montesquieu—as well as numerous other far more virulent examples—are moved by some combination of attraction and revulsion to Perrault's magnetic idea until they lay bare the misogyny embedded in the foundation of the Enlightenment.

Thus, in the wake of the conflict over cultural diversity, we can begin to appreciate the difficulty of evaluating the Culture Wars' outcome, of deciding which side was ultimately victorious. To claim victory for the Moderns, as do recent critics intent on blaming them for the excesses of today's intellectual life that they find most disturbing—from Hellenism's loss of authority to the religion of scientific progress—to claim victory for the Moderns is to fail to see how Pyrrhic numbers of their breakthroughs were.

Among the most disturbing phenomena in any Culture Wars– fin de siècle cycle is the process of blaming that inevitably seems to accompany the rumblings about civilization's end. In an act of homage to what is arguably women writers' most impressive contribution ever to the French tradition, the Moderns herald the superiority of female literary judgment. They succeed in provoking a complicated backlash, in the course of which, to evoke but a few brief examples, women are blamed for the spread of bad taste and bad writing, for all the perceived ills in the republic of letters. Confronted with the increasing prominence and quality of a genre of modern invention, the novel, the Moderns proclaim it the modern genre par excellence. In no time at all, critics are treating the novel as a contagious disease, a pernicious force responsible for the spread of idleness and the weakening of civic virtue. And, in a development never encountered before or since—until our own Culture Wars, that is—critics blame civilizations's end on changes in literary criticism, in the public for literature, and in the relative highness or lowness of the new cultural standards.

It can be objected, naturally, that even the most powerful backlash cannot take away the accomplishments themselves. It can, however, manage to hide them. Thus, in the eighteenth century, when French literary history was rewritten by supporters of the Ancients, women writers and the novel were virtually eliminated from its pages.[53] Le Mercure galant's originality and influence have always been underestimated. Even Perrault has never received the credit that is his due—for having imagined, in his Parallèle, an embryonic Encyclopédie, in which literature and the fine arts are considered alongside both the practical arts and the newly emerging scientific disciplines.

In such a case, what does it mean to be victorious?

3

A Short History of the Human Heart

Emotion is the most beautiful gift you can give.
—Advertisement, *Le Monde des livres,* 22 December 1994

INVENTING THE EMOTIONS

Sensibilité: Faculty of the sensitive [*sensible*] human being, traditionally distinguished from *intelligence* or *wit* [*esprit*] and from *will* → affectivity, heart, emotivity, fiber → emotion, passion, sentiment.
—*Le Grand Robert de la langue française,* second edition (1989)

Le Grand Robert's attempt to define *sensibilité* and to identify synonyms for it would, unless I am very much mistaken, be taken by French speakers today as an accurate account of the word's current semantic field.[1] This modern stability is founded, however, on a complex and turbulent origin. The process I have in mind begins some twenty years before the outbreak of the Culture Wars. It then becomes bound up with their unfolding to such an extent that the intellectual conflict and the linguistic process conclude at the same time. The process involved nothing less than a complete rewriting of the language of the emotions, the most extensive such revision ever accomplished in modern times. So extensive was this revision, in fact, that it seems on occasion as if the French writers, philosophers, and scientists who organized it were consciously attempting

78

to reinvent—if not the emotions themselves, at least the range of possibilities conceived of for the emotions and the very way in which emotional life could be portrayed by everyone from novelists to doctors.

The first French fin de siècle was a period of intense creativity in several domains that are not normally interrelated, or at least not to such an extreme degree: literature, philosophy, theology, medicine, and a science so new that it did not even receive a name in French until the middle of the following century, psychology.[2] At the same time as Ancients and Moderns were doing battle over the relative merits of their opposing canons and the meaning of cultural decline, linguistic innovators from what we now consider completely separate disciplines were inventing the same language for the emotions. During the fin de siècle, that language of affect was the foundation upon which were built a new literary aesthetic, a new discourse of moral philosophy, and a new discourse of the body. The efforts of these innovators should be seen in part as a reaction against the contemporary mood of decline and fall, but largely—in a complex movement whose contours should gradually become clear—as one aspect of the Modern drive to work at or beyond the limits of what Perrault had presented as the Modern condition, that of being at the end of the line. Perrault's heirs were poised at the conclusion of the first century in which a consciousness of that term's exact chronological confines existed. They were also poised at the end of history, in the vision of history presented by their chief spokesmen. For these innovators, it became necessary to imagine nothing less than a radically revised vision of the human heart. The heart thus reimagined proved to be the concept upon which a new era was founded, an idea whose influence became so pervasive that it is evident in every discourse essential to the age of Enlightenment. The Enlightenment, that paradigmatic age of reason, intelligence, and all the faculties of the head, would not have taken shape as it did, without the need, perceived more and more acutely from 1660 on, for a previously unexplored language of the heart.

The process of semantic innovation that I have in mind had roughly three phases. The initial phase was a failure, but a spectacular one. In 1649, Descartes begins his treatise Les Passions de l'âme by announcing that, since everything previously written about the emotions is worthless, he will write as if "I were dealing with a subject that no one before me had ever considered" (3:951–52).[3] Descartes's dismissal of the past serves as an appropriately radical inaugural gesture for the seventeenth-century French (re)invention of

the emotions. When semantic revolutions—that is, linguistic trans-
formations that originate with a conscious decision to impose a new
vocabulary—take place, they are for the most part confined to eso-
teric terms, such as the name of a new movement or style. In this
case, however, Descartes proposed a revolution in a domain no less
basic than the language of feeling or emotion. He begins his treatise
by explaining that the term featured in his title, *passion,* the then
dominant designation for a feeling or emotion, should be changed:
he suggests "les sentiments" (3:962) as a replacement, but explains
that he prefers to say "les émotions de l'âme" because this term
suggests that they "agitate and shake [*ébranlent*]" the soul "with
great force" (3:974).[4]

In these brief phrases, Descartes laid out the reinvention's first
phase: he showed what vocabulary should be replaced, what the
options were, and the advantages each presented. In the mid–
seventeenth century, there were two terms available to characterize
feelings—*passion* and *affection. Affection* was clearly subordinate to
passion: Furetière (1690) calls it "a passion of the soul." In addition,
passion, unlike *affection,* had its origins in scientific discourse: the
first definitions Furetière includes are from the domains of physics
and medicine. Finally, the terms' connotations distinguished them
in two different ways. First, *passion*—even though, as Furetière's
final definition clearly states, "it refers above all to love"—conveyed,
rather than a sense of emotional bonding, a sense of emotional *soli-
tude. Passion* is defined in terms of its effects on the feeling subject:
"it refers to the different ways in which the soul is agitated by the
variety of objects that present themselves to its senses" (Furetière).
Affection, on the contrary, is always shared, relational, as in Furetière's initial example: "Conjugal affection is stronger than paternal
affection."[5] Second, if *affection* was calm, stable, without upheaval,
passion was its opposite and designated "agitations of the soul"
(Furetière), the emotions as troubling, tumultuous forces that unsettle those who feel them.

Those very different resonances explain Descartes's preference for
emotion: the term's seventeenth-century semantic charge made it
the obvious heir of *passion.* He situates his discussion of affective
terminology in a scientific, in particular a medical, context (3:956),
a context entirely appropriate for *emotion,* then commonly used as
a synonym for "fever." Next, he justifies his preference for *emotion*
because of the term's connotation of "powerful agitation and upheaval in the soul" (3:962). In this, he is faithful to *emotion*'s etymological roots. In both French and English, the term's primary mean-

ing in the mid–seventeenth century was that of political or social agitation. An *émotion populaire* meant a political uprising with popular origins.[6] Then, in both countries, in midcentury the term was transferred from the political to the affective realm. It is difficult to view as devoid of significance the fact that, in the two nations for which the seventeenth century was marked by uprisings and revolts, the modern language of the emotions was explicitly generated from this spirit of political sedition. In its initial, Cartesian concept, the central term in our modern affective vocabulary in English connoted a form of inner turmoil as threatening as a popular uprising. Furthermore, since the seventeenth-century French revolt against the monarchy known as the Fronde had broken out only the year before Descartes published his *Passions de l'âme*, his attempt to shift *émotion* from the body politic to the body personal would have been perceived by his first public with the full force of its revolutionary implications.

Can this threatening conjuncture alone explain *emotion*'s totally different fate in French and in English? In England, no one tried to introduce *emotion* in that most revolutionary of years, 1649. According to the *OED*, the word is first transferred to the affective realm in 1660, the year that Charles II and his court returned to England from their exile in France. This shift in meaning could be seen as one way of burying the threat of political sedition. Indeed, it was as if a word could ward off political emotions: *emotion* quickly took root in England and was launched on the course that led it to become the central term of modern affective vocabulary.[7] In French, on the other hand, Descartes's overt attempt to revolutionize the emotions was a virtual dead end. In his wake, his suggested use of *émotion* was only rarely adopted; late-seventeenth-century dictionaries show barely a trace of its transfer from the realms of politics and medicine to that of feeling.[8] Even today, *émotion* used as a synonym for feeling is generally the last definition to be included in French dictionaries. At no time has the word been the primary French affective term.

Even if Descartes's categorical imperative ultimately proved to be a failure, he did strike a definitive blow against *passion*, which, during the century after his treatise's publication, gradually moved to the French emotional periphery.[9] Furthermore, Descartes had succeeded in bringing into the open something that was, as the decades to follow would ever more incessantly prove, a widely perceived need. During the period between *Les Passions de l'âme* and the outbreak of the Culture Wars, the second phase of semantic innovation took place. This time, numbers of collaborators were involved, and numerous suggestions were put forth. This time, both *passion* and *emotion* were shut out, in favor of a terminological blend that featured in particular *tendresse* and *tendre* (both as a noun and as an adjective) and *sentiment,* but that also included on occasion *sensible* and even, in what may well be its initial appearances in French affective vocabulary, *sensibilité*—all proposed as replacements for *affection.* From this phase, perhaps the most intensively creative moment in the history of the emotions in France, it becomes clear why Descartes's initial effort was doomed to failure.

In the final years of the Fronde and especially in the post-Fronde years, the modern affective revolution began in earnest. In its most striking departure from Cartesian theory and from other prior visions, for the first time in French the emotions are not portrayed as seditious forces. They are detached from the medical connotations according to which all dominant terminology was used only metaphorically to refer to the affective realm, while literally designating a bodily upheaval, such as a fever. During the second phase, all the terminology being tried out was initially without medical connotations.[10] The liberation from medical turbulence was, as will become clear, a necessary prelude to a complete reversal in the balance of powers between medicine and what would now be termed psychology—or what was then known as *la morale,* "the science that teaches us how to live our lives" (Furetière).[11] The replacements for *émotion* and *affection* acquired medical significance only once their implantation in the psychological realm had been assured. This uncharted emotional terminology then became essential to the innovative view of medicine that was being developed while the Culture Wars were unfolding—to such an extent that it seems inconceivable that the new language, along with the dramatically revised vision of the emotions' functioning that it introduced, did not determine to a significant extent the way in which the new medicine was defined. Then, once the bond between psychology and medicine had been reestablished, the new view of feelings and the new view of medicine triumphed together.

It is in the second striking departure from all previous theories made during the post-Fronde invention of the emotions that the essence of this renewed bond between psychology and medicine becomes clear. According to Cartesian theory, an encounter with passion is in essence not only a solitary experience but a painful or at least a not overtly pleasurable one: the emotions shake and unsettle the souls of those who feel them. The terms tried out in the wake of the Fronde are, without exception, relational, and the new emotional experience is always described in terms of a shared experience between subject and object, an experience that enlarges the subject's affective capacity. Indeed, by the time this vocabulary had succeeded in replacing all previous possibilities in French, the emotional experience is even conceived in terms of a mutual influence between subject and object. This move away from solitary upheaval is the second phase's most important innovation: more than any other quality, the emphasis on shared experience characterizes the modern reinvention of the emotions.[12]

In view of this new balance of powers, it is appropriate that the entire second phase should have unfolded under the guidance, no longer of a philosopher, but of a novelist, Madeleine de Scudéry. Indeed, in the development of her two ten-volume novels—*Artamène, ou le grand Cyrus* (1649–53) and *Clélie, histoire romaine* (1654–60)—the reader can virtually watch Scudéry presiding over this vast transformation. In *Artamène*'s initial volume, which appeared the same year as Descartes's treatise, Scudéry stakes out the same territory as Descartes, and she even tries out the same new term. On two occasions, Scudéry uses "émotion" in the psychological context in which Descartes sought to position it. Witness in particular this description of her hero on the day of his first encounter with his beloved Mandane: "Artamène has since admitted that, even on the day he fought the illustrious corsair, . . . he did not have as much emotion [*émotion*] as he felt [the day he met Mandane]. On that day, his great heart, which was never shaken [*s'ébranlait*] in the most terrible peril, was stricken [*saisi*] by an enormous fear" (235–36).[13] A vocabulary of upheaval associated with *émotion*'s then current meanings—"s'ébranler," "saisi"—bridges its passage into a new realm. That transition is actually made by means of the verb used with "émotion" in its new guise. First, Artamène *has* emotion, as one has a fever; then, he *feels* emotion—as if her hero, along with Scudéry's audience, had learned both the expression's new context and its implications for an enlarged emotional field. Finally, in the same passage Scudéry refers to Artamène's heart, the site that, as we will see, would soon replace the soul as the commonly accepted seat of the emotions.[14] However, it is as if Scudéry realized, already in 1649, that *émotion* would be only peripheral to the future of the emotions in French. Her preferred term is one rejected by Descartes, *sentiment,* but her semantic innovation seems almost accidental at this point.[15]

By the time Scudéry inaugurates her next novel five years later, her work with the emotions had become enormously more complex. In fact, it is evident from *Clélie*'s initial volume that both the process that led to the modern French language of the emotions and the early modern (literary) obsession with emotionality—from *sensibilité* to romanticism—were by now well under way. By far the term most visibly displayed throughout the volume is *sentiment*.[16] Scudéry's decision to feature a word transferred from the domain of the head to that of the heart—*sentiment*'s then dominant meaning was "an opinion"—is indicative of her belief that the emotions were forces that could be controlled.[17] Scudéry uses the term as a vehicle for the exploration of the vocabulary and the affective space connected with a wide range of emotions. Quite often, she makes her point by using *sentiment* in a passage in which she simply names a variety of emotions. Thus, in the moment during which Clélie first ponders Aronce's declaration of love, Scudéry first mentions "the *sentiments* of her father" (an instance in which the word clearly still refers to his "opinions") and then portrays her heroine's "mind filled with astonishment, anger, and sadness" (343). On occasion, she is more specific, noting, for example, "a feeling of friendship" or "a feeling of jealousy" (64).

However, it would be all too easy to overlook this generalized exploration in *Clélie*, in view of the affective territory for which the novel's initial volume is best known, Scudéry's attempt to dissect one emotion in particular: love—its origins, its development, and its effects. Here, her analysis takes a form so striking that it has always blinded readers to the full scope of Scudéry's involvement with the emotions. I have in mind the best-known scene in early French prose fiction, the staging of the *carte de Tendre,* or map of an imaginary land named Tenderness (fig. 3).[18] Scudéry's decision to map the emotions, or at least the emotions related to love, can be seen as the most decisive moment in the French reinvention of the human heart. With this gesture, the century's best-selling novelist made all those who held sway over the evolution of French taste and sensibility aware of the semantic revolution then taking shape. A true cultural cartography, the *carte de Tendre* functions at the same time as evidence of semantic drift and as early warning signal of a major shift in *mentalité*. Scudéry's map of Tenderness is as important in its own right as the Cartesian cogito. In its wake, no French speaker would ever be able to conceive of feeling in the same way again.

The *carte de Tendre* scene is staged as if to echo Descartes's message that everything previously written on this subject is useless.

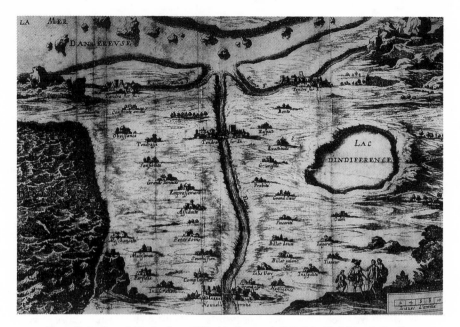

Figure 3. *La Carte de Tendre,* from *Clélie, histoire romain* (1654), by Madeleine de Scudéry. Reprinted by permission of Princeton University Libraries.

Several young friends are discussing what they feel for others and what these feelings should be called—*amour? amitié? tendresse?* Aronce declares that they should ask Clélie to sort things out because she "is able to talk about [tenderness] better than anyone ever has" (390). Clélie herself agrees with this assessment and explains why— in terms that uncannily prefigure the basic formula used by Marivaux, Du Bos, and all the sentimental theoreticians active by the end of the Culture Wars—"it's because my heart taught me how to talk this way; it's never difficult to say what one feels" (390). They then all press her with questions, and she promises them "the map of a country whose cartography has never before been charted" (393).

Scudéry's mapping of the emotions for the postseditious age thus definitively establishes the heart as their control center.[19] Her cartography also establishes the emotional hierarchy that is evident in all the new vocabulary: love is without contest the central emotion; it is defined by distinguishing it from friendship; other emotions find a place only in relation to these two.[20] Like Descartes, Scudéry's first objective is to find a replacement for *passion,* in particular in its function as a synonym for *love:* she hesitates between two idiosyncratic options and ends up promoting, not the one that became the next generation's favorite, *sensibilité,* but a term that has long since virtually been written out of the history of the emotions, but was for decades in the aftermath of *Clélie* the dominant synonym for amorous affection, *tendresse.*[21]

One of the map's primary functions is to link *tendre* and *tendresse* to more familiar affective terminology. Clélie's heart teaches her that all roads lead to *tendre,* including that of *sensibilité,* and the stops made along each way provide a context in which the uncharted vocabulary becomes clearer. When she explains her new language of the heart, Scudéry has her heroine interweave her innovations as though their meaning were already established—"tenderness . . . is a certain *sensibilité* of the heart" (211)—so that, in the end, any reader could not help but be convinced that all these terms make sense, that they already had a life outside this novel.[22]

And yet, from all that can be recovered today about the actual state of the language in 1654, it appears certain that nothing could have been further from the truth. To give this false appearance, Scudéry invented a technique, a type of semantic clustering, subsequently used by all those who continued her reinvention of the emotions. In clustering, new words are first linked to already familiar terms and then to each other, and finally each use of a new term is contextualized within a piling up of related vocabulary both old and new. As a result of clustering, these reinvented linguistic emotions were able to circulate in French well before their initial appearances traditionally have been dated by scholars.[23] A writer who wanted to integrate the innovative vocabulary but was afraid that its meaning might not be accessible to readers could cluster together related terminology so that the simple accumulation could suggest connotations for the new usage.

Clustering is omnipresent during the third phase of the affective reinvention, when, in the course of the half-century that followed Scudéry's inaugural gesture, this vocabulary edged toward semantic stability. Along the way, these words, which start out roughly as synonyms for *affection,* in the general sense of "an emotion," all come to be far more commonly used to replace *passion,* in the sense of "love." Hence the fact that far and away the two most common sources for the new language are novels (which portray love) and preachers (who condemn it from their pulpits). Here are but two examples, chosen from the initial period of the Culture Wars (1670–94), both of which show the new terms moving into their new meanings in the company of established terms. Thus, Sévigné, in a letter to her daughter from 9 February 1671, includes in a single sentence, in a veritable affective paroxysm, *sentiments, tendresse* (twice), and *sensibilité*, accompanied by "to love" and "to feel" (twice [1:152]). In an equally highly charged semantic outpouring from 1692, the celebrated sermonizer Bourdaloue piles on *tendre, sensible*, and *sensibilité*, in the company of both "to love" and "love" (each twice [49–50]). In the hope that the extraordinary innovativeness of these attempts will be fully appreciated, one statistic: *sensibilité* newly transplanted to the realm of the emotions appears only thirty-eight times in texts published between 1670 and 1695.[24]

Contemporary dictionaries confirm this impression of a barely emergent semantic field. This is clearest from the example of *sensibilité*, which, in its affective guise, is included solely in the last of the century's dictionaries, that of the Académie Française, in which the new usage would be clear only to those already accustomed to it: "*Sensibilité* of the heart."[25] Richelet and the Académie Française include examples for *sensible* that merely hint at the role the adjective was beginning to play in the reconfigured emotionality, as in the Académie Française's example of a person who is "*sensible* to others' sorrows."[26] On the opposite end of the scale is *tendresse*, the only term whose recent history is properly conveyed by all dictionaries. This is undoubtedly true because, as the *Dictionnaire* of the Académie Française suggests, the lexicographers could simply take their definitions from Scudéry: "It has no literal meaning, and figuratively signifies *sensibilité* to friendship or love."[27]

For these lexicographers, *sentiment* was key to the emotional exchange upon which the bond between psychology (*la morale*) and science was reforged. And, that bond once again in place, the reinvention of the emotions was completed, and the new emotional structures were ready to preside over the Enlightenment's first stirrings. The Académie Française defines *sentiment* as "all the movements of the soul." If we assemble elements from various definitions, the nature of these movements becomes clear. Literally, the term then referred to "the impressions that objects make on the senses" (Académie Française). In its most recent incarnation, it was being taken into the semantic constellation that was in the process of acquiring meaning: "He has tender sentiments for that young woman, in order to say, he loves her" (Furetière).[28] *Sentiment*'s then-primary figurative meaning, as defined by Furetière, indicates that this new language of love was linked to a revised view of love's functioning, a new view of "the movements of the soul": "the different perspectives [*vues*] from which the soul considers things, [perspec-

tives] that make [the soul] conceive different ideas or opinions."
Objects make impressions on the soul; these are the origin of feelings
or sentiments, which are the perspectives from which the soul in
turn considers the things that had initially attracted its attention;
and for which, by the end of the process, the soul has new feelings.

If we make two changes in this outline—put the heart in the
soul's place as the seat of the emotions and figure in a theory of
desire—then we have a succinct summary of the revised view of the
emotional process that was already solidly in place in science, and
in particular in some medical circles, by the time the dictionaries
were published.[29] A rather strange breed of medical theoreticians—
whose work should probably be situated somewhere between medicine and the most scientifically inclined psychology—took the rewriting of the emotions initiated by Descartes and Scudéry to its
logical conclusion both in medicine and in psychology. The influence was felt first in the domain of medicine, where the new emotional structure with all its ramifications played an essential role in
the most fundamental shift in medical philosophy in the early modern period.

During the second half of the seventeenth century, the basic theory governing medicine's view of the body was revolutionized. At
this time, the process was initiated by which medicine ceased viewing illness as tumultuous agitation, as upheaval within the bodily
space—as *émotion*—and began instead to view the body as more
interactive, both inside and outside its space. The new medicine was
a medicine based on attraction—of one organ for another, of one
body for another; it was a medicine of fibers and of nerves. The
medicine of *émotion* was being supplanted by the medicine of *sentiment* or *sensibilité*. By the end of the process, illness was portrayed,
no longer as the result of excessive violence, but as the result of
excessive feeling. The new medicine, like the new emotionality, like
the new literature created in Scudéry's wake, was governed by "the
moral philosophy of *sensibilité*."[30]

The work that first makes clear both this emerging conception
of medicine and its dependency on the revision of emotionality is
Guillaume Lamy's treatise, *Explication mécanique et physique des
forces de l'âme sensitive, des sens, des passions, et du mouvement volontaire*. It is entirely appropriate that the text in which this conjunction
initially becomes visible should have appeared in 1678, the year that
witnessed the publication of *La Princesse de Clèves* and the publicity
campaign in *Le Mercure galant* that initiated Donneau de Visé's
democratization of the public sphere. The issues fundamental to

Lamy's thinking are also central to the preoccupations of Lafayette's heroine: in particular, the question of whether desire and other emotions should be situated in the domain of the real or in that of each individual's perception of the real; as well as the question of the relational or the dialogic nature of the birth of the emotions. Both these issues are foregrounded in Lamy's definition of "the sensitive soul," in essence, the soul in its affective relations with others.[31]

"We have to realize that the sensitive soul perceives its objects; that it leans toward them, or turns away from them, according to whether or not they are attractive to it; and that it moves the body either to unite with these objects or to reject them" (4–5). Note first of all the new relation between the soul and sensitivity or sensibility. No longer simply the passive receptor of sensory impressions, "the sensitive soul" is now portrayed in an active role: it "perceives its objects," "it leans toward them," and so forth. Note also that this perception, true to the nascent medicine of *sensibilité*, is a drama of multiple levels of attraction.[32] Finally, as Lamy soon makes clear, this "qualité sensible" is a two-way street: we are moved and therefore formed in a certain way by the object of our emotions, and the object, in turn, "is shaped" so as to move us (11–13). Lamy's position is thus clear: the emotions have nothing to do with the real world; they fall squarely in the domain of the perceived world. In addition, Lamy lays the foundation for the most radically relational definition of the emotions yet, the first definition that allows us to understand how the reinvented emotionality could become the basis for a new vision of human subjectivity, a vision that, in turn, would prove to be the origin of the modern "science" of psychology.

All these definitions are firmly in place well before the end of the Culture Wars, in 1704, when Father Etienne-Simon de Gamaches published his *Système du coeur*. As his subtitle—*Conjectures sur la manière dont naissent les différentes affections de l'âme, principalement par rapport aux objects sensibles*—indicates, Gamaches has finally completed in the second domain, that of "the science of the heart," the affective reinvention initiated by Descartes and Scudéry. At his work's center is an extended theory of the functioning of *sensibilité* that demonstrates that it is precisely because the new emotions are relational, according to Scudéry's directive, that the fundamental Cartesian distinction between the real world and the perceived world is essential to their comprehension. According to what Gamaches terms "the law of reciprocal commerce" (250), "if external objects seem to us to be adorned with affective qualities [*qualités sensibles*], this is the case because . . . we attribute to them the different impressions that they make on us, or the different feelings [*senti-ments*] that they awaken in us by their presence" (178–79).

Gamaches's "system of the heart" is in effect an extended demonstration of how we transform the objects of our desire by our desire for them, and of how we are likewise transformed by the objects and by the displacement of our desire. The emotionality of *sensibilité* exists solely in the world of perceptions—and, furthermore, to the extent to which we are what we feel, we, too, are constructions of perceptions. It is a logical result of the attraction theory that subjectivity would be implicitly defined as a process of mutual attraction: we becomes ourselves in the eye of the other and through the other's perception, and that perception "originates" in our perception of the other.[33]

Perceived or imagined selves housed inside imaginary bodies—such was the long-term legacy of this process that unfolded over some sixty years. In it, medicine was only slightly out of step with the realignment initiated by "moralists" as a result of which perception came to dominate reality in their sphere: just a few years behind psychology, medicine, aided and abetted by the new affective terminology, was increasingly focusing attention on what could be termed perceived bodies, that is, bodily images or fictions that became, rather than any actual bodies, the site of medical speculation or theorizing.[34] I would never argue that the perceived body as a concept was invented by late-seventeenth-century medicine—each medical theory more or less successfully conceals its own fiction of the body within the folds, so to speak, of its speculation. The perceived body that allowed the school of medical *sensibilité* to flourish represents, however, a special case. To begin with, this fiction of the body as dominated by nerves and fibers and the "sensitive" interaction between like-minded parts was more intensely personified than other such images. Boulainvillier speaks, for example, of the "secret sympathies" that cause one organ "to take pleasure" in another (2:253). In addition, because it was totally dependent for its existence upon a vocabulary created by moral philosophy, this perceived body was by its very nature far more open to speculation and the different projections of *mentalité* that had created it than is usually the case with such medical fictions. Theoreticians from domains as diverse as psychology and philosophy had a far greater investment in the sensitive body than in its precursors, as treatises such as those by Lamy and Gamaches prove. As a result, the sensitive body was endowed with more interiority, with more affect, than other fictive bodies.[35]

This exceptionally powerful complicity between medicine and

fiction can be seen as the inevitable result of the unusual role reversal at the origin of the French affective revolution. Thus, on the one hand, Descartes, the representative of science, initiates his discussion of the vocabulary of the emotions by remarking that, whatever specific term one favored, "[the emotions] can be called perceptions" (3:962)—thereby distancing the affective realm from the real world and objectivity and directing it toward the territory of fiction. And, on the other hand, Scudéry, the representative of the novel, signaled her emotional reinvention with a gesture as exaggerated as her map of affectivity: in order to endow the false world, the world of perception, with truth and objectivity, it was necessary to externalize the soul or the heart, to project it in an apparently scientific manner.

By the time this half-century of linguistic creativity was over, the language and the fictions of *sensibilité* were fully operational. The emotions would never have been reinvented in French without a number of intense complicities, in particular that between scientific and moral discourses. The history of that complicity could be portrayed as the primal scene in the intellectual family romance that is philosopher François Dagognet's subject in his *Une Epistémologie de l'espace concret: Néogéographie*. Dagognet has three interrelated projects—proving that subjectivity is a historically evolving rather than a timeless entity; redefining psychology today as what he terms a "neogeography" or a "cartography"; and elucidating the relation of mutual and constant influence that he sees as the basic link between science and psychology. Given the centrality of psychology for Dagognet's project, it seems logical that the moment we have just been reviewing, that of the so-called social science's initial formulation, should confirm the structures he posits.

Nowhere is the suggestiveness of Dagognet's insights for the history that concerns us here more evident than in the manner in which he defines psychology and subjectivity. To *psychology*, he prefers in general the terms *neogeography* and *cartography*, both of which indicate what he sees as the discourse's fundamental (and necessary) instability. Thus, a cartography is a "configurational ensemble," while a neogeography is a "relational field [composed of] irradiations, numerous fragile paths, proximities and distances, an ensemble that can be said to constitute a personality" (174). Dagognet's definition of subjectivity is complimentary: "Subjectivity is not an entity [*un en soi*] that one can take or leave: it takes shape historically, progressively, thanks to the techniques and the concrete instruments that are reflected in it, giving it form through a series of return shocks [*chocs en retour*]" (173).

All Dagognet's definitions reveal an uncanny harmony with the field of affectivity as it was redesigned in the late seventeenth century. The relationality or interactiveness of the new emotions (what Dagognet calls "irradiations"); their particular situation as neither exterior nor interior, but as the internal externalized or the external internalized; their equally particular situation on the threshold between science and psychology (what Dagognet calls "the biopersonal" [170]); even the creativity of affective perception, according to which one becomes oneself in and through the other's perception, in and through one's perception of the other, through what Dagognet terms "return shocks"—all these find parallels in Dagognet's account of the history of neogeographies. However, my discovery of Dagognet just as my research on the emotions was coming to an end provided more than confirmation of my intuition that the seventeenth-century configuration could not be idiosyncratic. For, as Dagognet insists and as Lucien Febvre, Philippe Ariès, and Georges Duby had proclaimed before him, subjectivity does have a history, and everything indicates that the moment being played out during the Culture Wars was an essential turning point in that history's unfolding. Thanks to Dagognet, I became convinced that the common thread binding the reinvention of the emotions to contemporary scientific revisions to contemporary changes in the literary world and finally to the events of the second half of the Culture Wars was that these were all individual scenes in a drama with truly vast implications: this same period witnessed at the very least a radical redefinition of subjectivity—a redefinition so radical that it might be more correctly termed the invention or the formation of what we think of today as subjectivity.

In the case of the affective revolution perhaps even more than in that of the invention of the public sphere, it is crucial to note that the development of a culture of interiority did not, as Habermas's influential theory claims, have English and bourgeois origins. The wide-scale implantation of the new interiority in domains from medicine to literature was perhaps the most impressive of all Modern victories in the Culture Wars. This means that, just as was true for the creation of public culture, interiority's initial class politics were far more varied than is generally recognized. It also means that gender politics played a dominant role in the creation of the culture of interiority. In addition, because this culture first came into its own in the shadow of a fin de siècle, those gender politics were more intensely convoluted than has been the case at any time between the 1690s and our current sexually complicated decade.

The basic view of the sexual/gender politics that surrounded the new culture of interiority that has now become widely accepted in Habermas's wake is that of a relatively tranquil bourgeois domesticity. Women are granted prominence in this development because of the increased importance of domestic life and the family space. While this may have been true elsewhere—in England and in Germany, for example—nothing could have been farther from the case in France. The sexual and gender politics surrounding the rise of the French culture of interiority are far closer in their complexity and convolutedness to those of our age of so-called sexual revolution. In late-seventeenth-century France, women writers became prominent and suggested, for example, that interiority is synonymous with a woman's discovery of her emotions and in particular with a space for her desire. Other writers such as Perrault/Choisy (that strange "signature" will be explained shortly) undermined any easy use of sexuality or gender. Rather than tranquility, this interiority suggests the full range of desire's complexity.

This modern crisis in subjectivity forces us to return to the eternally vexed question central to the relation between words and things: can phenomena exist before the words to describe them? In this case, we must ask if the French *felt* differently once they had access to *émotion, sentiment,* and *sensibilité.* Evidence from domains as disparate as medicine, literature, and theology indicates that either this was the case, or at the very least that individuals became able, as we would now say, to access previously unrecorded affective possibilities.

What is important for my argument here is the fact that this newly configured psychogeography came to prominence just as the Culture Wars were unfolding. Given the prevailing mood, it seems only logical that developments in the biopersonal sphere quickly resonated not only in the literary world, but even in the realm of literary commentary. Thus, in contemporary literary works can be noted a simultaneous attempt, on the one hand, to develop techniques that foreground interiority and newly complex notions of subjectivity and, on the other, to fracture identity and to question the very possibility of a neatly defined identity—as though the new fullness of interiority somehow entailed a concomitant emptying out of interiority. In similar fashion, during their second phase, the Culture Wars were centered, no longer on progress and decline, but on identity issues. In fact, the issue that provoked the Ancients and Moderns to renew their hostilities was the initial formulation of a battle cry renewed by twentieth-century Moderns, the death of the author. In the inevitable backlash, the notion of an author took on a heretofore unheard of prominence: the denial of identity had clearly provoked the first true awareness of the usefulness of authorial identity.

From scientific speculation to literary criticism, the seventeenth century's end was an age, in this regard, much like our own, an age poised at the limits of subjectivity.

IDENTITY POLITICS

> All the other emotions [*sentiments*] subsequently become
> part of love, just as metals amalgamate with gold.
> —Voltaire, *Dictionnaire philosophique,* "Amour"

By the end of the Culture Wars, the Enlightenment's first major aesthetic philosopher, Du Bos, defined his *Réflexions critiques sur la poésie et sur la peinture* in remarkable fashion: he will write "as a philosopher" "a book that displays the human heart at the instant at which it is moved by a poem or a painting" (1:10). In 1719, a leading philosopher puts the heart at the center of his meditation on beauty and good taste because he believes that "the natural *sensibilité* of the human heart" (1:120), "that part of us that decides without consulting rules and compasses whether the object put before it is truly moving" (2:342–43), is the most trustworthy guide for aesthetic judgment. The key to understanding how a philosophy of the heart came to dominate aesthetic theory is found in the second act of the Culture Wars.

We left the Ancients and the Moderns on 30 August 1694, looking on as their leaders, Boileau and Perrault, kissed and made peace.[36] That public embrace had been prepared by extensive behind-the-scenes negotiations. The documents that survive prove just how precarious the peace thus obtained really was. The very debate that culminated in the alleged reconciliation also brought to the surface the grounds around which Ancients and Moderns would eventually renew their hostilities. A letter addressed to the chief negotiator, Antoine Arnauld, shortly after the successful completion of his mission shows the two leaders already at war over the terms of their agreement. Boileau complains that Perrault has been complaining that, according to his understanding of the deal, Boileau had agreed to suppress a particularly unflattering reference to Perrault from an already published work (Boileau, *O.c.* 567). Boileau claims never to have agreed to this, and he had his way. The reference remains.

The remark in question opens the third of Boileau's *Réflexions critiques sur quelques passages du rhéteur Longin*. Composed between 1692 and 1694, the first nine *Réflexions* had only just appeared at the time of the reconciliation. The contested passage, it is true, seems a far cry from a peacemaking overture. Boileau attacks Perrault for having published "the most inaccurate statement in the world" (498). He is referring to the third volume of Perrault's *Parallèle des Anciens et des Modernes, en ce qui regarde les arts et les sciences* (1692), in which the head Modern aligns himself with "the many excellent critics" who deny Homer's existence: "There never lived a man named Homer who composed the *Iliad* and the *Odyssey;* these two poems are only collections composed of numbers of shorter poems by different authors that were joined together" (3:31–32). Boileau cites Perrault verbatim, then dismisses his claim to be following the example of "excellent" precursors, in particular one of the seventeenth century's most respected theoreticians, Abbé François d'Aubignac. D'Aubignac would never have written such a thing, Boileau contends, because "he knew well that there have never been two poems as coherent, as unified as the *Iliad* and the *Odyssey,* nor poems throughout which the same genius is constantly revealed with such prominence" (499).

For once, Perrault was guilty as charged. Indeed, citing the authority of an unpublished treatise by d'Aubignac, he opened his *Parallèle*'s third volume with an extensive critique of the epics attributed to Homer.[37] His critique evokes all the major questions over which Ancients and Moderns would do battle at the turn of the eighteenth century, when, the new affective vocabulary by then firmly in place, the Culture Wars became focused on issues of identity, in particular, the reality of Homer's existence and the psychology of his characters.

The second phase of the French Culture Wars, sometimes known as the Quarrel over Homer, is generally presented as though it were a completely independent development, centered on an entirely new set of issues. Not only, however, did Perrault and Boileau set the basic terms around which the conflict was rekindled; their presence, and Boileau's in particular, was often evoked to preside over the new debates. In 1694, however, neither Ancients nor Moderns were ready to renew their hostilities over literary issues.[38] The fact that the peace officially "signed" that year was respected for over a decade can be explained in several ways, first of all by the successful implantation of concepts introduced as a result of Modern polemics, notably that of fin de siècle decline.

The century's end in France was marked by perhaps the most publicly perceptible type of decadence, climatic change: a series of unusually harsh winters, of which that of 1695 was the worst, resulted in ever more widespread famine for years on end. Literary Moderns feature signs of the times in their writing. Witness but one example, from the comtesse de Murat's 1699 fairy tale, "Le Sauvage," in which a fairy shows the heroine a magic room, "Destiny's study," from which "the fate of the world," and that of France in particular, becomes visible: "At the end of this century [*la fin du siècle présent*] the dimness [*faiblesse*] of the stars and the planets is causing complete disarray in the weather and in the horoscope of the century to come" (37).

The rhetoric of decline and fall so visible during the century's final years had been invented in the course of the controversy. Once the decadence the Moderns had forecast existed in actuality, however, literary conflict was forgotten for a time.[39] The questions around which Ancients and Moderns had originally gone to war—from the right of new publics to express literary judgments to the worthiness of modern authors to be compared to their ancient precursors—seemed no longer able to touch a public nerve once the atmosphere of decline had set in. The new set of identity issues around which it would all shortly begin again did not yet have the capacity to do so—even when formulated by Perrault and Boileau, the most successful leaders the two camps would ever find. From 1695 on, as we will see in the next section, what was felt to be a crisis in history inspired general concern. For the moment, however, here is the continuation of Boileau and Perrault's war.

Once the conflict did break out again, it seems apparent that, during its entire second phase, the literary controversy never again attained the status of true Culture Wars.[40] Once again, literary crisis was evoked as an explanation for societal change, and in particular for widely perceived decadence, but there is no evidence that the rallying cries of the new Ancients caused much alarm outside the academy.[41] This time, the literary war appears an exclusively ivory-tower dispute. This is hardly to say, however, that it was insignificant. On the contrary, as a consequence of the renewed hostilities between Ancients and Moderns, the institution of literature underwent a radical transformation, the consequences of which still affect the ways in which we negotiate that institution today.

During the conflict's second phase, party lines are often blurred:

Moderns by no means consistently argue, for instance, against the existence of Homer. By the time the hostilities finally came to a definitive end in 1716, however, it had all culminated in a major redefinition of literary and critical practice that can be accounted for in terms of party affiliation. In a variety of ways, the Moderns are followers of a doctrine of relativism, while the Ancients are resolute promoters of theoretical positivism and, to borrow an anachronism, of literary realism.

In the fifteen years between the public reconciliation and the renewal of the hostilities, various initiatives fell on deaf ears. Here are but two examples, one from the Modern camp and one from the ranks of the Ancients. D'Aubignac's treatise must have continued to circulate in manuscript, for when the Ancients finally took up the controversy where Boileau had left it off, they were obviously familiar with this work that was not published until the hostilities were coming to an end. It is incredible that response was so slow in coming, for d'Aubignac—pace Boileau—makes the most forceful formulation ever of the argument against Homer's existence. He devotes an entire treatise to the reasons why Homer was "an imaginary author," "no more than a name" (13–14, 7). Years would go by, however, before any Ancient was ready to take up that challenge. On the Ancient side, in 1699 the noted Hellenist destined to take over Boileau's role at the head of that camp, Anne Le Fèvre Dacier, published a translation of the *Odyssey*.[42] A decade later, the scholarly world would go to war over her edition of the *Iliad*. In 1699, however, Homer was not yet hot literary property, and Dacier's translation provoked no hostile commentary.[43]

And then, in 1710, it all started up again. That year, both Boileau and the woman about to assume his authority were preparing for publication works that, even though on the surface they seem to have nothing in common, share a crucial unity of purpose. In 1710, Boileau was dying. Rather than thinking of passing on the torch, however, he was busy with a final effort to shore up his authority, preparing "in all likelihood the last edition of my works that I will correct" (preface, n.p.). Boileau used this definitive edition of his works to craft the image he would leave to posterity. He played down, for example, his feud with Perrault as no more than "our poetic wrangle, extinguished almost as soon as it was ignited" (preface); he chose not to include the hostile letter written shortly after they had made peace but did print a subsequent letter that marks the most conciliatory moment in the long history of their exchanges (382–93; Adam and Escal ed. 568–74). As clear as the fact that

Boileau did not want to be remembered primarily as the adversary of Perrault, however, is the fact that he did want to be remembered in another adversarial role.

In the final months of his life, Boileau was working on the only major work published for the first time in this edition; he revised it and added a prefatory "discourse." This was hardly a new production, since Boileau initially worked on it in the late 1660s. As recently as 1707, however, he had still refused to allow its publication.[44] Virtually from his deathbed, Boileau decided it was at last time to give official life to his *Dialogue des héros de roman,* his attempt to mock the fledgling genre of the novel right out of literary existence.[45] Boileau clearly did not want to die without having seen to it that the *Dialogue des héros de roman* would stand as a pillar of his critical authority. He turned the manuscript over to his literary executor, Esprit Billiot, shortly before his death in March 1711. The following month, Billiot applied to have the *privilège,* the right to publish that had been granted Boileau, transferred to his name. The final preparation of this definitive edition of Boileau's works was slow, however, and it only appeared in early 1713.[46]

During the time thus lost, Anne Dacier made her move to take over Boileau's place. She published another translation of Homer, this time of the *Iliad,* and this time her endeavor was the gesture that rekindled the hostilities between Ancients and Moderns. In a long preface, however, she assumes only one of Boileau's adversarial roles, the other one: she lays out the essence of the arguments against the novel that, in early 1711, Boileau had not yet made public.[47] As she explains it, Dacier is concerned that there will soon be no audience for Homer because public taste has been corrupted by the reading of too many "vain and frivolous" novels. So bothered is she by the new prominence of the novel, in fact, that, before she discusses Homer, the next head Ancient devotes the preface to her edition of the *Iliad* to an extended diatribe against the values that novels allegedly introduce. Her vitriolic outpouring is vintage Boileau—*avant* (or *après*) *la lettre.* Readers "accustomed to the heroes of novels" come to expect that all literary heroes should be like them, "mawkish" and "bourgeois" (vii). Unless its reign is checked, in other words, the novel will threaten both the social stratification and the manly virtues upon which, the Ancients consistently proclaimed, French society depended for its strength. In the long history of the Culture Wars, Dacier is the only woman ever to assume the active role of producer of discourse, rather than being assigned the passive one of subject for debate. When a woman finally did intervene directly, however, she took the side of the Ancients, and her first announced objective in so doing was to take an extreme stance against the novel and against, therefore, the women writers who were its most prolific creators.

In the meantime, from his deathbed, Boileau explained the course of his career as a result of always having known how to give the public what it wanted: "I attribute all my success simply to the care I have taken . . . to be in tune with [the public's] taste" (preface). The striking conjunction between the rallying cries of the successive head Ancients suggests that both understood that the contemporary public was ready to concern itself again with literary conflict, and in particular that it was finally ready to respond to an attack on novels as a force for social corruption. If this was true in 1710 but had not been the case at the end of the first round of hostilities—in 1693, for instance—it could have been so because the fin de siècle had conditioned readers to look for culprits to blame for the perceived decline in civilizing forces. The novel, extending its domination over the literary scene with each passing year, would have seemed a likely suspect indeed.[48] The novel, in addition, was the principal site from which the affective revolution was being launched, and that revolution was bound up with every phase of the renewed conflict.

Dacier's critique confirms that, for her, novels are dangerous above all because of their association with one emotion in particular. Love—which she, in appropriately retrograde fashion, terms a "passion"—first corrupted modern society and then modern literature: "It is the soul of all our writing" (v). The ancients had understood that love could never be associated with greatness; hence Homer "was careful not to give love to his heroes" (v). The rewriting of the emotions carried out in the decades just prior to Dacier's treatise had aimed above all to portray a variety of emotions in their relation to love, foregrounding, therefore, love to the virtual exclusion of other emotions. The necessity Dacier obviously feels to banish love from all discussions of antiquity is an indication of the sentimental revolution's success. Ironically, Dacier's fear that the new interiority would invade her domain, too, caused just that infiltration to take place: during the controversy played out in her edition's wake, the role that literature should properly accord the emotions, and love in particular, was the one issue consistently debated that had never been raised by the first generation of Moderns.

Dacier's decision to open her translation of the *Iliad* with an attack on novels and the new affectivity is the first indication that the

second phase of cultural hostilities was in fact motivated by the
threat of interiority. After her inaugural pronouncement, identity
politics began to dominate debate within the academy. I will consider several of these issues and reconstruct briefly the role played
by each in a series of the principal contributions to the battle for
control over Homer—and, more importantly, to the battle for control over the institution of literature on the eve of the Enlightenment.

The Modern response to Dacier's challenge was slow in coming,
for the simple reason that it was the only appropriate one: with
the publication of another new edition of the *Iliad* (1714), Antoine
Houdar de La Motte established himself as the new Perrault who
would play opposite Dacier's Boileau. It would be hard to imagine
a more unlikely candidate for this role, since Houdar de La Motte
had no prior involvement with Hellenism. In fact, it seems likely
that it was Dacier's decision to center her attack on the literature
of *sensibilité* that attracted this particular adversary.[49] Houdar de La
Motte turns the "Discourse on Homer" that prefaces his translation
into a true Ancient-Modern polemic, reiterating the Modern position on Homer previously articulated by d'Aubignac and Perrault.
This was just the gesture for which the critical-scholarly world had
been waiting, for no sooner were party lines reestablished than participants rushed to close ranks behind their two leaders.

Indeed, the following two years marked the most active polemical
outpouring in the controversy's entire history. Dacier was so en-
raged at meeting opposition that she managed to get her lengthy
(more than six hundred pages) riposte, *Des Causes de la corruption
du goût*, into print before 1714 was over. Not to be outdone, Houdar
de La Motte brought out three volumes of *Réflexions sur la critique*
(1715) only months later. By this point, Abbé Jean-François de
Pons had already published a book-length attack on Houdar de La
Motte's edition (1714), and an anonymous Modern had contributed
a similar assault on Dacier's *Corruption* (1715). The year 1715 also
witnessed the publication of two of the most perceptive Modern
treatises: Abbé Jean Terrasson contributed a *Dissertation critique sur
l'Iliade*, and d'Aubignac's *Conjectures académiques, ou dissertation
sur l'Iliade* finally saw the light.[50] On the other side, Jean Boivin
published one of the least perceptive Ancient tracts, *Apologie
d'Homère et bouclier d'Achille*. And finally, Father Claude Buffier
and the Marquise de Lambert coproduced *Homère en arbitrage*, the
first of a series of attempts to moderate between the two positions.
The next year, Terrasson published a follow-up volume; Father Jean

Hardouin countered with his *Apologie d'Homère;* Etienne Fourmont added another moderating volume, *Examen pacifique de la querelle de Madame Dacier et de Monsieur de La Motte.*

The vast majority of all this frenzied production is incredibly myopic. Even when their titles hold out promises of wide-ranging discussion, these critics for the most part either simply attack the production of others line by line or produce a line-by-line defense of their own prior efforts. This refusal to see a big picture is never more irritating than in the Ancient tract that seems to have brought down the house of cards, Dacier's *Homère défendu contre l'apologie du R. P. Hardouin* (1716). Her obstinate defense of her view of Homer, commentary completely without overarching argument, is the ultimate example of the critical myopia with which three decades of intellectual controversy came to a sad end.

No one ever bothered to respond to Dacier's last challenge.

If one gets beyond the pedantic surface, however, it becomes evident that these admittedly petty quarrels raise issues with far from petty stakes. In the course of their disputes, the participants stumbled, as if by accident, on notions that were turned into critical dogma as a result of their debates and often reigned unchallenged until the beginning of our own Culture Wars. No subject for dispute had wider-ranging and more significant consequences than the existence of Homer.

Curiously, the two leaders at first miss the boat on this one. Dacier ignores the problem; in the preface to his *Iliad,* Houdar de La Motte in fact says that he personally believes that there was a Homer, and only mentions that "many" commentators have contended that he did not exist and that the poems are a composite of fragments by various authors (x). But this was enough for Dacier. In her *Des causes de la corruption du goût,* she quotes the new head Modern as if he had positioned himself against Homer's existence (37), thus providing the controversy that a second generation of Ancients and Moderns was clearly dying to find. The critical feeding frenzy of 1715 and 1716 is literally a battle *over* the body of Homer. In their desperation to cling to Homer's personal reality, Ancients come to believe that, to prove that Homer really existed, they have to prove that the epics are the work of one author; to prove this, it is necessary to prove that they are perfect works, as though the slightest imperfection in any domain, if generally accepted, would mean that the poems were not absolutely unified and therefore a composite of fragments by different authors. Increasingly, therefore, Ancients read every Modern critique of the *Iliad* as a death threat against its author. Here is but one example, naturally the most extravagant, that of the controversy over Achilles' shield.

It all began with an almost offhand remark by Houdar de La Motte: "I have to admit that Achilles' shield seems flawed; the objects that Vulcan depicts on it have no relation to the poem nor to Achilles, for whom it was made" (165). As though Homer's existence depended on this shield, Dacier characterizes it as "the most beautiful episode and the most perfect decorative detail that poetry has ever realized" (*Corruption* 375). This claim incited her followers to ever greater lengths. Thus, one of the most prominent Ancients, Jean Boivin, royal librarian and professor of Greek at the Collège de France (I give his titles because otherwise one is tempted to dismiss him as a crackpot), provided a book-length "apology for Homer" constructed along these lines: the *Iliad* is really the story of Achilles' shield; Homer had an actual weapon in mind; if, therefore, this real shield can be faithfully recreated, then Homer's existence can no longer be doubted. To this end, Boivin reimagines the shield in truly astounding detail—never suggesting for an instant that his presentation is anything but factual. He provides two double-page fold-out illustrations of his vision; he even gives the dimensions of each scene, concluding that the shield was composed of "two circles, each divided into twelve compartments, each containing a scene ten to eleven inches wide. All of this together will be four feet in diameter" (236–37).[51]

And, just to prove that this was not a controversy played out among a handful of specialists, but one of interest to a general audience, a reminder: the quarrel over Homer was recreated in the pages of *Le Mercure galant;* in particular, in October 1715, the editor asks his readers "if anyone can tell us if there really was a Homer, and if this time we can get a definitive yes or no" (238). For months after this, just as they had done on the subject of the Princesse de Clèves's conduct, readers wrote in to express their views.

If the battle over Homer's existence could be arrayed with the trappings of urgency for average readers, it was certainly not because they shared the scholars' vested interest in this basic literary property, but because this debate finally brought into the open certain notions that had been moving slowly into the public consciousness during the previous half-century. None of these was more important than what is now referred to as the authorial function. In the course of the controversy and with varying degrees of consciousness, scholars addressed questions such as the difference between a name (what d'Aubignac terms "a simple name") and an author's name, and the criteria used to determine authorial status (in this case, the qualities the *Iliad* had to possess in order to prove that it had been composed by Homer alone). To puzzle over the functions an author must play and to try to pinpoint the moment at which a name becomes an author's name was, by intention or by chance, to make one's readers hungry for what they were missing, to make them aware of the author and of the important role he could play in the literary process. When two generations of Moderns argued that Homer had never existed and that the epics attributed to him were really collections of anonymous fragments, this acted in fact as a protoformulation of what our modernity has termed the death of the author. This denial of authorial existence seems to have functioned as a necessary prelude to, if not the birth of the author, at least the author's emergence in a modern incarnation.[52]

Indeed, once the battle over Homer's body had created a new status for the author and the author's name, critics and commentators signaled their awareness of the heightened authorial function in a variety of ways. Increasingly, the fledgling genre of modern literary history came to be defined as the study of authors—the compilation of lists of the best authors, the establishment of authorial biographies, and so forth—as commentators began to respond to what was clearly a newly recognized need: for a man behind the oeuvre.[53]

The most concrete proof of the author's new primacy was the solidification of certain identities that are now seen as central to the French tradition but that had remained unstable until that time. In 1716, the Culture Wars died out along with the controversy over Homer's existence. The period just preceding and immediately following this divide knew an exceptionally high rate both of attribution of authors' names to works previously published anonymously, and of speculation about the identity of authors of such works. For instance, the first editions of Sévigné's letters that identify her on the title page appeared in 1725 and 1726.[54]

The example of "Lafayette" is perhaps the most intriguing. During the entire controversy surrounding her novel, Donneau de Visé and the other participants refer only to "the author of *La Princesse de Clèves.*" From 1678 to the end of the century, the most remarkable aspect of the novel's public history is the apparent general lack of interest in its author's identity. Indeed, the earliest public recognition of "Lafayette" as an author's name occurred only in 1710, when in the speech marking Houdar de La Motte's induction into the Académie Française, Callières referred to Lafayette as the author of

both *La Princesse de Clèves* and *La Princesse de Montpensier*.[55] Lafayette's name did not appear on the title page of an edition until
1780; however, the period from 1694 to 1719 witnessed the first
active interest in determining the author's identity and established
the bases on which the now accepted attribution was subsequently
founded.[56]

This crucial phase in the birth of modern authorial identity was
initiated by literary Moderns—and not only because their pronouncement of Homer's death was its catalyst. Initially, the Moderns had a particular stake in the recognition of authorial personae:
the ancient writers already had authors' names and what passed for
biographies; in order to constitute a new canon that could be proposed as an alternate to the established one, the Moderns needed
more than "simple names"; they needed full-fledged modern authors. Very quickly, however, this fundamentally Modern endeavor
slipped out of their control, for the establishment of absolute authorial identities was inherently compatible with the positivism of the
Ancient brand of literary commentary and just as inherently incompatible with the relativism of its Modern counterpart. To understand what this meant, it is necessary to pick up the battle over
Homer where we left it off, with the place of interiority in the *Iliad*.

Dacier's categorical dismissal of love from the life of the epic
hero provoked two types of response.[57] Some commentators, in the
manner of first-generation Moderns but with a twist that turns
Boileau-Dacier's attack on the novel against them, criticize epics for
displaying an excess of "violence and brutality" and only emotions
"that are evidently harmful to civil society," that "are contrary to
public happiness" (Terrasson 1:147–48).[58] True second-generation
Moderns show the effects of the sentimental revolution, and no one
more so than Houdar de La Motte, who counters Dacier's attempt
to limit the range of affect allowed in epic with a reading that situates
the emotions at the center of Homer's project: Homer sought above
all to "move" (*émouvoir*) his audience and, to this end, "he filled
his work with all the most touching natural emotions" (*Iliad* xxix).[59]
Houdar de La Motte, in other words, portrays Homer as a precursor
of the novelists who, during the entire unfolding of the Culture
Wars, had been gradually completing their takeover of epic's place
on the French literary horizon.

No one was more likely to understand the implications of his
argument than Anne Dacier, who begins her consideration of the
emotions by discussing generic boundaries, in particular that between history and epic. She quotes her adversary on the distinction

between the two: while history gives an accurate account of the lives of real people, epic "invents characters for the purpose of illustrating specific emotions . . . and it brings together in these characters all the visible signs of these emotions . . . in order to make us feel their nature" (Houdar de La Motte 56–57; *Corruption* 140–41). For Dacier, nothing could be farther off the mark: no more than the literary portrayal of the emotions, characters and plot that are merely fictional bear no relation to the world of epic as she sees it (*Corruption* 142).[60]

Dacier never deviates from a resolutely straightforward position, articulated time after time throughout her vast production: everything in the *Iliad*—every character, every event, every description—everything is real, that is, an absolutely faithful recreation of the reality of Homer's day. Furthermore, epic's inherent superiority to novel is founded on this exact transcription of reality: "The [epic] poet represents what is and not his view of the way things were. . . . Otherwise, his heroes would be like the heroes of novels, who have only a name in common with the person whom they represent" (*Iliade* xxiv).

To have admitted even the slightest deviation from this view of the epic's absolute fidelity to reality would have forced Dacier into a complete redefinition of Ancient critical practice. As it was, Dacier and her followers—notably Boivin—saw their task as simple, straightforward. Since the epic poet had left them with "an exact portrayal of everyday life [*moeurs*] in the period that he designated" (Dacier, *Iliade* xxv), the commentator does not second-guess, find fault, or judge in any way. All the commentator has to do is first locate all the parcels of reality embedded in the epic and then foreground those related to whatever aspect concerns him or her—from the way banquets took place to the decoration of palaces. The doctrine of the epic's absolute realism went hand in hand with a belief in the critic's total powers of recovery.

Nothing could have been more at odds with this positivism than the program for a revitalization of the critical process that Houdar de La Motte sets out in his Modernist manifesto, *Réflexions sur la critique*. As his title indicates, the head Modern understood that the crisis in the academy should provide a forum in which to discuss the definition and the function of the fledgling genre of literary criticism. The reflections that follow are a call to those involved in the production of literary commentary, challenging them to develop discourses to reflect the diversity of the new publics constituted as a result of the controversy. The plural is key here: to Dacier's vision of perfect unity—one reality, one truth, and therefore only one possible critical vision—Houdar de La Motte opposes a theory of critical multiplicity, of critical difference.

He contends that the Culture Wars have revealed the existence of two types of authors and of two different publics. The first category, observers as much as participants, is really attracted to such disputes only because they smell blood: they are out for "the trivial honor of winning" or "the malicious pleasure of watching authors drag each other through the mud." For them, the spoils of war are similarly straightforward: will Ancient authors dominate or their Modern counterparts?—or, as the question is put today, who's in and who's out? (*Réflexions* 3, 6). In Houdar de La Motte's description, none of the participation from this category is truly subversive: at most, one system would be negated and overthrown, only to be replaced by a new system with a different content but still the product of similar critical values. His second category is composed of those who seek debate precisely because they have a complicated vision of the truth, both of its nature and of what it means to possess it. For those who participate in Culture Wars from this perspective, "truth is just as welcome from the hands of others as from their own"; the goal of all the conflict is to obtain as many "clarifications [*éclaircissements*] about the truth" as possible, as many "different opinions about the same subjects" as possible, so that all involved "can be able to judge soundly" (5, 8).[61]

Indeed, even though in his own critical practice Houdar de La Motte never rises above type-A behavior—like Dacier, he devotes most of his energy to line-by-line attack and defense—the head Modern was at least capable of formulating a discourse of critical relativism truly remarkable for his day: he *almost* reaches the position of refusing to have the last word and of saying that criticism should reject closure.[62] At the very least, the last head Modern was clearly aware that the battle over Homer marked a watershed in the history of interpretive activity. By mid-1715, in fact, the innovativeness of the Modern position was so evident that a review of Houdar de La Motte and Terrasson in *Le Mercure galant* describes their contributions as "la nouvelle critique" (July 1715, 191).

Certainly at no prior moment in France had there been such a clear schism between two diametrically opposed visions of literary commentary and its objectives. In one camp, Dacier and the Ancients exalted a process founded on the critic's absolute authority, with the clearly circumscribed goal of recovering perfectly preserved reality capsules.[63] In the other, Houdar de La Motte and the Mod-

erns were groping more or less successfully toward a criticism that
they saw as both rational and relativistic, a criticism that recognized
individual perception rather than unmediated access to reality as its
founding value. The Modern position left the better-known and the
more brilliant legacy: it helped found the aesthetic theory that, in
the hands of practitioners from Du Bos to Diderot, was one of the
glories of Enlightenment thought. Once again, however, it would
be dangerous to conclude from this visibility that the Moderns won
the war.

The quarter-century that followed the battle over Homer was an
essential period in the formation of the modern French university.
The critics and pedagogues who were instrumental in this process
were overwhelmingly of the Ancient persuasion, and they guaranteed that the values of Boileau and Dacier would be passed on to
generations of French students. No work better illustrates this Ancient takeover of French literary pedagogy than the most influential
literary manual of the last decades of the old regime and the first
decades of the new one(s), Abbé Charles Batteux's *Les Beaux arts
réduits à un seul principe* (1746).[64] Just as Boileau and Dacier had
dictated, Batteux excludes all the genres, in particular the novel, considered dangerous for young readers because of their direct appeal
to the emotions. The model Batteux set up implicitly to perform
this exclusion and explicitly to guide future pedagogues in teaching
French literature is as positivistic as Dacier could have wished.

Batteux counters the theories proposed by Modern theoreticians
of aesthetics, notably Du Bos, by pronouncing that "there is only
one good taste, that of nature" (127). It is therefore easy to determine the great authors: they have "exposed" the designs of nature
in their works (145). (Dacier would have said that their works are
perfectly faithful to reality.) This doctrine immensely simplifies the
teaching-study of literature: the little parcels of nature (reality) in
great works are to be foregrounded; inferior works are shown to be
just that because the parcels embedded in them are judged unfaith-
ful to nature (reality). Thus, with Batteux's manual and works like
it, Ancient positivism secured the exclusion of all undesirable works.
A half-century after Perrault first went to battle on their behalf,
Modern (French) authors had at long last become the center of the
literary canon taught in France. The selection of authors and the
terms on which they were to be admitted, however, had been dictated exclusively by the Ancients.

Thus it was that a long struggle over public culture was reig-
nited and redirected by issues that had first come to the surface in

conjunction with the sentimental revolution. From Dacier's inaugural prohibition of love and Houdar de La Motte's inaugural proclamation of Homer's ability to "speak the language of all the emotions" (*Iliade* 17), the battle over Homer was very much a conflict over the emotions and their proper place in literature and criticism. The Moderns were clearly playing to the new public for these issues first reached by Donneau de Visé in the debate about *La Princesse de Clèves:* under Houdar de La Motte's guidance and by foregrounding the emotions as he did, they sought to show that all literature, even the classics of antiquity, can be related to the lives of modern readers. In addition, during the years between readers' first shock at recognizing, through the conversation between Lafayette's princess and her husband, the power of the new literary interiority and the end of the battle over Homer's authorial identity, issues related to the sentimental revolution were being played out with ever increasing complexity in new modern literary forms. As a result, the readers who followed the struggle between Dacier and Houdar de La Motte were a great deal more sophisticated in matters of the literary heart than the audience for Boileau and Perrault's battle had been.

MAPPING THE HEART

> The strange thing about life is that though the nature of it
> must have been apparent to everyone for hundreds of years,
> no one has left any adequate account of it. The streets of
> London have their map; but our passions are uncharted:
> what are you going to meet if you turn this corner?
> —Virginia Woolf, *Jacob's Room*

In June 1675, a French nun, Marguérite-Marie Alacoque, had a vision of Christ. He appeared as the Sacred Heart, that is, displaying his heart as burning "because it has loved men so much," and he asked the young nun to establish a cult devoted to the veneration of his heart (Le Brun 33). Alacoque was so successful in honoring this request that the entire tradition in modern Catholicism of devotion to the Sacred Heart is commonly said to have originated with her efforts.[65]

Devotion to Christ as divine incarnation of the loving heart had existed, of course, at earlier periods. In 1675, however, there were clear indications that the way had been prepared for a true spiritual movement centered on Christ's humanity and in particular on his interior life. The same cultural climate that created the need for a new affective vocabulary and a revised vision of emotional structure similarly deflected the course of seventeenth-century spirituality onto the terrain of personal interiority. The modern tradition of devotion to the Sacred Heart was made possible by the surrounding atmosphere of heightened affectivity as much as its initial flowering contributed to the contemporary emotional outpouring.[66] *Sensibilité* and the image of divine interiority can be considered parallel cultural constructions.[67]

A third image of the heart was also constructed in the course of the seventeenth century. William Harvey's discovery of the circulation of the blood (1626) was the foundation of our modern scientific vision of the heart. In Harvey's wake, a crucial period was inaugurated, as a result of which, by about 1670, a vast amount of new knowledge had become available about both the circulation of the blood and the structure of the heart. The key research was carried out in England, but new discoveries were quickly made available in France.[68] One of the roles Perrault clearly intended his *Parallèle* to play, for instance, was that of creating a new audience of nonspecialist readers, as Donneau de Visé had done for literary matters. Perrault wanted to open discussion to include scientific matters, modern discoveries in fields such as medicine, physics, and astronomy. Among all the scientific accomplishments enumerated, Perrault's fictive Moderns in the *Parallèle* are perhaps proudest, most convinced of their superiority over the Ancients because of recent discoveries in the science of the heart.[69] The seventeenth-century medical heart, or at least the vision of it that would have filtered down to a broad audience—the heart as the control center for the circulation of the blood; the heart as pulsing mass of "movements," nerves, and fibers—this heart was the perfect scientific counterpart to both the sentimental heart, site of the emotions, and the devotional heart, guiding principle of spiritual life.

For all those instrumental in the seventeenth century's affective and spiritual revolutions, the newly prominent medical heart was for the most part nothing more than an analogous construction of whose existence they were perhaps only vaguely aware, one whose suggestiveness for their own creations they, curiously, often failed to exploit.[70] Nevertheless, contemporary scientific discoveries and ongoing medical research helped make the heart a center of active cultural speculation. The convergence of discourse from domains as radically different as cardiology and mysticism guaranteed that the heart would be promoted as universal metaphor for interiority.[71]

In the final analysis, the heart was the only representation of interiority desired by the nascent age of *sensibilité*.[72]

More clearly than any other text, Perrault's *Parallèle* illustrates the heart's unrivaled status as cultural pivot able to facilitate connections among the various discourses essential to the Modern project. In several passages crucial to the articulation of his argument, Perrault makes the polymorphous heart the measure of Modern superiority. The most striking instance opens the *Parallèle*'s second tome, the crucial follow-up to the heavily attacked initial volume, in which Perrault had pleaded the Modern cause exclusively on literary grounds. He renews his attack by figuring in scientific progress on the Modern side of the equation. Rather than present science on its own terms, as he will in later volumes, however, Perrault introduces modern scientific discoveries only to the extent to which they reinforce the more literary types of progress upon which his defense of the Modern cause had originally been founded. Thus, he initiates a discussion of science in antiquity with astronomy: the ancients already knew just about as much as we do about the planets and the major stars; recent discoveries have made known both the satellites that revolve around the planets and many smaller stars. In similar fashion, Perrault continues, while the ancients knew "roughly" as much as we do about the central emotions, they never dreamed of the existence of the "myriad small sentiments . . . that accompany them like satellites." Indeed,

> Just as anatomy has discovered in the heart valves, fibers, and movements of which the ancients had no knowledge, in the same manner moral philosophy [*la morale*] has discovered attractions, aversions, desires, and repulsions unknown to the ancients. (2:29–30; see also 2:294)

In 1690, a crucial year in the Culture Wars, the first point at which combatants could take stock of the toll taken by the initial exchanges, Perrault claimed victory for the Moderns above all on the grounds of their superior knowledge of both the bodily heart and the heart that had been constructed to represent the new interiority. His unexpected reasoning shows that, for the principal architect of Modernity, who had initially been prepared to argue the doctrine of progress mainly, if not exclusively, on literary grounds, the greatness of Modern literature was determined by its ability to portray "the movements of the heart," the emotions great and small, "attraction and aversion, desire and repulsion." The grounds staked out by Perrault also indicate that the literary production that proved that progress existed was an aesthetic born at least in part as a discourse of the body.

To understand the enormity of Perrault's claim, an assertion intended to be every bit as aggressive as his proposition that modern authors were greater than their ancient precursors, one has only to compare the ideals promoted by French public culture on either side of the divide constituted by the sentimental revolution. When, in Pierre Corneille's *Le Cid* (1637), the hero's father, Don Diegue, confronts his son with a question that he intends as a probing of Rodrigue's sense of identity—"Rodrigue, as-tu du coeur?" (I.iv.i)— the heart is defined as the opposite of the site of sentiment, as a synonym for manly virtue, for courage. No other single line defines so succinctly the values considered appropriate for great French literature before the emotions had been reconfigured.

A literature of great men and their heroic deeds, in which their heroism was at least partly determined by their ability to resist love—this was the preferred subject matter of French public culture when Scudéry began her dissection of "the anatomy of the amorous heart." Scudéry, as we have seen, was undoubtedly the single most influential force behind the semantic revolution. In her own novels, however, she did not take the necessary next step, that of exploring the new affective code's potential to create the illusion of an interior life for her characters. Scudéry's characters revel in the virtually interminable unraveling of the nuances of love and other emotions, but they dialogue more as detached moralists than as concerned participants. In addition, they appear always to have access to fully conscious feelings. At no point does their discourse on the "myriad small sentiments" force them into moments of self-exploration or self-confrontation, struggles that would reveal these characters to readers in the process of discovering or redefining their identities. As it stands, Scudéry's characters, in the manner of postmodern literary figures, do not for all intents and purposes have hearts, in the sense of an interior life or an internal being.[73]

Indeed, readers would have to wait a full quarter-century after Scudéry's novels for a work in which her project is fully realized. In *La Princesse de Clèves,* Lafayette proves that the creation of an affective language and the formulation of an ethics of *sensibilité,* a new code to govern human relations, inevitably culminate in a literary enterprise that retraces the birth of an awareness of the self.[74] With Lafayette's novel, the seventeenth-century construction of the heart came into its own in literature. In the manner of the authorial personae generated as a result of the controversy over the author's existence, Lafayette's heroine can be seen as the fulfillment of debate about the birth and the consequences of interiority.

In key scenes of the novel, we witness the princess quite literally discovering the existence of basic emotions and, in the process, implicitly acknowledging her prior affective emptiness, a crucial original absence of feeling. In the course of the novel, the princess becomes the first character in French literature to achieve at least the rudiments of what is recognizable as an interior life. *La Princesse de Clèves* is known as the first modern French novel. If we bear in mind Perrault's equation between literary modernity and superior knowledge of the heart, we may well wonder if Lafayette's work was originally promoted to this status because it features what could be described as the process by which a character quite literally comes to discover her affect. Lafayette is the first novelist to describe a character's reaction to a situation, not as a series of fully formed propositions, but as a succession of emotions. She took the psychologically hollow characters that had previously populated the novel and filled them out with internal "flesh." She thus gave the novel interiority and psychology.

Lafayette imagined a heroine who, we are asked to believe, is at first unable to recognize the most basic emotions, or even to know if she herself is feeling them. Witness, for example, the earliest extended conversation between the heroine and her future husband, a true "anatomy of the amorous heart," in which she tries in vain to convince him that she experiences a complex emotion, that is, one that "troubles" her at the sight of him. (He remains convinced that she feels nothing more complicated than "a feeling of modesty," rather than a true "movement of the heart" [50–51].)[75]

Indeed, the princess's entire trajectory is charted out as an emotional apprenticeship. This is first evident on the level of vocabulary, for Lafayette's heroine acquires key terms as a result of every major shift on her interpersonal horizon. Perhaps the most striking such acquisition occurs as a result of her discovery of a love letter that she believes to have been addressed to the man with whom she has fallen in love. As soon as she reads the letter, she begins to reflect upon the discovery that she is not the only woman in Nemours's life.

The sentence that holds the key to her feelings at this moment is an extraordinary formulation, even for this novel in which the emotions are laid bare almost as a matter of course: "She was fooling herself, however; for this torment, which she found intolerable, was jealousy in all its horror" (99). As though to convey the impression that the princess is literally conceiving of its existence for the first time, the passage is awkward, as when the emotion is named: "[It] was jealousy." The passage stresses the complexity of this coming to affective knowledge by never fully clarifying the status of her realization. The birth of jealousy is part of an interior monologue. The other moments of emotional growth are clearly designated as taking place within the princess's head: "It seemed to her that this suffering was made particularly bitter because of . . ."; "she now saw that . . ." (99). In the case of jealousy, however, the boundary between narrator's knowledge and character's knowledge is not clearly established: "She was fooling herself." It is as if, in the process of learning "jealousy," in the process of the coming to consciousness of what was not conscious, the princess is obliged to divide herself into a knowing self and a self still fighting the new knowledge. The acquisition of new affective vocabulary, Lafayette's novel consistently suggests, is a process that forces the novice self to test the limits of its being.

In addition, Lafayette structures her novel around these scenes of affective acquisition. What is perhaps the most unsettling instance of this phenomenon is centered on the moment at which the heroine finally understands what her husband had been trying to explain in their earliest emotional exchange. "One cannot express the sorrow she felt at knowing, because of what her mother had just told her, the interest she was taking in M. de Nemours: she had never before dared admit it to herself. She saw then that the feelings that she had for him were those that M. de Clèves had so much asked for from her" (65). While the scene is one of self-knowledge—"she had never before dared to admit it to herself"—it is not yet a moment of semantic acquisition. The princess still cannot name what she is feeling and resorts to the understatement "interest" and the euphemism "[the feelings] that M. de Clèves had so much asked for from her." The scene ends, however, with the princess ready to take the next step on the road to knowing "love." She resolves to tell her mother "what she had not yet said to her" (65).

This is one confession the princess does not make, however. When she arrives, her mother has a fever, so she puts off their conversation (65–66). A few pages later, her mother is dead, after having made it clear that she understands the nature of her daughter's feelings, after having told her, just as her future husband had done, what emotions she should and should not have, but without having actually given those sentiments a name. For the princess and for the novel, the implications of this progression are clear: the mother dies

as soon as, and therefore because, her daughter experiences an expanded emotional life, an emotion that "touches [her] soul" (50).

In her final attempt to foreground the new affectivity, Lafayette
makes her heroine's development coextensive with her acquisitions
of emotion. To do so, she invented a literary technique, the interior
monologue, so visionary that it would only truly be exploited in
the nineteenth century. To make her intentions clear, rather than
smoothly enfolding reflective passages within the novel's action, she
literalizes them, making them the stylistic equivalent of a separate
space. The novel's first interior monologue, in which the princess
admits to herself her "interest" in Nemours, is a classic example
of this strategy. Her mother tells her certain things that provoke
reflection. That reflection cannot take place immediately, however,
for the primary artifice in Lafayette's presentation of interior monologues in effect renders thought incompatible with either dialogue
or action. In this case, someone arrives, and the princess is able to
do what she apparently has to do in order to think: "Mme de Clèves
went home and shut herself away in her study [*cabinet*]" (65). Once
the princess is absolutely alone, the monologue, and her affective
progress, can begin.

Lafayette's artifice, the suggestion of a radical separation between
reflection and action, makes the discovery of the emotions part of
the process by which an individual comes to understand a more
complex notion of interiority and exteriority, of the self. The novel
thus prefigures Francis Hutcheson's attempt, in his 1728 treatise on
the emotions, to spatialize the acquisition of affect—"something
different from *ourselves,* . . . a body which we do not call *self,* but
something belonging to this *self*" (161).[76] In *La Princesse de Clèves,*
the interior monologues, during which the princess is always literally
"shut off from" the outside world, signal her gradual acquisition of
a space for interiority, of a heart. As the novel unfolds, this space
becomes progressively larger, when the monologues become far
longer and stylistically more complex. The princess is also able to
integrate interiority more successfully. Thus, for example, by the
time she has returned to the court after a period of mourning for
her mother, she receives a visit from Nemours during which she is
able briefly to reflect on the feelings provoked in her by what he is
saying while he is still in the room (85), a variation that indicates
a growing acceptance on her part of the necessity of this interior
space.

The princess's development of interiority is not premised on a
wide-ranging exploration of the emotions. Instead, it reinforces the

foundations laid by Scudéry when she made the rediscovery of affectivity an integral part of the project of the novel. In *La Princesse de Clèves*, the heart and interiority are in the final analysis synonymous with the exploration of one emotion alone, love.

John Boswell begins his *Same-Sex Unions in Premodern Europe* by remarking that "to an observer of the modern West's cultural monuments it would probably seem that romantic love was the *primary interest* of industrial society in the nineteenth and twentieth centuries" (xix). To witness the birth of interiority in French literature is to witness the origin of the radical shift in focus for the monuments of public culture whose apogee Boswell describes here. Beginning with *La Princesse de Clèves*, the novel proclaims that love is the center of our affective life and that it is by the ability to love, and to attract love, that an individual's worth can be evaluated.

This sentimental revolution was prepared in the years just prior to the Culture Wars, but it was truly won during the conflict's initial phase. At that time, the generation of historical novelists who rose to prominence in Lafayette's wake promoted, with increasing fervor and decreasing subtlety, the message that the capacity for interiority, and for love in particular, rather than courage and great deeds, should be seen as the measure of human merit. Since, furthermore, this dramatic readjustment in literary values was being proposed just as the literary public was undergoing a process of rapid broadening and democratization, romantic love's centrality was broadcast to the first audience for French culture worthy of the designation public.[77] The two most impressive Modern accomplishments came together in spectacular fashion to suggest the dawning of a new age—of individuality, of interiority, of heightened affectivity.

Boswell concludes his opening remarks on the prominence of romantic love in the modern West by calling attention to the phenomenon's exceptional status: "Most human beings in most times and places would find this a very meager measure of human value" (xix). Already in the seventeenth century, this was a common response to modern literature's new focus, all the more so because the implications of this revised vision went far beyond the depictions of a fictive princess's discovery of love. *La Princesse de Clèves* and all the subsequent novels that were constructed according to Lafayette's model featured the repercussions of the interior life of a great many princesses, and princes as well, often those whose existences were firmly grounded in historical record. Thus, Lafayette surrounds her fictive characters with historical figures as well known to her contemporaries as Henri II and Mary Stuart, figures she portrays as obsessed with love in different ways. The women tend to talk about it incessantly, and the men are driven by their passion to alter their own lives and even those of their subjects. In the model Lafayette imposed as the first modern novelist, love is consistently portrayed as the prime motivation behind the great events that shape a nation's course and for which its great men are known. At the French court, "love was always mingled with affairs of state and affairs of state with love" (45), according to Lafayette's best-known maxim. The new prose fiction, which swept the nation along with the Modern program, reconfigured the long-dominant model for public culture.

This cultural revolution could hardly have been launched at a more explosive moment. The conflict that generated the most intense anxiety during the actual fin de siècle period is referred to as the crisis in history. Critics on both sides of the Ancient-Modern divide argued that the discipline was in dire need of reform and that there was widespread distrust of contemporary historians whose accounts were considered unreliable.[78] Beginning just after Boileau and Perrault's public embrace in 1694 and continuing until the outbreak of the Dacier–Houdar de La Motte battle in 1711, commentary concerning the crisis in history took two forms.[79] Commentators in the first camp, who can be seen as Moderns whether or not they explicitly designate themselves as such, attack contemporary historians because of a range of inadequacies: they were lacking in discernment; they invented their alleged facts, failed to verify their sources, and were incapable of true research; they chose subjects not worthy of their or their public's attention, and so forth. Commentators in the opposite camp do not so much defend contemporary history as they counterattack, trying to lay the blame for the lack of confidence in contemporary history at the feet of either historical novelists or of those historians who were accused of presenting an overtly novelistic view of history.[80]

The case against the historical novel received its most eloquent formulation at the height of the fin de siècle crisis about historical reliability. In his *Dictionnaire historique et critique* (1697), Pierre Bayle denounced "a problem growing more important every day" because of the success of what he termed "the new novels" (*nouveaux romans*).[81] The "new novelists" have so successfully simulated actual historical writing that "they have thrown a thousand shadows over real history," and readers are now unable to "separate fiction from true fact" in their production (*Dictionnaire*, article "Nidhard," n.C, 2:666).

Bayle's fin de siècle anxiety about the historical novel's dangerous ability to confuse readers becomes understandable in the context of the crisis in history. At a time when history was being judged unreliable, novels might be considered more so—especially if, as was the case, they foregrounded motivations not previously recorded and they concentrated on a type of history guaranteed to appeal to a public eager for interiority, a behind-the-scenes history of great men and great events in which great men are portrayed as motivated by familiar human emotions.[82] The model Lafayette created for the novel, or so Bayle suggested, threatened to create a new history, so much more appealing than other available models that readers could choose to believe that the vision presented by the "new novels" was truly historical.[83] The history whose outline they were the first to suggest is one that commentators are still calling for today, a history of the emotions or a history of the heart.[84]

History itself furnished perhaps the ultimate proof that Bayle's anxiety was justified. Before the Culture Wars had ended, there were clear indications that one of the ways in which historians were combating the belief in their inadequacy involved taking on the novel on its own ground by inventing types of history more open to affective concerns. Thus, in 1712, Abbé Louis Le Gendre inaugurated the tradition of what soon came to be called "the history of private life" with his *Les Moeurs et coutumes des Français dans les différents temps de la monarchie.* Le Gendre helped originate a crucial shift in historical focus, whereby attention was displaced from monarchs to the nation and its culture. Even when he does discuss the kings of France, he uses more developed descriptions of their private lives to characterize their reigns.[85]

Still other signs of the new novel's influence are evident, even in the most traditional type of history then practiced, histories of the French monarchy. One has only to compare the style of such accounts before and after the Culture Wars' divide to realize just how evident the incursions of "histoire sensible" became. In his *Histoire de France et l'origine de la maison royale* (1679), Father Adrien Jourdan describes, for example, in great detail the reign of Childeric—his battles and conquests, the plots against him—paying almost no attention to his affective life (598–620). The vision of the same period found in Abbé Paul-François Velly's *Histoire de France,* the canonical account for much of the eighteenth century, is startlingly different. In the manner of the historical novelists, Velly begins with a brief portrait of Childeric: "He was the most handsome man in his kingdom: . . . born with a tender heart, he gave himself over entirely to love, and this was the cause of his downfall" (41). Velly

call this reign "like something out of a novel [*romanesque*]" (43)—
and indeed, in this account, it is often straight out of one of the
new novels, a reign during which all political and military activity
is inspired by love interests.[86] Once kings with "tender hearts" and
novelistic reigns had begun to preside over the most widely read
account of the French monarchy, it must have been evident that
history, too, had fallen under the spell of *sensibilité*.

Even as these first steps in the direction of a history of the emotions, a portrayal of private life, and an awareness of the self as an
affective construct were being taken, however, a literature was coming into existence remarkable above all for the depiction of characters who may well be the first true precursors of heroes generated
by the nineteenth century's fin de siècle. These heroes are recognizable by either their lack of identity or by the "sharp rupture of an
identity."[87] It was as if, no sooner had psychological depth and self-
awareness become values for the novel, than writers began to imagine a literary self whose very definition toys with the notions upon
which the stability of identity was founded.

The boldest such attempt, a work that still seems incredible even
in our postmodern age, seems to have been the product of a most
unlikely collaboration. In 1695 and 1696, *Le Mercure galant* published two versions of a short story, "Histoire de la marquise-
marquis de Banneville."[88] The publication was anonymous, and the
indications concerning its author's identity provided by Donneau
de Visé are contradictory. For its first edition, the story opens with
a preface by the woman identified as its author, who describes her
effort as a perfect example of women's writing (543–44). For its
second edition, Donneau de Visé justifies the publication by remarking that "the woman who wrote it left out several episodes"
(*Le Mercure galant*, August 1696, 171). Midway between these two
publications, Donneau de Visé had included another story in his
periodical, "La Belle au bois dormant," introduced with the claim
that it was from the pen of "the same person who wrote the story
of the young marquise that I shared with you a year ago and that
won so much praise" (*Le Mercure galant*, February 1696, 74).

This elaborate cross-referencing becomes a problem, however,
when readers remember that the author of "La Belle au bois dormant" was none other than Charles Perrault.[89] "La Belle au bois
dormant" is the ultimate Modern work: it was the first published
example of the most important genre to be created in the aftermath
of the conflict between Ancients and Moderns, the genre that Perrault invented while he was still completing the *Parallèle* and his

struggles to prove Modern supremacy and as his contribution to the fin de siècle years, the fairy tale.[90] "Histoire de la marquise-marquis de Banneville" could, therefore, be considered a typical example of women's writing only if women's writing is defined as Perrault did, that is, as quintessential modern writing produced by either men or women. Donneau de Visé's comparison between the two tales was surely an attempt to link Perrault with "Histoire de la marquise-marquis de Banneville." Without it, no contemporary reader would have associated the rather staid public servant and head Modern with perhaps the most outlandish publication of the classical age.

Modern scholarship generally considers the work a collaboration between Perrault and François-Timoléon, abbé de Choisy.[91] The association between Choisy and this work is easy to see: Choisy was the most prominent and the most successful cross-dresser in an age in which the phenomenon was hardly discreet; "Histoire de la marquise-marquis de Banneville" is a tale in which the central characters, cross-dressers all, alternately dupe their public and are in turn duped by other practitioners of their art. Along the way, the story offers abundant commentary on both the relation between dress and sexuality and the relation between sexuality and identity.

Surely no other work from any age prior to our own has ever demonstrated with such insistence that the self exists only to be performed and has glorified in no uncertain terms the liberating potential of cross-dressing.[92] "Histoire de la marquise-marquis de Banneville" takes the issues of interiority and identity debated during the Culture Wars to such extreme conclusions that the tale could be seen as portraying the death of the fragile new self exposed in Lafayette's novel, the lesson that this self must be fiercely protected behind masks and facades, or even the unraveling of every stable notion of interiority—to replace them with the image of a "self" self-made to be as slippery, as elusive a creation as possible. If Perrault truly had a hand in its production, then the head Modern may be said, just as in the case of "century," to have understood that each of the Moderns' inventions was destined simultaneously to be undone. In this case, Perrault initially praised modern literature's new interiority in the work that made the fin de siècle inevitable and then exploded all commonly accepted definitions of identity in the first true fin de siècle literary work.

In the manner of Lafayette's heroine, the young marquise is raised in isolation by a widowed mother and only confronts the centers of power when she is already an adolescent. Like the princess, she is initially "completely ignorant about her state" (550).

This ignorance is, however, truly unsettling, for the young marquise does not know that she is in fact—a marquis. When her father was killed in battle, her mother, who was then pregnant, decided that, whatever the child's sex, to avoid a repetition of its father's fate she would raise it as a girl. And thus it came to pass that—with the aid of "iron bodies" that from childhood "corrected" and "constrained" the young body to produce hips and breasts (544–45)—when the dowager marquise de Banneville arrived in Paris, she had a twelve-year-old "female" beauty in tow.

The example of Mariane, the young marquise-marquis, defines sexuality as that of which she is ignorant, her "state" (550, 558). With this terminological choice, the story suggests first that sexuality is changing, something to be acquired, as opposed to something stable and inalterable because it is there from birth.[93] In the seventeenth century, a "state" was the opposite of a permanent identify, such as class (condition), acquired at birth. In his Dictionnaire (1690), Furetière says that état "is used for the different rungs that distinguish people according to their office or profession." In addition, an état, once again as defined by Furetière, was inherently performative, a way of being defined acted out in large part through dress: "In France, one can only know the state of individuals by their lifestyle, by their clothing."

In "Histoire de la marquise-marquis de Banneville," sexuality is fully a state in both senses of the term. Mariane's maleness is exchanged for femaleness as if she were changing professions, and the change is accomplished largely by means of dress. The story devotes the bulk of its descriptive energy to clothing and jewelry, to dressing as a performative act, and to the vociferous admiration provoked by displays of sartorial splendor. Mariane is by no means the only character to perform her sexuality in such spectacular fashion. The story goes to great lengths to explain that cross-dressing is equally, and just as successfully, acted out by men. The first of Mariane's admirers to attract her attention is a "beau jeune homme" (551), a young marquis who parades the trimmings of masculinity and who turns out to be a marquise.

The frontier between maleness and femaleness is so permeable, in fact, that the story features a conversation between Mariane and her mother's best friend in which they are discussing the beauty of the young marquis, whose "true" sex they have not yet discovered, and conclude: "Why doesn't he dress as a girl?" (551)—for, as Mariane is quick to point out to him, "you wouldn't be the first, for young men today arrange themselves [s'ajustent] as girls" (552). Indeed, the principal justification for the tale's second edition is to include the story of another such "arrangement," that of a beautiful princess, in "reality" prince Sionad, whose elaborate self-transformation is recounted in the most lavish detail (*Le Mercure galant*, August 1696, 207–36).

The process of self-adjustment, while elaborate, is consistently characterized as natural. When someone suggests that the princess-prince should stop "forcing himself" and return to male garb, he responds with astonishment: "force myself [*me contraindre*]. . . ? I have never forced myself" (*Le Mercure galant*, August 1696, 226). Once properly readjusted, their behavior is free and without restraint because it has become literally second nature to them. Witness the terms in which Mariane's mother finally reveals her biological sex to her: "Yes, my child, . . . you are a boy. . . . Habit has given you another nature" (*L'habitude a fait en vous une autre nature*) (559). By this she means that these new tranvested identities are not only second nature but are as important as nature itself, that the identities that they choose to perform are valid, permanent identities, the only ones to which the public will have access.

No matter how perfectly it is performed, however, second nature does not erase biological nature. Mariane and the young marquis fall in love. This initially generates enormous anxiety about the possible consequences of their attraction, but in the end all potential problems are quite simply resolved. They marry; they reveal the bodies behind the iron bodies—and each is thrilled with the "destiny" that led them to each other (563). They decide to take full advantage of their double nature. As the happy husband sums it up for his new bride on their wedding night: "Enjoy, beautiful marquise, all the charms of your sex, and I'll take advantage of all the freedom of mine" (563)—by which he means that, even though they are both delighted with the new pleasures they have just enjoyed as man and wife, they will continue in public to "enjoy" a different kind of sexual performance.[94]

It is hard to avoid the temptation to read this curious tale in the context of current debate around sexuality and gender. For example, a work that closes on a scene in which "sex" is used as a synonym for cross-dressing would seem to confirm Marjorie Garber's view of transvestism's centrality as the sexual category that destabilizes the very notion of sexual category.[95] In addition, this text, centered on a clear distinction between a fixed biological (natural) difference and a variable behavioral (acquired) difference, would seem a tailor-made illustration of Thomas Laqueur's theory of the "making of

sex" and Michael McKeon's more recent formulation of "the emergence of gender"—all the more so since it dates from precisely the
period both identify as the crucial turning point in the creation of
our modern categories.

"Histoire de la marquise-marquis de Banneville" is, however, far
cannier than the presentation of late-seventeenth-century material
by these theoreticians leads us to expect.[96] Premodern texts, Laqueur
argues, are marked by the absence of "what we would call core gender identity, the sense that infants acquire early on of whether they
are boys or girls" (138). One would think this to be so with Mariane—until the key final scene when, on her wedding night, "she
no longer doubted that she was a boy" (563). The story should not
be misread, however, as simply reaffirming in the end the triumph
of biological difference and "core gender identity." "Histoire de la
marquise-marquis de Banneville" proclaims—flaunts might be a
more appropriate verb—a more modern view: since no fundamental
incompatibilities and absolute rules govern sexual categories, a person
can have it all at the same time—biological identity, core gender identity, and his-her own "naturally" constructed identity.[97] In the world
of "Histoire de la marquise-marquis de Banneville," sexuality is simultaneously an *état,* something that can be recreated at will, and a
condition, something fixed at birth. Identity can be performative and
stable at the same time. The natural self can be "constrained"; social
constructions of masculinity and femininity are flaunted, played with,
bent—and noble families will still get an heir.

The story of the two young sexual performers will probably remain anonymous. It is, nonetheless, tempting to think of Perrault
turning from his leadership of the Culture Wars to team up with a
cross-dressed ecclesiatic to produce this tale in which all the *jeunesse
dorée* of France seems to spend its days bending gender. The tale
could be seen as an over-the-top takeoff on the Ancients' worst fears
of rampant promiscuity and permeability, on Boileau's fin de siècle
nightmare of the French nation destroyed by the forces for social
change unleashed by the Moderns.

It may also have been intended as a cautionary tale to those Moderns who were propagandists for the new affectivity with its vision
of the self generated through its relation to a sympathetic other.
Mariane does discover her heart and her interiority in a spontaneous
movement at the sight of her marquis (551); when the lovers are
separated, she pines away with what her doctor diagnoses as an "illness of the heart" (*Le Mercure galant,* September 1696, 135). The
tale suggests, nevertheless, that self-construction is a more impor-

tant project than self-discovery, and above all that identity is not easily known and never transparent.

No amount of questioning, however, could stop the spread of the image of the heart as the full measure of identity. From the first classic of *sensibilité*, Anne Bellinzani Ferrand's *Histoire des amours de la jeune Bélise et de Cléante* (1689) to Gamaches's "system of the heart" (1704), in which *sensibilité* is pronounced "the foundation of all the qualities we want to find in others" (52), to the first novel of *sensibilité's* most nuanced portraitist ever, Pierre Carlet de Marivaux, *Les Effets surprenants de la sympathie* (1713–14)—by the end of the Culture Wars, it was widely accepted that, in the emotional exchange that was the essence of the affective revolution, each sensitive heart recognized simultaneously its own emotions and those of its secret sharer.[98] This was the dream of transparency, an idealized vision of identity politics according to which perfect self-knowledge was synonymous with perfect knowledge of the other, whose wide dissemination helped the French across the first fin de siècle divide.

It may be possible to conclude from the fin de siècle's fascination with "anatomies of the amorous heart" that it was an age like ours, desirous of interiority and engaged in the collective creation of an obsession with affective precision because it was terrified of emotional emptiness, of the possibility that many people who resemble Lafayette's princess existed—individuals not fully in touch with their hearts and so frozen by affective paralysis that they only realize what they are/were feeling after the fact. No matter what its origin, once it had been implanted, the desire for interiority did not disappear, even in the face of the triumph of other forces originally brought to prominence by the Moderns, reason and progress. Indeed, just as *sensibilité* was reaching its full glory in Marivaux's novels of the 1730s, in particular *La Vie de Marianne* (1731–41), commentators were already beginning, by complaining that the French no longer had a heart, to reveal a longing for a resurgence of emotionality.[99] Witness the example of René-Louis de Voyer, marquis d'Argenson, who in his *Essais* (1736) records a dire vision of a nation increasingly dominated by individuals who no longer value the heart: "The heart is a faculty of which we are depriving ourselves more every day because we do not use it, and all the while we are sharpening our minds and wits [*l'esprit*]. . . . Today, we are losing that beautiful part of ourselves that is called *sensibilité*. Love, and the need to love, are disappearing from the earth. . . . This is what I observe in those of my age and those born after me. The heart is being overcome by paralysis."[100]

4

Culture or Civilization?

Civilization: All the social phenomena—religious, moral, aesthetic, scientific—common to every great society.
Culture: All the intellectual and aesthetic aspects of a civilization.
—*Le Grand Robert de la langue française* (1989)

Today, the definitions given in the epigraph are standard for two of the terms that have dominated the polemics between twentieth-century Ancients and Moderns—Western civilization versus cultural studies, to give the most obvious example. The same dictionaries that propose these definitions also tell us that "culture" and "civilization" are recent inventions, terms that only began to be used in French at the turn of the nineteenth century.[1] The dictionary would thus encourage us to believe that the adversaries in the first Culture Wars had no words with which to express these interrelated concepts. If we allow the dictionary to guide our thinking, we will, therefore, be forced to conclude that the concept of civilization could have had no relevance for seventeenth-century debates, because our precursor Ancients and Moderns simply did not think along these lines.

But they did, or at least they began to do so as a result of the forces unleashed by the Modern proclamation of superiority over their Ancient precursors.

In January 1687, Perrault concluded his reading of *Le Siècle de Louis le Grand* to his fellow Academicians by declaring that none of the Modern accomplishments would have been possible without

> the greatest of Kings
> To whom we owe that immense splendor
> Which illuminates our century and France. (25)

In that single sentence, Perrault highlighted the two notions upon which the new intellectual horizons opened up by the Moderns would be founded. Just as, in the usage Perrault imposed, *century* indicates the chronological literalness necessary for both the myth of progress and the notion of decline and fall, so "France" points to a novel geographical precision, a conception of territory that proved essential to the reconfiguration of what Norbert Elias terms "the civilizing process." As a crucial opening move in the Culture Wars, a sense of French intellectual territoriality, of the inherent French-ness of this civilizing process, was promoted. The Moderns thus succeeded in making the "France" of "our century" synonymous with the birth of "culture."

Prior to Perrault's cataclysmic invasion of the republic of letters, *culture* was used to refer only to what is now usually termed agriculture: "the effort necessary to render the land fertile through plowing" (Furetière). Then, no sooner were the hostilities declared, than *culture* was suddenly jolted from the cultivation of the earth to the cultivation of the intellect. This time, the innovative usage was not invented by Perrault, but by the other major early Modern leader, Fontenelle. The year 1688 witnessed the appearance of the two most significant Modernist polemics in the history of the Culture Wars, the initial volume of Perrault's *Parallèle* and Fontenelle's *Digression sur les anciens et les modernes*. The *Digression* features a textbook example of semantic slippage, the process by which a term's transfer from an established usage to a metaphorical one is facilitated for the neologism's first audience.

To make *culture*'s new function clear, Fontenelle imagined a canny blend of cultivation of the soil and cultivation of the mind. He begins with a discussion of plants and climates and concludes with a meditation on what would now be termed cultural difference:[2] "Different ideas are like plants or flowers that do not take equally well in all types of climates. . . . Perhaps the fact that orange trees do not grow as easily here as in Italy indicates that there is in Italy a certain way of thinking unlike anything we have in France" (126). The link between intellectual activity and the cultivation of plants thus firmly established, Fontenelle introduces his key word.

It is undeniable that . . . the climatic differences that have an effect upon plants necessarily also have an effect upon minds. In this case, the effect is, however, less important and evident, because art and *culture* are capable of far greater impact on minds than on soil, which is a harder and less malleable substance. Thus a country's way of thinking [*les pensées*]

is more easily transplanted to another [country] than is its flora, and we
would find it less difficult to adopt the genius of the Italians in our works
than to make orange trees grow [in France]. (126; my emphasis)[3]

Thus, *culture*'s implantation into French took place in a passage
that affirms the primacy of a country's intellectual climate—rather
than, for example, such diverse manifestations of what Fontenelle
terms its "physical universe" (*monde matériel*) as its native flora or
agricultural traditions—in determining a nation's sense of its speci-
ficity. In addition, the passage affirms in particular the existence of
France as an independent cultural entity by contending that there
is a certain way of "thinking" and a certain type of "intelligence"
(*esprit*) that are inherently French and unlike those that characterize
either earlier civilizations (he gives the example of Egypt) or other
contemporary traditions (for instance, that of Italy).

As with other Modern linguistic innovations such as "siècle,"
even as it creates "culture" Fontenelle's inaugural inscription undermines the status of such related notions as cultural absolutism and
cultural supremacy. Thus, he concludes his reflection on comparative national cultures, on cultural difference, by affirming his belief
that in the long run climate would not prove to be the determining
factor in the development of culture "as long as all minds are culti-
vated to the same extent." There have not yet been works of genius
from either the coldest or the hottest zones, Fontenelle admits, but
this does not mean that "we may not still hope to see one day great
authors who are Lapp or Negro" (126–27). Fontenelle warns, in
other words, against any belief in inherent cultural superiority. In
addition, his treatise frequently reiterates that it is impossible to
predict how civilization will evolve, what peoples will keep the flame
alive, or even whether the entity "culture" for which he was attempting to win recognition would always continue to exist. Fontenelle concludes on his most forceful formulation of cultural relativism, by speculating that the scholars of the future, "who might even
be Americans," might well totally lose respect for any and all past
cultural traditions, might reject anything that could be considered
ancient, including, of course, the seventeenth-century Moderns
(136–37).

Fontenelle's *Digression* thus both introduces *culture* as a term and
lays claim to the concept of culture as an inherently Modern phenomenon. Already in its initial appearance in French, *culture* is comparative and multiple: the term was said to reveal national characteristics precisely because it indicated, not a continuum, a heritage

passed on from one civilization to the next, but rather a tradition native to each individual soil.

In a now classic formulation, Elias exposed the semantic tensions that, he contended, had caused "culture" to be constructed in opposition to "civilization." In Elias's view of the relation between the two terms, *civilization* expresses just what is missing from Fontenelle's inaugural inscription of *culture:* the term was created to signify "the expression of Western consciousness," "Western national feeling" (12). *Civilization,* still according to Elias, translated the self-satisfaction of those peoples whose national frontiers and national characters were definitively set, and it provided, furthermore, the foundation for the belief in the superiority of Western traditions essential to the colonizing enterprise (*Civilisation* 23, 85). Rather than the multiplicity of differences inherent to *culture, civilization* stressed the sameness among those peoples who, it was believed, shared a common heritage. For Elias, at its origin the concept of civilization is an English and, above all, a French preserve, a term linked to a process founded on the essential aristocratic values of politeness, civility, courtesy, and good taste. "Culture," on the other hand, which Elias considers an inherently German concept, was, according to his theory, a bourgeois invention, designed in particular to stress the national differences erased in the aristocratic view of the civilizing process wrought by *politesse* (*Civilisation* 14, 20–21). In this view, "culture" was born as a national reaction on the part of a people who experienced national unification only much later than their more Western counterparts, a people whose national frontiers were for a long time far less stable than theirs. "Culture" was thus a reflection of the consciousness of a nation still trying to delimit its political and spiritual frontiers, still wondering just how to define its national character (15).

I rehearse Elias's argument in some detail both because it has recently become so influential that it seems impossible to discuss the pairing of culture and civilization without reference to it, and because I fully agree with his view of the fundamental tension between the two concepts. We part ways in significant fashion, however, when considering the development of that tension. Elias's history of the primacy of "civilization" and his view of "culture" as a reactive creation ignore both the invention of "culture" in French decades before the initial occurrence in German and, therefore, the original involvement between these two concepts, an involvement that was far more intricate than Elias's point-counterpoint scenario indicates.[4]

This is not, however, to take exception with Elias's view of *culture*'s original semantic charge. Already at its inception in a very different context from the nineteenth-century German context Elias describes, culture can be seen as a concept constructed in opposition to civilization—even though the actual term *civilization* would not be invented for another half-century.[5] This oppositional structure is most remarkable, not for the fact that there is no trace of the invention of the word *civilization* during the years of the Culture Wars, but for the fact that "culture" came into existence with its oppositional charge at precisely the same time as the concepts upon which "civilization" would subsequently depend for its existence were coming fully into their own. Unlike "culture," which sprung fully formed into its French existence, the concept of civilization can been said to have been coming to life for decades before the word itself was coined. During that time, the concept was expressed by a constellation of interrelated terms, each of which indicated various elements of the total semantic charge of *civilization:* chiefly, *civility* and *politeness* and its variants such as *polir* (to polish or refine), but also several terms often closely related to these two, such as *society* (in particular when used in the phrase *société civile*, which meant something close to "civilized society"), *manners* (*moeurs*), and *taste* (*goût*).[6]

During the years just prior to and during the Culture Wars, all these terms were implicated in forging a belief in the existence and the necessity of the civilizing process. A few brief examples from contemporary dictionaries demonstrate that this semantic constellation was successful in playing this role largely because, just as was happening with the new affective vocabulary, the words were constantly used to refer to each other, as if the meaning of all the terms but the one being defined was already clear. This system of cross-referencing functioned to lend supplemental meaning to each member of the constellation. Thus, the Académie Française defines *honnête* as "civil, polite" and *to civilize* as "to make civil, *honnête* . . . refine [*polir*] behavior [*les moeurs*]." In similar fashion, Furetière says that *politeness* means "*honnête* and civil behavior" and provides this example for *society:* "Men started to form societies in order to live more politely." This elaborate cross-referencing indicates that a cluster of concepts revolving around politeness, civility, and *honnêteté* was viewed as the foundation of the process as a result of which society and its inhabitants became more refined.

Only in scattered phrases do the dictionaries give a more precise idea of what this process of refinement entailed. The Académie

Française, for example, states that "*honnête* conversation in worldly circles is a necessary prerequisite for civility" and repeats more or less the same formula for *politeness;* it also declares that "the study of belles lettres refines young men." In his examples, Furetière makes explicit the class-bound nature of the civilizing process: "Only peasants have no civility"; "Peasants are not as civilized as bourgeois, and bourgeois [are not as civilized] as courtiers." In addition, refinement is not only an aristocratic preserve; the process is also inherently under French control: "It is impossible to see a higher level of politeness than that which exists at the Court of France" (Furetière). Finally, because they have succeeded in raising refinement to this new level, the French are presented as having taken up the civilizing flame first brandished by the Greeks, who, in the Académie Française's definition of *to civilize,* are described as "having civilized the barbarians."

The core civilizing vocabulary also proclaims that there is only one good taste, and that it, too, is at present an inherently French phenomenon. The genealogy of good taste proves definitively, furthermore, that the French are the heirs of the Greeks. In the list of examples Furetière provides to illustrate the concept of the best taste, the juxtaposition of the Greeks and the French implicitly makes this point: "The taste of the Greeks was surest in the domain of architecture. Poussin's paintings have captured the taste of many." When the Académie Française concludes its characterization of taste by calling it "the general character of a century," the phenomenon is once again confined within the double set of limits—chronological and geographical—of Perrault's Modernist manifesto. Indeed, the vocabulary that indicates that the civilizing process was inherently French is most widely diffused at precisely the moment at which France, under Louis XIV's guidance, was undergoing an obsession with its frontiers, trying to guarantee that they would reach perfect limits.

Hence the passage that culminates in Perrault's praise of France and the seventeenth century begins with a eulogy of its monarch's military genius, in this case, his ability "to extend his frontiers as far as he wishes" (*Siècle* 23). The semantic strain that culminates in the mid–eighteenth century in the creation of "civilization" is indeed, as Elias declared, an expression of the superiority of French taste, knowledge, and behavior presented as the ultimate expression of Western civility. It is also, as Elias intuited, the expression of France's confidence in its new national limits, a confidence necessary for it to extend itself beyond those limits through the creation of colonies. The French civilizing vocabulary came into existence just as the country's colonizing enterprise was undergoing a period of reorganization and expansion: when Perrault read *Le Siècle de Louis le Grand* to the Académie Française, the *code noir,* the legal code drawn up to legislate the institution of slavery in the French colonies, was barely a year old.[7] It was to this sense of national intellectual superiority—the French as modern heirs of the Greeks in their civilizing role—and to this sense of national entitlement—the conviction that France could now openly expand its territory across the sea because it was itself territorially complete—that Perrault played in the *Siècle,* in the hope that French protonationalism would guarantee the success of his polemic for modern superiority.

There is, however, a second tendency evident in the seventeenth-century vocabulary related to the civilizing enterprise, one that prepared the way, not for the eventual creation of "civilization," but for Fontenelle's invention of "culture." Indeed, in the case of the civilizing vocabulary outside the core group, almost all the examples from contemporary dictionaries point not to the isolated supremacy of something that could have been called French civilization, but rather to a multiplicity of separate but equal national cultures. In fact, perhaps the biggest surprise encountered when dealing with this case of semantic slippage concerns the degree to which distinctions are maintained between the contiguous but conflicting tendencies, one of which culminates in the civilizing vocabulary, the other in "culture."

Witness, for example, the Académie Française's treatment of *moeurs* as "the different customs and laws of each nation. . . . Each nation has its customs." And, in the same vein, Furetière's definition of *nation,* which demonstrates that terms in this category reinforce each other not through cross-referencing but through the repetition of one basic idea: "Collective name, used for a great people inhabiting a defined area of land, enclosed within clear limits. . . . Each nation has its own individual character. . . . Someone should take on the important task of composing a comparative study of the behavior and customs [*moeurs et coutumes*] of all nations." In its presentation of *nation,* the Académie Française adds to the core definition the fact that all the inhabitants speak the same language, then gives these examples: "The French nation. The Spanish nation. A nation's temperament, character [*esprit*], genius." According to the terms of their own self-presentation, the French were thus in a class by themselves as far as "civilization" was concerned. In the domain of culture, however, they saw themselves as simply one nation among many, all equal in their cultural difference—"each nation has its own individual character."[8]

This, then, is the binary situation out of which our modern civilizing vocabulary developed. Long before Kant proclaimed the creation of *Kultur* in opposition to *Zivilisiertheit* to reflect the desire of a national bourgeoisie to liberate itself from French cultural domination, even longer before Germaine de Staël recreated *culture* and *civilisation* in French under the influence of Kant's German usage—long before the terms entered the second phase of their oppositional history retraced by Elias, a primal opposition already divided them.[9] Even as *civilization* was first being intuited as the label that would proclaim French superiority most effectively, but well before it was invented, *culture* was already being used, by the mix of bourgeois and aristocrats who composed the Modern ranks, to signify not so much a reaction against "civilization," a simple desire to replace one concept with another, but an entirely different way of handling the business of culture.

"Civilization" seemed to lead inevitably to the barbarians-at-the-gates mentality—witness Dacier's proclamation of the Académie Française as "the rampart of language, knowledge, and good taste" (*Corruption* 32), as though that learned body were a defensive system separating the civilized within from the uncivilized hordes without. It also seemed to lead, inevitably and ironically, to a status quo mentality—what we have is working because we are the best, so we shouldn't change a thing. Witness once again the example of Dacier, warning ominously (and providing unwitting confirmation of Perrault's claim that the Modern style of 1687 was the most perfect aesthetic moment ever) that "foreigners have been criticizing us for allowing the good taste of the last century to degenerate" (*Corruption* 13). For "culture," on the other hand, there were not really any gates, much less any barbarians.

At the core of the Modern program were three cultural values: an openness to cultural difference; an insistence on reflecting upon the criteria for inclusion and exclusion, rather than simply practicing a new form of inclusion; and a defense of the right to individuality. Thus, Perrault may have criticized Homer's barbarity, but he never used this type of argument against non-French moderns. In the *Parallèle*, one of the most intriguing passages is centered on a discussion of how French monumental architecture could be made receptive to foreign conventions. The friends consider a project for the completion of the Louvre by adding on apartments "in the style of each of the world's nations." Not only would each architectural style be imitated, but furniture and appointments would be exactly duplicated, so that "all foreigners would have the pleasure of being able in a sense to encounter their own country in ours" (4:273–74). Coming in the aftermath of the nationalistic official competition to add onto the Louvre, Perrault's project—featuring both foreign styles and intimate spaces borrowed from other architectural traditions—is the antithesis of the definition of architecture as reflection of the glory of France and its monarch that was the dominant vision of the Versailles era.[10]

Perrault's successor, Houdar de La Motte, is the best representative of the Modern desire to create a debate about culture that would not be primarily a contest to determine cultural superiority. His *Réflexions sur la critique* is above all a plea to his public not merely to be interested in which argument seems correct, but to try to discover the multiplicity of points of view possible on a given subject (1:3–8). In the final analysis, both these principles were made to serve the cause of the ultimate Modern cultural precept, the defense of individual genius: all culture, individual culture as much as cultural tradition, is formed not by simple repetition of existing cultural monuments, but by such a thorough assimilation of the past that the resulting cultural mosaic is completely original.[11] Rather than seeking to create a culture viewed as the last word, all these Modern positions aimed to present culture as an ongoing historical process.

The existence of such an open and flexible approach to culture at the moment at which French cultural imperialism was coming into its own might well seem little more than a fine irony. Once again, however, I will permit myself a moment of speculation, first, concerning the origins of French cultural imperialism in the late seventeenth century and, second, about what might have happened, had the Modern vision ever received a concrete application. During the Culture Wars' years, the foundations were being laid for what was destined to become the official model for the transmission of French culture. One may take as a founding date for this practice 1661, the year of Cardinal Mazarin's death.

In his will, the former prime minister provided a vast sum for the construction of the Collège des Quatre Nations, a school for the instruction of sixty adolescent male students. Despite a name that suggests what we would term diversity, the school Mazarin endowed had as its mission the first state-sponsored attempt at using pedagogy to eliminate all the categories of difference that, as we have seen, were reflected in *nation*'s connotations in the late seventeenth century. Its students were to be chosen from the four territories France had most recently conquered. The *collège*'s mission was straightforward indeed: Mazarin believed that it was not sufficient simply to make land French through conquest; provinces would only "become truly French through their own desire [*inclination*]" (quoted by Franklin 145). In order to generate that desire, Mazarin planned to give the selected sons of the elite from each province "a completely French education" so that they would subsequently "take what they had learned back with them to the country of their birth, . . . where they would convince others to obtain the same instruction and acquire the same feeling" (quoted by Franklin 145). That feeling, as Louis XIV made clear when he subsequently drew up the documents founding the *collège,* was "to win their hearts and to make them truly French" (quoted by Franklin 161).[12] Until 1684, the project did not get beyond the construction stage. In was only between 1684 and 1688 that the institution's educational policy was established.

It may have been a mere accident that the first institution designed to make students French through the imposition of French national culture as a replacement for their individual regional cultures finally opened its doors in October 1688, at the height of the conflict between Ancients and Moderns, even though the money for its creation had been bequeathed a quarter-century before. It is tempting, however, to see some significance in the timing of what can be seen as the foundation of the official French cultural policy with respect to foreigners living on French soil, what is now known as assimilation: foreigners were taught French culture in the belief that this would make them want to give up their own native traditions and aspire to live as the French did.

What was the content of the culture on which this central civilizing mission hinged? We know that the *collège* had ten classes: one in mathematics, one in rhetoric, two in philosophy, and six in the humanities—which meant, according to educational practice at the time, that literature would have formed the center of its definition of French culture, for works that we would consider literary were almost always the basis for instruction not only in literary matters but in subjects we would know by other names today, history or political science, for example. The works thus promoted were not, however, works of *French* literature, for, in accordance with dominant pedagogical practice of the day, all instruction took place in Latin.[13] In fact, the only exposure to actual French culture in this "completely French education" occurred at mealtime, when students sometimes had Géraud de Cordemoy's highly traditional *Histoire de France* (1685–89) read aloud to them (Franklin 105).

In 1688, the Moderns had not yet had the opportunity to demonstrate what practical consequences their program might have for education in France, how radically it might change the definition of French culture. They had only had time to set off an uproar, to unleash the Culture Wars, as a result of which, with extraordinary rapidity, Ancient supporters began issuing ominous warnings about the catastrophic consequences a Modern victory could have on pedagogical practice in France. Witness the version of this doomsday scenario that Perrault placed in the mouth of his fictive Ancient, the Président, in the second volume of his *Parallèle*, already in print in 1690: if the Moderns have their way, the Président insists, "it is impossible to imagine the disorder that will befall the Republic of Letters, that of education and of the school system [*les collèges*]. . . . People will be told that all they have to do is to study the good taste of this century, to comply with [its directives], and to read the newspapers of France, Holland, and England to keep themselves abreast of the latest discoveries. . . . That will certainly be an easy way out, and one that will eliminate the need for long hours [of work]" (2:297). In the face of such dire warnings to the effect that to make French culture truly French would signify the end of civilization in France, it is impossible to imagine that, in 1688, any official educational institution could have granted modern (French) literature a significant role in its course of study.

Such hesitancy seems all the more comprehensible if we bear two additional factors in mind. First, the issue of a national culture is never more sensitive than at the time of its formation—all the more so because that moment almost inevitably coincides with the moment during which the nation is in the process of attaining definitive territorial limits.[14] Second, many of those involved in the Culture Wars seemed to have known instantly that pedagogy was destined to become one of the most controversial cultural issues. It is tempting, therefore, to imagine that, in 1687 and 1688, those involved in making the final decisions about the functioning of the most official pedagogical institution in the seventeenth century decided to define an education in Frenchness as one that shut out works written in French.

Certainly this was, or was destined to become, the official Ancient view of literature's role in the civilizing and nation-building process. No Ancient ever waxed more eloquent on the subject than Dacier, who maintained that the mission of "fortifying the young" against the Modern "poison" was the principal motivation behind her decision to enter the fray (*Corruption* 9). The "poison" she had in mind was the promotion of modern literature, an enterprise whose success she describes in terms infinitely more dire than those Perrault imagined for his Président: "A nation's [*état*] young men [*jeunes gens*] are its most sacred possession; they are its base and its foundation. . . . If false principles are allowed to corrupt their minds and judgment, . . . bad taste and ignorance will ultimately triumph, and the humanities [*les lettres*] will be doomed—the humanities, which are the wellspring of any just government" (9–10). This argument—a nation depends on its youth for its survival, and any nation that wishes to guarantee it future strength must stringently monitor its young people's exposure to the great (i.e., ancient) books—thus developed, Dacier proceeds to her diatribe against modern literature and then to her defense of classical literature and of Homer in particular.

Contemporary pedagogical theorists—even those not completely of the Ancient persuasion—advised pedagogues to follow Dacier's principles. There is no more convincing example of this practice than the most influential work on education of the early eighteenth century, the four-volume *De la manière d'enseigner et d'étudier les belles-lettres, par rapport à l'esprit et au coeur* (1726–28), composed by Charles Rollin, former rector of the University of Paris and professor of eloquence at the Collège Royal.[15] Rollin—who foregrounds education's role in the civilizing process and whose rhetoric is heavily weighed with the vocabulary of "civility" and "politeness"— presents himself as something of a moderate, and he at times can be seen as paying lip service to the Moderns. In particular, he proposes that children should study the French language before they learn Latin and Greek (1:3) and contends that works written in French should be made part of their education: "Our own language provides us with a large number of excellent works, suitable for developing their taste" (1:18).

Rollin, however, devotes only a few pages in four volumes to the canon of these "excellent works" written in French—and with good reason: "The very limited amount of time that can be devoted to studying them . . . obliges us to decide on only a small number of works" (1:18). He eventually spells out the extent of his commitment to modern authors: he advises pedagogues to devote at most a half-hour a day—or perhaps every other day—to works written in French (1:34–35). He admits that this isn't much but contends that they can't afford to allot any more time to French authors because there is so much else to study.

Rollin's treatise proves just how successful the Ancients had been in excluding French authors from the definition of Western civilization that was put into place at the moment in French history still considered to have marked the golden age in the development of French national culture.[16] What is most intriguing about the degree to which they were successful in this endeavor is the absence of evidence indicating that there ever existed a Modern threat to the values of French pedagogy to be combated.

True, in 1686, the year before the Culture Wars began, Abbé Claude Fleury published his *Traité du choix de la méthode des études*, the most widely read pedagogical treatise ever to defend what can be considered the Modern perspective, slightly *avant la lettre*. No educational theorist of the classical age placed greater emphasis on the French language than Fleury. Alone among his contemporaries, he believed that grammar and Latin were two different subjects (174). In fact, he made the revolutionary statement that, by grammar, he had French grammar in mind and even contended that it wasn't necessary to know Latin in order to learn any of the subjects he discusses (209).[17] Even in the case of students who did know Latin, priority was always to be given to the French language. (Fleury gives the example of oral exercises in rhetoric, which were always to take place in French [241].) Fleury was not only Gallocentric: he was, once again alone among his contemporaries, profoundly egalitarian. Well over halfway into his treatise, he pauses to reflect that, until this point, he has been discussing "subjects that should be made available to everyone, women as well as men, rich and poor alike" (170). He subsequently devotes a special section to "studies for women" in which he vigorously condemns the narrowness of the education generally given them in his day (264–70).

Fleury's treatise was reedited for nearly a century and a half, so he obviously reached a sizable audience.[18] He did not, however, convince the audience with the power to change the situation along the lines he prescribed. For well over a century after the publication of his treatise, there is no evidence that education in France was seriously influenced by any of Fleury's ideas. During that same time span, Fleury did not even exercise a visible influence on any of the pedagogical theorists who follow in his footsteps. Witness the example of the next major post–Culture Wars publication after Rollin's, Abbé Nicolas Gedoyn's *De l'éducation des enfants*.[19] Gedoyn has mastered all the protonationalistic pedagogical rhetoric; he even re-

alizes that proclaiming the superiority of the French language—
"this language that has gained influence over all others; this language that is spoken at all the courts, that has become, or nearly
so, the universal language of Europe" (31)—is a logical part of that
rhetorical package. Gedoyn is not prepared, however, to make room
in the canon for works written in French. Timidly, he prescribes a
sort of parallel education: students would learn both classical languages and French, and they would study an ancient author in tandem with a modern writer.

Indeed, even the most inflammatory of the second-generation
Moderns, Houdar de La Motte, fails to make a much stronger case
for the place in the classroom of works in French. In a statement
that would have been welcome at many moments in today's Culture
Wars, he refuses to frame his discussion of the canon in terms of
who's in and who's out.

> The point is not, as many people imagine, and as the outraged defend-
> ers of antiquity seem to believe, whether we should be scornful of the
> ancients or value them, forget about them or hold onto them. There is
> no question but that we must respect and read them; we simply have to
> decide whether we shouldn't give ancients and moderns equal consider-
> ation, whether we shouldn't . . . erase from all works, so to speak, their
> author's name, in order to be able to judge them on their own merits.
> (*Réflexions* 1:31)

In Houdar de La Motte's vision, the goal of this equal-weight strategy would be to produce courses of study in which ancient and
modern authors are read together and with a double goal: that of
learning about ideal literary structures (*des modèles de toutes les
beautés*) and that of using the classical texts to show that their formal
beauties should not blind us to the fact that "we find in them examples of every kind of error [*faute*]" (*Réflexions* 1:29–30). From Perrault's earliest critique of Homer on, the Moderns had spoken of
Homer's "errors" to signify the ways in which his work reflected
the values of an age that did not respect the standards for "civilization" in which the French classical era was coming to believe.
Houdar de La Motte advocated a pedagogy that would have considered the ideology of classical texts along with their rhetorical perfection.

To review the development of pedagogical theory during the Culture Wars is to take stock of the extent to which the scenario circulated by the Ancients with respect to the imminent Modern takeover
of the educational curriculum (what we call today the canon) seems

largely to have been a put-up job. This is one area in which the
Moderns never made radical demands, one area in which they
fought for changes that would have been not only modest, but also
fully compatible with the needs of the nascent concept of French
culture, in the sense of a body of knowledge that must be imparted
in the same fashion to each student in order to guarantee his assimilation into the ranks of the French. The Modern defeat in this area
was undoubtedly brought about as a result of the success of the
Ancient propaganda campaign and, therefore, the willingness on the
part of the French of the late seventeenth and the early eighteenth
century to be persuaded that modern literature was dangerously
subversive reading for the youth of the day and a threat to the cultural fabric just beginning to bind their nation together.

Their defeat must also be attributed to the Moderns' own lack
of foresight and to their failure to work together in order to realize
the kind of broad-scale, concrete pedagogical project that would
have served to demonstrate the practical value of their views on
education. Fleury's treatise may have illustrated positions compatible with the Modern program, but its appearance on the eve of the
Culture Wars was merely a sign of the times, and Fleury never
aligned himself with the Moderns. No Modern spokesperson ever
bothered to compose a work of educational theory. No Modern ever
took time from polemics to found an educational establishment,
for example, a *collège* that could have made Mazarin's dream of a
"completely French education" a reality.[20] This defeat was perhaps
the most serious loss suffered by the Moderns. It signified that the
premise behind which they had originally closed ranks, the recognition of the greatness of a specifically French tradition, would not
be admitted in the pedagogical arena and would not, therefore, become part of French culture, before the end of the ancien régime.[21]
It can, therefore, honestly be said that the Moderns fought the Culture Wars for nothing.

The Modern pedagogical failure is particularly painful to contem-
plate. By handing over this essential territory to the Ancients without a struggle, the Moderns lost the opportunity for a dramatic
transformation of the history of culture in France. They surrendered
control over the imagery and the mythology of the civilizing process
to those who viewed civilization as an eternal flame to be kept burning and intact, rather than as a hybrid energy with multiple points
of "origin," an uncertain trajectory, and no perfect nature to be
maintained inviolate. As a result, the French continued to reject the

possibility of a culture that would be specifically French (Modern) and to maintain the goal of being always, eternally Ancient, as free of individuality and of all traces of specific ethnic traditions as possible. The most important of all Modern challenges—to the nature of the very entity, culture, that they initially defined—was so completely forgotten that Fontenelle's conviction that there would be great Lapp and Negro writers one day seems in the long run a mere aberration.[22]

And yet, had this not been the case, had the Moderns decided to join ranks not only in theory but in practice and to work for practical changes—in pedagogical technique, in the curriculum, in winning the right to education for new publics—they might have succeeded in putting an entirely new definition of French culture in place. They just might have challenged the rise of the civilizing process and have altered thereby the entire future of the involvement between "culture" and "civilization." Elias (and Kant before him) would never have been able to identify "culture" as the mark of a German revolt against French hegemony, for the prior subversion from within the French system itself would have remained visible.

This reflection on the fate of culture and opportunities missed brings me both to the original point of departure for this study and to what I early on realized would be the thoughts with which I wished to conclude my attempt to reread the late seventeenth century in terms borrowed from our current cultural conflict. From the beginning, I operated as though the following basic translations were acceptable:

1. When late seventeenth-century authors spoke of belles lettres and the relative pedagogical merits of ancient and modern authors, they had in mind a meaning close to what is conveyed today by the use of *canon;* in these two radically diverse contexts and allowing for the full extent of all historical, political, and institutional differences, speakers felt the need for what can be considered the same concept and for roughly the same reasons.

2. When the Ancients had recourse to the set of terms that denoted the civilizing process—in particular, civility, politeness, and taste—they were seeking to convey a message about that process with telling similarities to that transmitted by the phrase "Western civilization" in our current conflict.

3. When seventeenth-century Moderns invented "culture" or when they used the terminology linked to it (*nation, moeurs*), they

meant something very close to what their heirs today wish to project when they turn to adjectives such as *multicultural* and *transnational.*

The intellectual process in which the various seventeenth-century commentators were involved—from the invention of modern forms of literary history and literary criticism to the foundation of the entire modern educational system—was in its infancy during the period I have been discussing, whereas, in all its many facets, it has reached an intense level of complexity today. To many observers, it seems as if we are now at the end of a line and that all these institutions, the university in particular, are in dire need of reform.

I first became aware of the conflict that would become so divisive in our republic of letters in an almost accidental fashion. I began to remark that the person seated next to me on a plane would be as likely to be reading Allan Bloom's *The Closing of the American Mind* as what I considered more standard travel fare, for instance, the latest John Grisham novel. Initially, I admit, I was amused and pleased at this development and imagined that my professional concerns might be of interest to an audience outside the academy after all. In no time at all, of course, as other volumes began popping up instead of Grisham, my amusement gave way to concern about just what all these academic outsiders might be looking for—or just what they thought they were finding. For me, the decisive moment came in late 1990 and early 1991, when I realized that the only news that managed to put an end to the stream of letters to the editor that continued the debate on Alvin Kernan's *The Death of Literature* in the *International Herald Tribune* was the outbreak of war in the Persian Gulf.

It is naturally tempting to consider the national obsession with Bloom and his followers as a simple transfer of anxiety: a nation concerned about its increasing internal disorder and its increasing loss of international prominence shifts some of its frustration onto an area that seems more controllable. This reasoning is undoubtedly true to a certain extent. The entire phenomenon of the Culture Wars cannot be written off so quickly, however—and the example of the seventeenth century warns us against just that. It is, of course, easy to agree with those who, like Louis Menand, refuse to take campus politics seriously and contend, for example, that the canon will never be the instrument of any real social change (49). It is just as easy to agree with John Guillory's claim that schools do not transmit a

"national culture" but a "school culture" (38). And it is also easy
to share the conclusion, most recently put forward by Gregory Jusdanis, that we have only become obsessed with multiculturalism in
America now that there is no real ethnic culture left, only an ersatz
commodity (55–56).

All these valid points should not, however, allow us to forget that
the true importance of "culture" and "civilization" lie in the domain
of words rather than in that of things. Those paired concepts, and
all the related civilizing vocabulary as well, function above all to give
the impression that a sort of symbolic function exists and that it
serves to unify the citizens of a nation and therefore to keep the
nation strong. How else can one explain the fact that Louis XIV and
Mazarin, possibly the two most brilliant political mythmakers of all
time, having realized the role that a "completely French education"
(read "canon") might play in the process of national unification,
then proceeded to give absolutely no thought to the content of that
education, to how one would make it "completely French"? The
first individuals to have put the notion of a canon explicitly at the
service of the creation of a national cultural fabric may well have
believed that it did not matter what that fabric was made of, as long
as those to be unified with its threads were confident of its existence.

A definition similarly without content, as well as an equally vital
role, has been assigned to such notions as Western civilization in
the course of our Culture Wars. When the Culture Wars were declared with the simultaneous publication in 1987 of Bloom's volume
and E. D. Hirsch's *Cultural Literacy*, two very distinct conceptions
of civilization, and of cultural warfare, became clear. On the one
hand, there is Hirsch, for whom it is all very much a matter of
things, that is, the list of cultural facts he obsessively works and
reworks, as though it were possible to define with absolute precision
every detail of what one must know to be American. To the traditional Ancient precept that the sharing of identical information en-
sures "domestic tranquillity" (Hirsch xii), Hirsch adds what he
terms an "anthropological theory of education" and a guiding rule:
"All human communities are founded upon specific shared information. Americans are different from Germans, who in turn are
different from Japanese, because each group possesses specifically
different cultural knowledge" (xv). All this means simply that
Hirsch proposes a literalization of Mazarin's dream: he would transform the American educational system into a giant Collège des Quatre Nations and, in so doing, be far more logical than his seven-

teenth-century precursors: his curriculum to guarantee cultural
literacy would be composed solely of American works; no foreign
content would corrupt this completely American education (107).[23]

Allan Bloom's involvement with culture, on the other hand, is
totally bound up with its mythmaking capacity. To this end, he takes
over Dacier's role as intellectual whistle-blower and concentrates his
energy on the denunciation of America's cultural ills. In images that
recall Dacier's characterization of the Modern "poison" 's threat to
the social fabric, he portrays the politicized contemporary university
as capable of destroying the nation's very foundation: "When there
are no shared goals or vision of the public good, is the social contract
any longer possible?" (271). For the greater part of his book, Bloom
simply rants and raves—about, for example, the cultural threat
posed by rock (which plays for him the role Dacier assigns opera),
against feminists, against the 1960s. When, late in the game, he finally gets down to his solution, it is startlingly vague. The university
is the only place where today's students will be exposed to the civilizing process, and this is best handled by means of "the good old
Great Books approach": "A liberal education means reading certain
generally recognized classic texts, just reading them, letting them
dictate what the questions are" (344)—as though society could be
so easily made whole again. As our Culture Wars have unfolded,
however, Bloom's vagueness has prevailed over Hirsch's cultural
precision. Today as in the late seventeenth century, establishing belief in the existence of an American cultural fabric—and above all
belief in the fact that its existence is now threatened—has proved
more appealing than paying close attention to the actual composition of that fabric.

Thus, exactly three centuries after Perrault initiated the conflict
that propelled France toward a fin de siècle, Culture Wars broke
out again. This time, however, instead of a Modern initiative, aimed
at changing not only the questions that could be asked but also the
way in which they could be asked and even the ranks of those who
could ask the questions, the controversy was provoked by Ancients.
Small wonder, then, that culture would first become a crucial notion, not for its ability to unsettle received ideas of intellectual capital, but solely in its mythmaking capacity, in this case, to serve as
early warning signal of the imminent decline and fall of America.[24]
This was surely the case because of the fact that, in this capacity,
"culture" proved remarkably effective in selling books. The huge
commercial success of the first volumes encouraged others to jump
quickly into the fray. No one jumped more quickly or contributed

more efficiently to an acceleration of the threat-to-civilization rhetoric than did the head of the National Endowment for the Humanities, Lynne Cheney.[25] It was Cheney above all who, in her 1988 *Humanities in America,* made the crucial shift from "culture" to
"Western civilization" and initiated the portrayal of America as on
the verge, not only of coming apart as a society, but also of abandon-
ing its role as current keeper of the civilizing flame (8, 12), thereby
taking full advantage of the civilizing vocabulary's potential to ad-
vance the Ancient cause.[26]

Cheney's use of Ancient rhetoric had positioned her in the right
place at the right time, and a twist of fate completed her elevation.
Virtually as soon as Dick Cheney was catapulted to national prominence during the Gulf War, the coincidence that gave America a
husband-and-wife team simultaneously in charge of the nation's defense and the nation's humanities served as the pretext for a telling
semantic escalation, one for which George Will apparently deserves
credit. In an 22 April 1991 editorial for *Newsweek,* "Literary Politics," Will formulates an already familiar warning: "The transmission of the culture that unites, even defines America . . . is faltering."
In his praise of Lynne Cheney for her attempts to check that faltering, he terms her our "secretary of domestic defense" and concludes
by suggesting that the two Cheneys play at least equally important
roles: "The foreign adversaries her husband, Dick, must keep at bay
are less dangerous, in the long run, than the domestic forces with
which she must deal." Will thus first suggested that, in addition to
the battles it wages overseas, America is also literally at war against
forces seeking to undermine national security from within. This vision of actual Culture Wars proved so attractive that a commentator
for the *Los Angeles Times* soon had a quote from Lynne Cheney's
precursor, William Bennett, to make the point in a neater package:
"Between her and her husband, they have the entire defense of
Western civilization as their responsibility" (Allan Parachini; July
5, 1991).

It is surely no accident that 1991 witnessed both the literalization
of the Culture Wars' metaphor and the official consecration of the
most successful of all Ancient terminological inventions, *PC.* First
used in 1988, *PC* was invented at the conflict's inception, but its
presence became widespread only once education's civilizing function had been renamed "the defense of Western civilization."[27] This
was so because this catchall term could serve to designate the new
barbarians at the gates, all those who made the task of "the secretary
of domestic defense" such a vital one. In an 11 April 1991 editorial

in the *International Herald Tribune,* William Pfaff become one of
the first to connect the two vocabularies: he informs his readers
that "politically correct" professors of literature are attempting to
destroy the foundations "upon which Western education and Western civilization rest."

From this time on, commentators could dismiss with the unruly
lists of culprits that one notes in early studies such as Bloom's and
Kernan's—in which, for example, blame was laid equally on femi-
nist critics and deconstructionists, as though their goals were identical—and simply lay all responsibility at the feet of the forces of PC.
At no point, apparently, has anyone felt the need to be more specific
about just who was doing exactly what to bring about the end—of
literature, of the American mind, of Western civilization—not even
in the one precise example ever to be widely discussed. I have in
mind Stanford University's Program in Cultures, Ideas, and Values,
what came to be known simply as the Stanford course in Western
culture.

The Stanford course should have provided a perfect opportunity
for a full airing of the pedagogical consequences of the choice between civilization and culture. Any examination of the relevant documents demonstrates clearly that the program's coordinators intended to make one type of substitution: instead of courses
illustrating the tradition of Western civilization, they imagined a
group of courses that would explore "culture," in a use of the term
perfectly faithful to Fontenelle's initial conception.[28] They never intended, as every commentator who rushed to attack the program
in print claimed, to break Houdar de La Motte's cardinal rule and
make a new canon by eliminating ancient works and replacing them
with modern ones.[29] The Stanford faculty had the misfortune of having engaged in debate about the "civilization"/"culture" alternative
in 1987 and 1988, at the very outbreak of the Culture Wars. Their
program thus provided an all-too-convenient example of the excesses in which, according to the Ancients, the Moderns were engaged on a regular basis. Their program became enshrined as the
perfect illustration of every new term invented to characterize the
subversive work against the social fabric binding America allegedly
being carried out inside the university.

With the electronic means available today, it has become easy to
do what is nearly impossible for earlier periods, to retrace with absolute precision the development of terminology. In this case, it is also
possible to reconstruct the creation of a national panic, the process

by which a society is led to believe that those responsible for the education of its future citizens are engaged in a gigantic plot to lure them away from their nation's civilizing mission. Moderns have made significant attempts to demonstrate the extent to which Ancients have been careful to keep a concept such as Western civilization content-free and to employ it with no regard for the actual history of its function in American education.[30] They have also investigated the history of higher education in the U.S. and have demonstrated the extent to which our current structures are recent creations, put into place for the most part only in the late nineteenth century.[31] Their research constantly reminds us both that the history of "Western civilization" as an American pedagogical institution is very short indeed and also that the phrase has never had either a precise or a stable content.

To those who might think that the character of our Culture Wars has by now completely changed and that the conflict has shifted focus and is centered, no longer on issues of civilization, but on problems that can be considered under the currently fashionable label "family values," I offer but one counterexample. On the surface, Dinesh D'Souza's most recent contribution to the Ancient cause, *The End of Racism,* would seem to indicate that he, like William Bennett, has moved away from his previous exclusive focus on the university as the origin of America's ills. Underlying his argument about the history of civil rights in America, however, is a use of the dyad culture-civilization so highly predictable within the context of Culture Wars commentary that, for all his apparently new range, he ends up in a familiar process of blame laying. Thus, according to D'Souza, once the "civilization gap" that exists between blacks and whites in this country is closed, racism will become an insignificant problem. In D'Souza's theory, the main obstacle to progress in closing this gap has been created by those he terms "cultural relativists." Cultural relativists, in his view, are all those who, guided by the mistaken conviction that all cultures are equal, fail to teach those on the far side of the "civilization gap" to aspire to a higher level of civility. Thus, as a result of this latest round of table-turning, Moderns in the university are seen as responsible, no longer only for bringing civilization to an end, but even for preventing it from taking root.[32]

Even though, therefore, we may seem a long way from the time when Allan Bloom and Lynne Cheney were the powers to be reckoned with, in reality, we are still locked in the same cycle in which

Ancients use *civilization* to praise and *culture* to blame—for an ever broader spectrum of ills—while Moderns make "culture" the foundation of their attempts at self-definition.

Perhaps the most distressing fact about our current Culture Wars that becomes evident when they are compared with the seventeenth-century conflict is the extent to which the controversy, initiated by the Ancients, has remained under their control. Thus far, Moderns have remained on the defensive and devoted most of their energy to responding to attacks. There have been virtually no Modern efforts to take control away from the Ancients and to enter the fray on an equal footing, by defining the issues around which debate will be centered and setting the terms in which it will take place. Unless they are able to do so, no hard facts, no surveys—for example, the Modern Language Association's 1990–91 survey of 527 English departments, which indicated that the canons of American and English literature as they are taught in American universities today remain very classic indeed and show remarkably little influence of recent curricular debate—will be able to change the public perception that a radical takeover of our universities has been staged.

When seventeenth-century Moderns were charged with conspiracy to derail the civilizing process, they were guilty, if not as charged, at least with having consciously attempted to revolutionize every aspect of the business of literature as it was practiced in their day, whereas twentieth-century Moderns strike me on the whole as being not guilty enough.[33] One of the editorials presenting Lynne Cheney as the defender of Western civilization ends on this thought: "If you want to reform academia, it's a wonderful time to move in."[34] This is undoubtedly true and will continue to be the case for some time to come.

As I was working on this project, I was constantly reminded that the Quarrel between the Ancients and the Moderns could be taken for a cautionary tale. At every turning point, Moderns were so eager to invent new audiences that they neglected the essential step of taking time away from their individual, newly public performances to collaborate on practical applications for their ideas. In similar fashion, today's Moderns have all too largely avoided the pedagogical arena. True, new courses have been created, for the most part in specialized "studies" programs—black studies, gay studies, women's studies. True, these courses have helped encourage the creation of new special audiences, new publics for literature, to such an extent that it is becoming more and more common to speak of a black public sphere, a gay public sphere, and so forth.

And yet, as one survey after another demonstrates, changes introduced in these specialized courses have to date had remarkably little effect on the way business is done in the big, general courses in which the vast majority of undergraduates receive their only exposure to literature. Moreover, it may well be that the time for thinking in terms of new canons, or alternate canons, or bigger canons, or even what once may have seemed the ideal solution—"multiple, conflicting canons"—is past, that these issues, which may have been essential to the initial moments of Ancient-Modern conflict, are ones that we can no longer afford to spend time debating if we are to be prepared for the restructuring that will inevitably occur in the controversy's aftermath.[35]

The most useful concept for bridging the gap between the *Firing Line* debate mentality and willingness to undertake the spadework necessary to prepare for the future after the conflict is one that has been all too rarely advanced in either of the Culture Wars: what we teach our students is far less important than the way in which we teach them. In this case, the actual canon proposed matters less than provoking both an awareness of the criteria for inclusion and exclusion, as well as an awareness of the ways in which institutional power has been negotiated through the system of canonicity. In 1715, at the origin of canon formation in France, Houdar de La Motte was moving, albeit timidly, toward the position that Ancient-Modern commentary should be restructured in this way. If our Culture Wars are not to be dismissed as a mere tempest in a teapot, we must take a stand on this more supple terrain, in our negotiations of canonicity as critics and, above all, as pedagogues.

Witness the example of Ross Chambers who, in "Irony and the Canon," encourages teachers to sidestep the power plays that he sees as inherent to every negotiation of canonicity, so that any attempt to alter the canon inevitably supports the system it strives to overturn (18). He proposes that we devote our pedagogical energy instead to instructing our students in an irony that "negates, or can negate, the system without denying its own involvement in that system" (21). Chambers gives "tactical" examples of how such an irony can be used to help us avoid continuing simply to replicate the canonic system's primary function, which he defines as that "of forming taste"—and Chambers is nearly alone today in adopting *taste*, the key early modern term in the founding debates about canon formation—so that we can concentrate instead on creating a pedagogy aware of the system within which it functions, a pedagogy that seeks to keep students alert at all times to what is at stake in any process that results in the shaping of taste (20, 23). The ideal pedagogical practice, according to Chambers, would expose the function of systems such as the canon without being co-opted by those systems. This is certainly a fine line to tread, but there may be no simpler way of breaking out of the deadlock system of point-counterpoint, which duplicates in our course offerings the structure of a *Firing Line* debate.

Already in 1715, Houdar de La Motte had similar insights, in particular the insight that a discourse intended above all to destabilize other discourses is itself in turn open to destabilization. The true Modern discourse, in other words, can never be a last word. In his own work, however, Houdar de La Motte was unable to live up to the potential of this insight: he allowed his *Réflexions sur la critique* to be trapped within the system he denounced by turning it into a simple attack on Dacier. Imagine the possibility thus lost: the year 1715, poised on the edge of the Enlightenment, in the course of which thinking in so many crucial domains was to be revolutionized—but not in that of pedagogy and of pedagogical criticism, which only began to catch up with the Moderns' insights in the nineteenth century and in many ways have not yet fully risen to that missed occasion.

As far as our Culture Wars are concerned, we still have a long way to go before we find ourselves in the position of 1715—you've no doubt long since understood that I don't take these chronological encounters lightly. Nevertheless, signs already abound indicating that our period is moving ever closer to revolutionary change in domains ranging from warfare to the nature of work. In all these domains, it appears that we may be witnessing the end of a long phase in the history of the phenomenon in question, the foundations for which were laid during the seventeenth-century Culture Wars. In addition, commentators even suggest that the history of each phenomenon may to a certain extent have come full circle so that it now presents important similarities with its pre-Enlightenment phase. In the history of warfare, for example, this would mean that we are entering an age in which the increasing reliance on increasingly sophisticated technology—the history of whose advances can be said to have begun in the closing decades of the seventeenth century under the great military genius of Louis XIV's reign, Sébastien Le Prestre de Vauban—will finally be curtailed, at the same time as more "primitive" types of combat stage a return. In the history of work, technological advances appear increasingly to be forcing us to return to conceptions of what the phenomenon entails and of how it is carried out that predate the Industrial Revolution.[36]

In addition, many commentators predict that equally cataclysmic upheaval will soon be upon us in the areas central to my presentation of the seventeenth-century Culture Wars, and that, as a result of this upheaval, the structures put into place in the course of the first fin de siècle will soon be reborn in a radically new guise. Thus, it is now forecast, for example, that technological advances may soon make newspapers as we have known them since the late seventeenth century obsolete.[37] It is also predicted, to cite the example relevant to chapter 3, that we are on the threshold of a revolution in the emotions and in subjectivity, a revolution that will also take us back to the Culture Wars' era because it will be founded on a repudiation of the Cartesian conceptions that were the inspiration for the seventeenth-century rewriting of the emotions.[38]

Perhaps the most convincing of the recent anti-Cartesian studies is Antonio Damasio's *Descartes' Error*, which he presents as an attempt to correct Descartes's most influential "error," "the Cartesian idea of a disembodied mind" (250), and to propose the project of a new mapping of the emotions, one that would take advantage of recent advances in neurobiology in order to locate their sites in the brain and their effects on the body. In the terms of the revolution Damasio proposes, emotion, rather than thought, is the primal component of the self.[39] In addition, like other commentators, Damasio believes that, just as happened during the Culture Wars, the revision of the emotions will have important effects on the evolution of medicine.[40]

A final tendency in recent commentary that also suggests that we are on the verge of an affective revolution is the growing body of work devoted to warnings about the threat posed by current technological developments to the functioning of the emotions. This school of theorists—most prominently, Clifford Stoll in *Silicon Snake Oil* and Mark Slouka in *The War of the Worlds*—rather than heralding the brave new world of virtual or cyber emotions, argue that the new feelings are only ersatz and should not be confused with traditional emotions, the speed of whose production cannot be artificially altered. These commentators warn that increased contact with virtual emotions will provoke a backlash—a backlash I associate with the affective revision so widely predicted—as people begin increasingly to believe that life in cyberspace is not a life and to feel the need for "real" exchanges.[41]

Everything suggests that—like the newspaper, the workplace, and the affective realm—the university is on the brink of sweeping transformation. Faced with that prospect, there are, in effect, three courses open to us. We can, in the most solipsistic scenario, take advantage of the new technology for our personal research alone and ignore its implications for any radical institutional change that may be ahead—remain blind, in effect, to the prospective academic revolution. We can, in the most conservative scenario, be attentive only to the dire predictions about the threatening impact of changes ahead on our way of academic life, and try to barricade ourselves inside our scholarly fortress—and hope we're no longer around by the time the university has been restructured. For, if the first Culture Wars are any indication, without active intervention, that restructuring will take place according to Ancient dictates and will make the university of the twenty-first century a very conservative institution. Or, in a final scenario, we might find ways, as teachers and as scholars, of using a revolutionary moment to our advantage. We can learn from the lessons of the last Culture Wars: we can work together to imagine a pedagogy and a criticism worthy of Modern theoretical aspirations. This new pedagogy will have to account for factors that fuel the conservative backlash—in particular the menace of economic instability, even collapse. In particular, at a time when financial crisis will threaten every aspect of our scholarly lives, we will have to be powerfully creative, if we wish to avoid finding ourselves, once we are on the other side of the Culture Wars' divide, in moral bankruptcy.[42]

If the Moderns are to be blamed, at least they should give their critics something to blame them for, an actual, large-scale threat to existing pedagogical practice.

NOTES

PREFACE

1. This portrayal of literary politics is indebted to Carl Schmitt's analysis, in *Political Romanticism,* of the passivity of those who poeticize the political and of the ways in which their political activity implicitly legitimates the status quo.

2. Habermas, indeed, does not even go to the sources himself, but merely cites the work already done on *public*'s history in French by Erich Auerbach (31)—who, in turn, relied solely on late-nineteenth-century historical dictionaries for his findings.

3. The ARTFL (Trésor de la langue française) database, whose American diffusion is directed by the University of Chicago, was developed by the Institut national de la langue française with the goal of producing a new historical dictionary. Previous historical dictionaries, compiled about a century ago, derived their view of the state of the language at the early modern period largely from the works then proposed as the classic texts of French literature. For the ARTFL database, on the other hand, texts were selected on the basis of their linguistic richness. There were limits to this policy of inclusion. The lexicographers were to a large extent forced to cite authors whose works had already been computerized, rather than being able to computerize either as complete a range of texts as possible or their ideal selection of texts. Imperfect though it may be, this database is nonetheless far more inclusive than previously available linguistic models. It also makes it possible to formulate one's own questions with a degree of precision never before conceivable, so that one is now able to compare, for example, all the appearances of *culture* between 1670 and 1695.

4. In contrast, some commentators today are already worried that our fin de siècle will become such a pure media event that "we will never grasp the meaning of what is about to happen" (D. T. Max, *New York Times,* 10 October 1995).

CHAPTER ONE

1. Poussin's *La Danse de la vie humaine* (1638–40) is the archetypal representation of the dance of time when *siècle* meant "age" and when France was still on classical time.

2. In the so-called nominalist/realist debate over whether words generate phenomena or whether a phenomenon can exist only if it has a name, I take the position that a name (and, in particular, consistent terminology, the same name at all periods) is not essential for a phenomenon's existence. The invention of the term *fin de siècle* only in the late nineteenth century does not mean that the phenomenon thus designated did not occur before this time. It is equally obvious that the phenomenon I describe as the first fin de siècle is not identical to its nineteenth-century incarnation. I will argue that the phenomenon of fin de siècle decline was at least widely apprehended—even if it was not so often clearly articulated—two centuries before the term we now use to designate it was invented. I will also argue that in the seventeenth century the pervasive sense of decline that is essential to a fin de siècle did generate a term, if not exactly to designate this consciousness, at least to demarcate it: *siècle*, which came to be generally accepted in the sense of a period of one hundred years as a result of the seventeenth-century conflict I will be describing here.

3. As far as the evolution of time is concerned, Watteau's *L'Enseigne de Gersaint* (1720) can be seen as the visual counterpart to Poussin's *La Danse de la vie humaine*. Here, the transition to modern time has been completed. The portrait of Louis XIV, the monarch whose unsurpassed reign provoked *siècle* to become synonymous with regnal glory, is being boxed up. By 1720, as crucial texts of the end of the Culture Wars will teach us, that intermediate meaning of *siècle* was also being, as it were, boxed up and was disappearing from common usage. Never again would the term be limited simply to the reign of a particular monarch.

4. According to Hillel Schwartz, the term *fin de siècle* was first used in 1885 or 1886 (159). Leo Braudy has called the 1690s the first true fin de siècle in Europe in general. His definition of a fin de siècle has, however, very little in common with the terms I will set forth here.

5. One extreme in the usage of Culture Wars is represented by Richard Bolton, who, in his *Culture Wars: Documents from the Recent Controversies in the Arts,* uses the term to refer exclusively to the public outcry that has surrounded the sponsorship of artists such as Robert Mapplethorpe. In his *Culture Wars: The Struggle to Define America,* on the other hand, James Davidson Hunter is interested solely in the conflict inspired by issues such as abortion and homosexuality and feels that controversy over artistic or cultural issues such as education is not an essential part of today's crisis.

6. The best twentieth-century example of this permeable frontier between societal change and literary change used as the basis for such allegations is found in Allan Bloom's *The Closing of the American Mind.* In the section of part 1 entitled "Music" Bloom evokes the familiar equation between rock music and substance abuse. By part 3 of his study, rock and therefore substance abuse have been metonymically linked to literary theory. The first scene of Molière's *Dom Juan* (1665) relates the use of tobacco to the Ancient-Modern divide and characterizes tobacco as an agent of societal change. On tobacco's (threatening) novelty at that time, see Vigarello (131–33). On late-seventeenth-century French laws against the selling and the consumption of tobacco and on attempts by the police to drive tobacco dealers out of business, see Delamare (1:495). Sévigné's correspondence in the 1670s (in 1671 in particular) testifies eloquently to the

seriousness with which chocolate, then very recently introduced in France, was taken because of what were believed to be its addictive powers.

7.   I choose to begin the "turn" of the seventeenth century in 1685 because of two transformational decrees published by Louis XIV that year: the revocation of the Edict of Nantes, which ended freedom of religious expression, and the *code noir*, which began the official regulation of slavery. Other dates have been proposed—Hazard, for example, uses 1680. The Revolution provides a convenient beginning for the following century's "turn," though, once again, this is not the only possibility: 1778, which marked the symbolic end of the Enlightenment, because of the simultaneous deaths of Rousseau and Voltaire, is also used on occasion.

8.   I hasten to add that I do not intend these pages as still another contribution to the quest for the origins of modernity that has become such a widespread obsession on the part of specialists of early modern literatures in recent years. Even if I am obliged to use generally accepted notions of periodization and markers such as modernism, I do so in the hope of complicating rather than reinforcing the new history of the birth of our modernity. And, rather than the linear view of literary history on which the search for modernity's origins is of necessity based, I prefer to think of literary history, in a sense closer to Lucien Febvre's view of history, as having, not originating markers, but central points from which a movement can be shown to radiate both forward and backward. (See also philosopher François Dagognet's theory of "irradiations" [174], as well as the section from *The Education of Henry Adams* from which I take the epigraph for this chapter.)

9.   Voltaire himself (rather than subsequent literary historians) was responsible for the term. For example, he referred to the proceedings surrounding the trial and execution of the Protestant Jean Calas as "cette étrange affaire" (this curious business) (89). The irony of Voltaire's phrase serves to highlight the peculiarity of the use of *affaire* in all such contexts: the word undermines the seriousness of the very legal matters it is used to designate.

10.   Like *affaire*, *querelle* theoretically has the potential to label weighty matters. The Littré dictionary, for example, includes the definition "animated dispute consisting of either bodily, verbal, or written combat." When the war is a war of words, however, the speaker often uses *querelle* to deprecate the phenomenon being described. Note the example of another of Voltaire's phrases cited by the Littré dictionary, this time from his *Dictionnaire philosophique* (1764): "a miserable literary quarrel." For a reading that stresses the continuity of seventeenth-century *querelles*, see Timothy Reiss.

11.   The participants in the quarrel of *Le Cid* may have been the first to use on occasion the term *querelle* to refer to the controversy in which they were engaged, thereby inventing the usage later favored by literary history. See the documents in the Gasté edition, for example, 225, 241, and 357.

12.   The Quarrel that was played out, under the control of the newly created Académie Française, around Corneille's *Le Cid* in 1637 came closest to reaching a more general audience. It was during this dispute that the phrase *the public* appears to have acquired for the first time in French its modern meaning of "an audience." See the Gasté edition, most strikingly, 355.

13.   At all periods, many stances have been taken in the controversy over

the right to judge. To cite but one recent example, I think of Edward Said's attack on Paul Johnson's contention that a random sample of people would prove better judges of political matters than a representative group of intellectuals (Said 14). What interests me here is first of all the fact that conflict over the right to judge is a central issue during Culture Wars, and second the fact that this becomes the case after Moderns propose that the judgment of nonprofessionals might be the surest. By the end of the French Culture Wars, for example, Abbé Jean-Baptiste Du Bos suggested in 1719 that the instincts of average readers should be preferred to those of professional scholars because average readers followed their hearts rather than their heads (2:351).

14.   See, notably, the most widely read contemporary periodical, *Le Mercure galant,* February 1715, on "cette affaire" (186). All this terminology was as yet uncodified; seventeenth-century dictionaries link neither *querelle* nor *affaire* to the domain of literary controversies. The copy of Anne Dacier's *Des Causes de la corruption du goût* (1714) in the Arsénal Library in Paris contains a sheet glued into the front of the volume that confirms my description of the contemptuous connotations of *querelle* at the period. The note describes the controversy's last round in 1714–15 and concludes: "This important conflict . . . degenerated into a literary quarrel."

15.   In 1761, Irailh featured what he named the Quarrel of the Ancients and the Moderns in his three-volume history of literary controversies. Irailh (whose authority was probably founded solely on the enormity of his compilation!) seems to have been responsible for the success of the term *querelle* in French literary history. In one way, however, literary history has recognized the exceptional status of the seventeenth-century Culture Wars. Irailh includes subsequent disputes in the same category, but never again did the title stick. The Querelle des Anciens et des Modernes remains known as the last of the *querelles,* the *querelle* that broke the mold.

16.   French lexicographers have traditionally stated that the phrase *opinion publique* was not used before the eighteenth century and have credited Rousseau with the first usage. As early as 1665, however, on the eve of the outbreak of our *affaire,* Cardinal de Retz speaks of "those phantoms that public opinion creates to frighten vulgar souls" (5:544). One of the key participants in the final round of the Culture Wars, Antoine Houdar de La Motte, appears to have been the next to use the phrase in his most important contribution, the 1715 *Réflexions sur la critique,* in which he specifically linked public opinion to literature and literary criticism (114). Shortly over a decade after the controversy's end, the phrase begins to appear with some regularity. (These findings are taken from the ARTFL database, which, I repeat, does not contain all the works published in French in a given period.)

17.   In considering previous fins de siècle (I use the standard French plural), I will be privileging, as do many commentators, the French incarnation of the phenomenon.

18.   Braudy considers an integral part of the seventeenth century's end in England to be what he terms a "national identity crisis," which he describes as the transition from a nationalism defined by a single class into one in which various classes realize that they have a stake in the country's definition (67). The situation I have in mind in France is far more complicated. The French

"identity crisis" of the 1690s is also class related, but it is much more a crisis provoked by gender-related concerns—and, furthermore, the specter of what we now term race is also visible as a source for anxiety as early as the 1680s. Recent studies, such as those of Braudy and Levine, demonstrate that in England conflict between Ancients and Moderns essentially began as an offshoot of the ✓ French Culture Wars and was therefore an early-eighteenth-century phenomenon, rather than an integral part of the fin de siècle. This can explain why England's "identity crisis" was more narrowly focused than France's.

19.   *Sensibilité's* origins are generally situated in the early eighteenth century. A literary historian (Paul Hazard) and a historian (Lucien Febvre), each of whom refers to the literary phenomenon in an aside, made me realize that *sensibilité* began as a fin de siècle movement.

20.   Other critics—Elaine Scarry, for instance—stress certain attributes quite different from those highlighted by Schwartz for the century's end, but they share with him a belief that all fins de siècle are in essence the same. Scarry's characterization of the fin de siècle is unusual and appeals to me because she stresses literature's role, and in particular its generative role: "When . . . one draws a picture of human will based on the *poetic* legacy of final decades, a very different portrait emerges: the many poems already evoked here . . . suggest that the end of the century inspires inaugurating linguistic acts, words, lines, passages, plays that invigorate the language not just of the next century but of a period far into the future" (10). Scarry does, however, maintain that the last four fins de siècle have all been played out in similar fashion. Daniel Milo denies the status of fin de siècle to all pre-nineteenth-century manifestations of the phenomenon because of his claim that the notion of the century was created by the cataclysmic upheaval of the French Revolution: according to Milo, the century had to be accepted as the basic chronological marker before the fin de siècle could come into existence. Now that the fin de siècle has been created, however, Milo implies that they will all be alike. Milo underestimates the complexity of the seventeenth-century material he cites, and he fails to see, in particular, *siècle's* emergence in its dominant modern usage.

21.   Although Ariès does no more than hint at the consequences for *mentalités* history of this radical shift in interest, the so-called end of the Enlightenment presumably would also mean at least a dramatic realignment, if not an "end," to this methodology as it has traditionally been defined.

22.   On the notion of such a quarrel in contemporary philosophy, see Stanley Rosen's *The Ancients and the Moderns: Rethinking Modernity,* a work also important for my argument here because of Rosen's attack on the Enlightenment: "In my view, the most visible and important sign of [today's crisis of confidence] is the contemporary relevance of the quarrel between the ancients and the moderns. I mean by this that the champions of antiquity, after having been relegated to the status of ineffectual aestheticism, are today enjoying a renaissance. As it seems to me, this is due to the extreme rigor with which twentieth-century spokesmen for the Enlightenment banished the ancients from a position of respect" (15). On the notion of a recurrent, global quarrel between Ancients and Moderns, see Latour (10) and Hartman (239). See also Vassilis Lambropoulos's discussion of thinkers of the last two centuries who act as if the quarrel had never ended (for example, his reading of Leo Strauss [316]) and

for his view of the ways in which recent controversies over literary theory can be seen as repeating the positions of the original Quarrel (90, 117). Lambropoulos, in a complex and fascinating reading, presents every victory of the Moderns as a victory of the Hebraic model and the Quarrel's most significant long-term legacy as a continued "campaign of anti-Hellenism" (91).

23. Margreta de Grazia convincingly analyzes the ways in which the Renaissance has come to be assigned in English new literary history a role parallel to that played by the Enlightenment for French intellectual history. In particular she claims that this scenario also reveals the same obsessions with modernity and periodization that I am discussing here.

24. Perrault is best known today as the author of classic fairy tales. Our modern image grossly undervalues his contributions to the late-seventeenth-century intellectual ferment, both in the form of the Modernist polemics I will discuss here and in the form of compilations, in particular the two-volume *Les Hommes illustres qui ont paru en France pendant ce siècle* (1696–1700).

25. The idea of science as universal panacea was touted in the seventeenth century, most insistently by the writer who was undoubtedly the century's most imaginative vulgarizer, Charles Sorel. As early as 1634, Sorel launched his campaign with *La Science universelle:* "With the coming of a universal science, the golden age of humanity will begin" (297). Sorel published expanded editions of *La Science universelle* throughout the 1640s, and in 1655 he renewed his claims in *De la perfection de l'homme*, in which he argued that widespread acceptance of scientific method would lead to human perfection. None of Sorel's proclamations became influential during the Culture Wars, when humanity's perfectibility was evoked first and foremost in terms of pedagogy, as a function of what persons had read.

26. Perhaps because he sensed the implications of this scenario for progress as far as his personal fate was concerned, Louis XIV himself was apparently resolutely opposed to the concept. He is reported to have said: "I become involved with things that seem new only in order to hinder progress" (quoted by Guitton 2:181).

27. The precursor Moderns, whom I discuss in chapter 2, reveal no more awareness of this implication of progress than does Perrault in 1687. For instance, Desmarets de Saint-Sorlin in his 1674 *Le Triomphe de Louis et de son siècle* compares Homer's age to springtime, Virgil's to summer, and his own to "the fertility of a happy autumn" (31), making no mention of the less prosperous days that by implication inevitably lay ahead. The Moderns were only in 1688 able to recognize, or at the very least became able to admit, the notion of the decline of civilization.

28. I cite Perrault's *Parallèle* in the original edition. Since the latest edition, by H. Jauss, reprints the original edition, readers will also be able to refer to it.

29. In his history of illness and wellness, Georges Vigarello notes that the invention of the idea of progress gives birth to a heightened anxiety about the body's capacity for degeneration (162). The year 1688 clearly marked a turning point in the process by which the Moderns created the first fin de siècle, the moment at which they were suddenly aware of the anxiety implicit in their rhetoric of perfectibility. The other major contribution from the Modern camp that year, Fontenelle's *Digression sur les Anciens et les Modernes*, is also permeated

with the sense that the golden age has now ended: "We have to admit . . . that this good time has been over for a few years" (243).

30. None of the Moderns ever allows for the possibility of rebirth. Their view of progress and its history, spelled out in greatest detail in Perrault's *Parallèle*, is, therefore, linear and committed to irreversible decline, rather than based on cyclical reversal, as was generally the case in their classical precursors.

31. The debate over the value of tradition is another issue recurrent in times of Ancient-Modern positioning. Witness, for instance, the quarrels within twentieth-century modernism, in particular that between T. S. Eliot and W. C. Williams, over whether tradition should be considered a burden or a gift.

32. Other interpretations of "century"'s chronology include that of de Grazia, who contends that the notion of a fin de siècle was inconceivable in Renaissance England to begin with because the idea of a century as a historical dividing unit was not yet in place.

33. In French, the collection of one hundred things was called just that— in poetry, for instance, notable examples of what could be considered a fin de siècle phenomenon of the sixteenth century include the *Livre des cent ballades* of Jean le Seneschal and others (1389) and Christine de Pizan's *Cent ballades* (1395–1400).

34. Perrault's phrase, "the end of the wars of the League," is, conveniently, a bit vague, since different dates can be assigned the status of an end to this long conflict. The final battles in the wars of religion took place in 1593; 1595 was the year of the pontifical absolution that signified the real end of the League; in 1598 the Edict of Nantes defined the status of Protestants in France.

35. In a subsequent work, *Les Hommes illustres qui ont paru en France pendant ce siècle*, also closely involved with the new meaning of *siècle*, Perrault reveals the parallel awareness that his century's end had to be established as close as possible to the year 1700. The work's first edition in 1696 includes all seventeenth-century figures deemed illustrious who had died by that time. Perrault then published a second edition in 1700, enlarged to include those who had died in the intervening years. The relation Perrault establishes between cultural decadence and physical decline—the century was in its old age because artistic progress had passed its apex—indicates that Perrault also intuited the notion of the anthropomorphizing of history that de Grazia sees as the key element in the creation of the first fin de siècle (38). De Grazia, however, considers this phenomenon to be impossible before the appearance of a nineteenth-century (Hegelian) sense of history. I cannot claim that Perrault's anthropomorphizing tendencies reach the level of complexity found in subsequent examples, but he nonetheless instinctively adds this element to his fin de siècle "package."

36. Dictionaries confirm that Perrault's usage had become dominant by the end of the century. The Académie Française's 1694 dictionary gives as the first definition of *siècle:* "Course [*cours*] of a hundred years." Furetière's 1690 dictionary gives the same primary definition—"a measure of time that lasts one hundred years"—then follows it with an example that illustrates the complicity that was quickly established between literary periodization and the modern sense of a century: "We refer to as *contemporary* authors those who live in the same *century*." Only much later does Furetière mention the previously dominant usage: "The Ancients divided time into four ages, which they called the golden

century [*siècle d'or*]," and so forth. The modern use of *siècle* can also be noted in other contributions to the Culture Wars. See, for example, Gueret (180–81).

37.   The collection was published anonymously, and is generally attributed to either Fontenelle or d'Aulnoy.

38.   Barthes's essay, "Les Deux critiques," was first published in 1963 in *MLN* and was reprinted the following year in his *Essais critiques*.

39.   There could be no exact equivalent of today's academic criticism at the turn of the eighteenth century. Barthes defines it as the preserve of those who teach at universities, and the French educational system in the early modern period possessed little of the institutional prominence and organization it has since achieved. The seventeenth-century Culture Wars played a major role in initiating the definition of the modern French university system, a process that unfolded throughout the eighteenth century and was finally completed under Napoleon. Ancients such as Goujet were the first true academic critics, in Barthes's sense of the term; they were all pedagogues, and their commentary was resolutely positivistic and constructed in opposition to the ideology of openness developed by the Moderns. I explain in the following chapter how literary pedagogy was practiced in institutions such as the university at the time of the Culture Wars. For the time being, I will use *pedagogical* as a synonym for Barthes's *universitaire*.

40.   Perhaps the surest sign of the belief in that absolute difference between centuries is provided by the return to optimism that can be noted in the first years of the new century, even among those who had served as the early leaders of the Moderns. Already in 1702, for example, Fontenelle was proclaiming that progress was once more operative in the sciences and the arts: "All the sciences and all the arts . . . have acquired renewed vigor in [this century] and have begun what may be thought of as a new development" (*Histoire*, preface, n.p.). The atmosphere of decline seems to have evaporated as if by magic once 1700 had come to put an end to the fin de siècle.

41.   In speaking of Du Bos in these pages, I will refer to him as a theoretician of aesthetics, even though I realize that, once again, I am speaking of a phenomenon that had not yet been named. Alexander Baumgarten is generally credited with the invention of "aesthetics," in 1735. It is to Du Bos that Voltaire directs the preface to *Le Siècle de Louis XIV*.

42.   "I will use [century] to signify an interval of sixty or seventy years" (135).

43.   Another major French cultural document absolutely contemporaneous with Du Bos's treatise, Watteau's *L'Enseigne de Gersaint* (Gersaint's Shopsign) from 1720 (fig. 2), can be seen as a related commentary on the new sense of time that had been put in place during the fin de siècle. Louis XIV's portrait is being packed away, as if it were no longer of commercial value. Never again would *siècle* simply be the age of a particular monarch. In addition, the careful lining up of paintings in the shop's interior seems to echo Du Bos's affirmation that the new use of *siècle* served above all a categorizing function.

44.   Note that the American variant of the fin de siècle for which the expression was coined was referred to as the Gilded Age, a phrase that, for all its connotations of superficiality, nonetheless carries no implications of decadence and decline.

45.   This is Blau's formulation: "When the radical activism of the sixties

abated or went underground it surfaced again in *theory* as a new erotics of discourse. The lifestyle desires and polymorphous perversity which were celebrated at Woodstock and seemed to be savaged at Altamont also went under, retreating across the Atlantic, and entered the high intellectual traditions of continental thought, given the *ideology* they were charged with *not* having in the sixties. . . . If you ask, then, of literary theory what Stanislavski asked of actors who were building a character or Freud asked of women who were eluding ego psychology: *What does theory want?*—it wants, at the simple level of living . . . what the students used to want, or thought they wanted" (7).

46. I feel able to include cultural history in the category "literary criticism" or "literary theory" because those opposed to its methods consistently justify their hostility with reference to what they see as cultural history's excessive preoccupation with literary matters.

47. Woven through the fabric of the seventeenth-century Culture Wars was a remarkably similar theoretical dream, the possibility of being beyond sex in one's thinking. Perrault first expressed the notion that, to think as a Modern, it was necessary to think as a woman (*Parallèle* 1:30). In one of his *Pensées,* Montesquieu gave the notion perhaps its clearest formulation: "There is only one sex, and we are all women in our thinking" (389). Just prior to the Culture Wars' unfolding, these theoretical musings were given at least some semblance of reality in the cross-dressed adventures of Abbé François-Timoléon de Choisy, whose memoirs recount what is surely the first tale of what we now know as gender bending. In 1695, just after the public reconciliation between Ancients and Moderns, Choisy coauthored with none other than Perrault a short story, "Histoire de la marquise-marquis de Banneville," published in *Le Mercure galant* (February 1695). The story, which I discuss in detail in chapter 3, features men who dress and live as women, and women who dress and live as men; it portrays sexuality as a force to be controlled and altered, as performative rather than natural.

48. The Swatches, presumably a male and a female model, feature lovers who express their longing through tears as weighty as the diamonds that fall from the eyes of Coppola's Dracula.

49. Andrée Putman, an equally influential French designer of the facade of postmodernism in America, recently used a nearly identical phrase to explain her disavowal of her earlier, more visually complex minimalism: "These days, the less you see, the better you feel" (*New York Times,* 26 October 1995).

50. Since any new sentimental outpouring would presumably take place largely through such electronic circuits as bulletin boards and e-mail, it would leave, unlike the epistolary explosion of the turn of the eighteenth century, few traces.

CHAPTER TWO

1. In the first edition (1873) of his historical dictionary of the French language, Littré includes this meaning as number 14 and characterizes it as "outmoded."

2. I cite the text of Sévigné's letters from the edition prepared by Roger Duchêne. However, I will also give the date of each letter, so that readers may refer to other editions.

3. Whereas I have relied on the ARTFL–University of Chicago database for expanded linguistic coverage and have supplemented it in many cases with examples from my own reading, I am naturally aware that additional examples probably predate my findings as well. However, it is convenient, at the very least, to situate, even in a provisional manner, the term's inaugural appearance in the context of a literary controversy. See Hélène Merlin's study for an examination of many of *le public*'s seventeenth-century incarnations, in all of the term's various meanings. She notes numerous appearances of the term that have not been previously studied; she also suggests a critique of Habermas and of all sociologically informed readings of seventeenth-century literary material. Her analysis of the concept's significance during the quarrel staged around Corneille's *Le Cid* is particularly useful.

4. See the Gasté edition of documents from this quarrel, especially 152–55, 224, 355, and 418.

5. Like Auerbach, on whose research he relies, Habermas so devalues late-seventeenth-century French society that he is unable to grant any importance to the function of criticism at that time: "Although one sees here the first signs of that combination of economically unproductive and politically functionless urban aristocracy of eminent writers, artists, and scientists (who frequently were of bourgeois origin) typical of the *salon* of the eighteenth century, it was still impossible, in the prevailing climate of *honnêteté*, for reason to shed its dependence on the authority of aristocratic noble hosts and to acquire that autonomy that turns conversation into criticism and *bons mots* into arguments" (31).

6. In the case of *public opinion*, Habermas acknowledges that the term has a French origin—Rousseau's 1750 *Discours sur les arts et les sciences*—whereas in fact the phrase can be noted in French as early as 1665. The two standard studies of "public opinion" are by Keith Baker and Mona Ozouf. Both follow Habermas's lead and situate the phenomenon's origin in the mid–eighteenth century. See chap. 1, n. 16 on *public opinion*'s history in French.

7. On the role played by the nobility in the formation of this new enlightened elite in the eighteenth century, see Chartier, *Les Origines culturelles de la Révolution française* and Daniel Roche (in Goubert and Roche). See also Darnton on the class and the class politics of the *philosophes* ("The High Enlightenment" 17–40).

8. I realize that I am thereby going against the grain of a major strain in contemporary theory, which proposes on the contrary that class, rather than gender, was the most significant factor in numbers of key early modern debates. See most recently Michael McKeon and Ozouf (*Les Mots des femmes*).

9. See Robert Darnton ("In Search of the Enlightenment"), for example, on the opposing ways in which historians of the Enlightenment—he contrasts the approach of Peter Gay with that of Annales' historians—have dealt with phenomena and thinkers of the seventeenth century's end.

10. I have in mind here both recent work on what is known in France as the history of the book and what is becoming known in this country as the materiality of the text—in other words, research that privileges the history of readers and reading, as well as the history of the conditions in which books were produced. Both fields of inquiry are always indebted to the pioneering work of French cultural historians, in particular, that of Roger Chartier—who

in turn acknowledges a debt to the pioneering recent work of English bibliographers. Among American historians of the book, Robert Darnton has been particularly influential. The aspect of this history that concerns me in particular, the creation of public literary opinion, has not been considered in any detail by French specialists of the history of the book.

11. The two standard histories of the Querelle des Anciens et des Modernes remain those by Hubert Gillot and Hippolyte Rigault. For a rapid overview of the Quarrel in France and in England, see Gilbert Highet. For additional information on the participants in the Quarrel, see the most recent editions of Perrault's *Parallèle des Anciens et des Modernes,* in particular that of H. R. Jauss. See also Noémi Hepp's *Homère en France au XVIIe siècle.* Robert J. Nelson gives an excellent, brief overview of the Quarrel. Vassilis Lambropoulos's reading of the Quarrel, from the English perspective, often comes to similar conclusions as mine, but in a very different context and on the basis of very different evidence.

12. The January 1687 meeting had been called because Louis XIV had just been operated on for a fistula. The Academy had been assembled to express its joy at the king's recovery.

13. Perrault foregrounded for his original audience the document's overtly political character by electing not to read it himself but to have it read by Abbé Louis Lavau, perhaps the Academician with the most meager intellectual credentials. Lavau owed his seat in the Academy solely to his ability to broker political influence. He had negotiated, for example, a spectacularly upwardly mobile marriage for the daughter of Louis XIV's minister of finances, Jean-Baptiste Colbert.

14. If the act of assigning the name by which the opposite faction will be known—and, furthermore, assigning one's opponents a name with negative connotations—is a move to take power, as twentieth-century practice seems to indicate (the example of *PC* immediately comes to mind), then, with this act, Perrault struck a first strategic blow. He established, in the name of the Moderns, the names always used to refer to both camps. Previous uses of similar terminology indicate that the hostility that created the controversy was in the air from the late 1660s on. Previous usage, however, never achieves the polemical charge found in Perrault's. For instance, Gabriel Gueret, in *La Guerre des auteurs anciens et modernes* (1671), uses *ancient* and *modern* only as adjectives, rather than making them into the nouns that Perrault would transform into rallying cries. In the preface to *Iphigénie* (1674), Racine refers, not to "the moderns," but to "some moderns" (*des modernes*), whose judgment on ancient authors he condemns. For additional early uses of related terminology, see Gillot (216).

15. *Petite histoire* "explanations" are all founded on allegations of personal animosity among key players. Thus, Segrais, an important Modern, is reported to have hated Racine and Boileau, key Ancients, because he found them "smug and scornful" (Boileau, *O.c.,* ed. Adam and Escal, 1003 n. 20).

16. *La Comparaison de la langue et de la poésie française avec la grecque* (63). Perrault acknowledged neither this borrowing, nor any of the numerous ways in which he profited from Desmarets's pathbreaking discourse. Ironically, the chapter from which the line Perrault makes into *the* modernist slogan is taken is devoted to issues of imitation and plagiarism. Desmarets contends in particular that French poets are "too imaginative . . . to reduce themselves to

adorning their works principally by looting the ancients" (64). In addition, Desmarests seems even to have foreseen just what would happen. Shortly before his death in 1676, he asked Perrault to take up his cause: "Come defend, Perrault, France which is calling you; / Come fight with me that rebellious troop, / The assembled enemies who, weak and mischievous, / Prefer Latin works to our own songs" (cited by Rigault 113).

17.   Gillot (524–25) lists all the reasons from the domain of political history that can be evoked in this context. According to his description of the state of the country's affairs during the unfolding of the Culture Wars, France became more and more of a military underdog on the European scene. At the Treaty of Ryswick (1697), it accepted significant territorial loss. And the Treaty of Utrecht (1713–14), simultaneous with the controversy's last gasp, was a triumph for England.

18.   Longepierre concludes his eulogy of interpretive security with an attack on translation in which he declares that we can know a literary text only in its original language and that translations are only simulacra of the "true" texts (55). The controversy over the value of translations played a major role in the war's final phase (1711–16).

19.   Lumières: Personal insight or enlightenment. Perrault's usage in 1687 of this key Enlightenment vocabulary may have been the first indication of the role played by the Culture Wars in preparing the way for the "siècle des Lumières."

20.   "Le Génie" was initially published in the July 1688 issue of Le Mercure galant along with an announcement of the forthcoming appearance of Perrault's Parallèle. Its appearance there was an early indication of the unwavering support that Le Mercure's editor, Donneau de Visé, would always demonstrate for the Modern cause. Perrault dedicated the poem to his fellow Modern, Fontenelle.

21.   Most notable is the fact that the newspaper with the broadest coverage of the contemporary scene, Le Mercure galant, includes only one reference to the controversy, when, in the July 1688 issue, Donneau de Visé published Perrault's "Le Génie."

22.   At the time of the publication of the first nine reflections in 1694, Boileau tried to package them as the promised response to Perrault's 1687 attack with the title "Réflexions critiques sur ce Rhéteur où l'on répond aux objections faites contre quelques Anciens" (O.c. 1095–96).

23.   The Dialogue des héros de roman was composed in the late 1660s; Boileau had made no attempt to publish it since that time. The first edition Boileau claimed to have authorized was prepared for publication only shortly before his death in 1711.

24.   In 1683, Fontenelle inaugurated what was destined to become an important genre throughout the literary war, the dialogues des morts (dialogues of the dead). He imagined a series of paired exchanges in which a famous figure from antiquity and a counterpart from a more recent century meet to debate their views on a given subject. The genre proved an ideal format for airing the issues that divided seventeenth-century Ancients and Moderns.

25.   Adam agrees with Desmarests's theory. He presents L'Art poétique (1674) as coming directly out of the period that led to the literary war, the early 1670s when Desmarests was publishing a series of ever more aggressive pro-Modern tracts (Histoire 3:131, 141).

26. The earliest formulation of this notion is found in the preface to *Ibrahim, ou l'Illustre Bassa* (1641). The preface is widely considered to have been composed by Georges de Scudéry, whereas the novel is felt to have been a collaboration with his sister, Madeleine. On the preface, see Henri Coulet, vol. 1. Coulet reprints the preface in volume 2.

27. In a letter to Racine dated 26 May 1687, Boileau lends credence to Adam and Escal's view that his loss of voice was hysterical and suggests that he feared that his malady had a particularly feminine nature. He provides thereby indirect confirmation both of my sense that the threat of feminization was his greatest personal obsession and of my theory that he used his attack on what he always presented as a feminine genre as a homeopathic remedy for what ailed him: "I see only people who claim to have had the same malady as I and who were cured of it, but in addition to the fact that I do not really know if they are telling the truth, they are for the most part women or young men who have nothing in common with a man of fifty" (*O.c.* 735).

28. Donneau de Visé couches the two reviews in fictive letters "that fell into my hands, addressed to a person of quality" (January 1677, 27). The fiction was undoubtedly designed to protect him from Pradon's powerful benefactors. Donneau de Visé's preference for Racine is based on the fact that Pradon completely eliminated the question of incest that, according to Donneau de Visé, "it was absolutely necessary to treat" (31).

29. A warning to readers: the following section contains a number of especially long notes necessary to support the claims on which my argument is founded. Readers may wish to follow the argument and read the notes separately. The novel gained ground rapidly and steadily during the final decades of the seventeenth century. The decade between the publication of *La Princesse de Clèves* and the outbreak of the Culture Wars was a particularly crucial one for the genre's development, a fact documented by Maurice Lever's excellent bibliography, *La Fiction narrative en prose au XVIIème siècle*. The novel's rise at this period was jointly determined by women writers and by *Le Mercure galant*. In 1678, along with Lafayette's novel, also appeared the comtesse de Salvan de Saliez's *La Comtesse d'Isembourg*. Catherine Bernard began her career as a historical novelist in 1680; her second novel appeared in 1687. Anne de La Roche-Guilhen began her steady production of historical fiction in 1683. Catherine Bedacier's first novel appeared in 1687 (*Les Amours du Cardinal de Richelieu*—a particularly appropriate choice of historical focus for the year of the explosion in the Académie Française). The most prolific woman writer of the second half of the century, Marie-Catherine Desjardins (known as Madame de Villedieu) published three titles during this period alone. Whereas no woman writer published a novel during the two years before *La Princesse de Clèves*'s appearance, in 1687 alone three novels by women came out. From then to the end of the century, the frequency of their publication, as well as the number of women writers publishing, continued to grow. Also during the period between 1678 and 1687, *Le Mercure galant* contributed directly to the novel's rise. Lever includes (correctly) many of the stories (*histoires*) that first appeared in the newspaper (many were subsequently republished elsewhere) in his bibliography of the seventeenth-century novel. Donneau de Visé began including these stories from the time of the paper's inauguration in 1672, but their appearance

became *far* more frequent from 1677 on. This undoubtedly indicates Donneau de Visé's sense that, on the eve of *La Princesse de Clèves*'s publication, the time for the new genre had come.

30.   Indeed, it was in the aftermath of the seventeenth century's last two literary *affaires*—the debate surrounding the publication of *La Princesse de Clèves* and the battle between Ancients and Moderns—and as a result of the publicity the novel received during these conflicts that French writers, in particular male writers, began to move in important numbers from the stage to the novel, thereby signaling the end of theater's rule over the French tradition. In 1721, to note the first major example, Montesquieu marks the true beginning of his career with *Les Lettres persanes,* whereas a generation before he would have chosen a work for the stage. (His first literary efforts, which were never published, were plays, written when he was a student.) There are indications that in America today we may be witnessing the end of the long period during which the novel's dominance has been virtually unchallenged and during which a taste for grand narratives has reigned. Numerous critics seem to believe that the novel is at a dead end, as bankrupt as tragedy was felt to be at the seventeenth century's end. Others believe that we may be witnessing a return to, if not tragedy as it was in previous incarnations, at least some primacy of the theatrical. Witness Vincent Canby's characterization of Tony Kushner's *Angels in America* as "a bold attempt to create a theatrical epic, a slangy American equivalent to *Paradise Lost* and *Paradise Regained*" (*New York Times,* 15 February 1995). Far more numerous, however, are the critics who warn that all traditional artistic media will be sacrificed to the reign of technology.

31.   Let me repeat that my use of "average" is conditioned by the possibilities for readership open in seventeenth-century France. There were very few average readers in today's terms, because such individuals had no access to formal education. When I speak of average readers, I have in mind readers previously excluded from a reading process that was in any way public. Earlier, this process of evaluating literature was more exclusively Parisian and took place in more exclusive settings—the academies and the salons in particular—and was open to the participation only of aristocrats and those bourgeois who lived as though they were aristocrats. The making public of the business of literature that I have in mind here opened the process of judgment to a readership far more numerous and far more varied in socioeconomic and geographic terms.

32.   I will refer to *Le Mercure galant* as a newspaper, whereas technically it would be more correctly designated a periodical. I want to stress, however, *Le Mercure galant*'s exceptional status among early French periodicals: in a variety of ways, it was the first true ancestor of the modern daily press. French periodicals before *Le Mercure galant* were clearly intended to perform very different functions. *La Gazette,* founded by Théophraste Renaudot in 1631, operated under tight official control. It was devoted above all to reporting military and court news. The *Muse historique,* edited in verse by Jean Loret from 1652 to 1656, contained a mixture of court and literary news similar to *Le Mercure galant*'s. However, each issue was very short (only about four pages), and the paper had quite limited circulation. (Loret claimed he edited it for only a dozen people.) *Le Journal des savants,* begun by Denis de Sallo in 1665, was devoted exclusively to scholarly concerns—it announced the latest books, gave an idea of their con-

tents, mentioned scientific discoveries—but it reported them not for a general audience external to the republic of letters, as Donneau de Visé tried to do, but strictly for a scholarly audience. It was also short (twelve pages) and a weekly publication. It was never critical of the works discussed and, in the course of its long history, was often a semiofficial organ. When Donneau de Visé began publishing in 1672, *Le Mercure galant* appeared every three months. It was immense (three hundred pages) and expensive, three livres. (N.B.: It is virtually impossible to calculate the exact value of such figures. Here is a stab: according to Audiger [*La Maison réglée*, 1692], one could "live like a noble" on forty-eight hundred livres a year; the secretary of an important aristocrat earned three hundred livres per annum, as did the person responsible for the education of the aristocrat's children [32, 103].) Publication was sometimes irregular until 1677, when Donneau de Visé completely reorganized his operation. When regular publishing resumed in 1678, Donneau de Visé restructured both the paper's price and its format. (It seems likely that he sensed that the controversy he was about to create around *La Princesse de Clèves* would be a major success and wanted to cash in on its profits.) From 1678 to 1714 (the entire span of the Culture Wars), *Le Mercure galant* appeared as a monthly of between three and four hundred pages. Every three months a supplement, known as an *extraordinaire*, of five hundred pages, was published. Most of the paper's content was political and literary; Donneau de Visé included more literary—in a broad sense of the term—news than anything else. But he also published information on fashion, new songs, society games, and so forth. The paper must have been highly successful because several clones sprang up in provincial cities—notably Lyons and Toulouse. According to the contract drawn up for his copartnership with Thomas Corneille in 1680, whereby they split the profits, Donneau de Visé earned a handsome salary, another proof of the paper's commercial success: six thousand livres—which was increased to fifteen thousand livres in 1697. For additional information on early newspapers in general, see Bellanger (1:137–41). See also Martin and Chartier. For additional information on *Le Mercure galant*'s readership, see Vincent.

33. "Il est vray, Visé vous assure / Que vous avez pour vous Mercure; / Mais c'est le Mercure Galant" (*O.c.* 263).

34. We have precious little exact information about the circulation of early French newspapers. We know very little about such basic issues as print runs and precise readerships. Here are the available facts about *Le Mercure galant* relevant to its role as I see it. The earliest information on print runs dates from 1778, when the paper had some two thousand to twenty-five hundred subscribers (accounts vary). Before that, it is hard to determine the number of its readers. The market was limited because of illiteracy, but as the *Histoire générale de la presse française* (ed. Bellanger) argues: "The number of illiterates should not be overestimated" (159). It is almost certain that the paper, in part because its issues were lengthy and therefore relatively expensive, never had vast numbers of subscribers. However, the particular format Donneau de Visé chose for *Le Mercure galant* may well provide the best indication of why circulation figures, even if available, would vastly underestimate the paper's readership. Whereas *Le Mercure galant*'s most serious precursor, *Le Journal des savants*, was published in quartos, the most common format for scientific works, indicating Sallo's

desire to appeal to a scholarly readership, *Le Mercure galant* appeared in volumes small enough to fit in a pocket (in duodecimo). This was the format in which contemporary novels most often appeared. These volumes could thus have been easily carried about and produced whenever conversation relating to one of *Le Mercure galant*'s topics came up. As many of the letters from his readers published by Donneau de Visé indicate, much, possibly even most, reading of his paper during its early years was *group* reading, when a circle of friends gathered together to read the paper and debate the issues raised in its pages. The *Histoire générale de la presse française* confirms that the practice of public reading and oral retelling of news read in newspapers was widespread (161).

35.   See Vincent's "*Le Mercure galant* et son public féminin" for an attempt to define as much as possible the composition of the paper's female readership.

36.   Letters to the editor received before the 1678 campaign are far less complex. Each letter simply contains one person's opinion, rather than being structured around controversy and collective debate. It was only when the novel and the newspaper joined forces that Donneau de Visé was able to create a literary public.

37.   The history of that campaign and excerpts from its important moments are included in Maurice Laugaa's *Lectures de Madame de Lafayette*.

38.   Readers familiar with *La Princesse de Clèves* will recognize in this question the essence of the novel's central dilemma. The swift response to Donneau de Visé's literary game, in which readers debated the conduct of Lafayette's characters, proves how quickly her novel found a wide audience. At the same time, Donneau de Visé's readers follow his lead—note that he refers to "a virtuous woman," rather than to the princesse de Clèves—when they relate the conduct described in the novel not to what they feel would be the appropriate behavior for a fictional character, but to what they feel to be the proper conduct for men and women in real life. The critical judgment Donneau de Visé inspired remained as resolutely personal as he had intended it to be.

39.   Since some of the reading collectives sign their letters with fictive names, it is not always possible to establish their readers' social origins. The activities described in the letters, however, are rarely those associated with an aristocratic life.

40.   These primitive interpretive communities were obviously more or less consciously continuing practices of collective reading and writing that had been initially developed by the Parisian aristocratic public that gathered in the salons. Donneau de Visé transformed formats devised within closed societies into public practice by introducing them in the most public print medium of the day. On the use of collective writing in the salons, see my *Tender Geographies* (60 and 93–99).

41.   The literary criticism generated in the wake of Lafayette's novel was by and large far from sophisticated. However, major commentators such as Fontenelle played on occasion a role in Donneau de Visé's project. In addition, I do not cite the far more professional criticism produced during the quarrel, Jean-Baptiste-Henri du Trousset de Valincour's *Lettres à Madame la marquise* *** *sur le sujet de "La Princesse de Clèves"* and Abbé Jean-Antoine de Charnes's *Conversations sur la critique de "La Princesse de Clèves"* (both 1678). These two book-length considerations of the novel go far beyond the exercises in personal

judgment to which the letters in *Le Mercure* are for the most part limited; they clearly indicate the transition from commentary to criticism. Indeed, when the critical production generated around Lafayette's novel is considered in its entirety, as is necessary in order to obtain a sense of the quarrel's scope and significance, it becomes apparent that commentary of varying degrees of sophistication contributed to create a major turning point in the history of literary criticism in France: by the end of the Culture Wars, all the major modern forms of criticism were clearly in place.

42.   See Lambropoulos on the history of taste as a democratic concept (117–20).

43.   In the entries Donneau de Visé devotes to the quarrel over the two competing plays, he gives not a hint of the format he will introduce, just a few months later, for the next literary controversy. His coverage of the last important theater quarrel contains not a single critical scene.

44.   For an account of the relationship between the simultaneous rise of the newspaper and of the novel in England, see Lennard Davis, chaps. 3 and 4. As Davis describes it, the English phenomenon is very different from the French development. Nevertheless, Davis's characterization of what he terms "the nexus between news and novels" (191) confirms a sort of primal affinity between the newspaper and the novel.

45.   When Donneau de Visé set up his equation between the Moderns and the novel, he was predicting Perrault's position in the *Parallèle*, where he has his Modern (the abbé) argue that the novel is the Moderns' greatest contribution to literature and the literary domain in which they surpass the Ancients most clearly (2:127–30). Perrault cites Huet as sharing his opinion.

46.   The union of *Le Mercure galant* and *La Princesse de Clèves* made possible by far the most significant instance of this broadening of the literary public, but the phenomenon was not limited to this most visible incarnation. I discuss later in this section the proliferation of new periodicals in the years between 1678 and the outbreak of the Culture Wars. See note 29 for information on the novel's rise during the same period.

47.   Adam contends that Boileau began work on Satire X after the publication of volume 3 of Perrault's *Parallèle* (*Histoire* 5:61). Boileau would thus have had time to assimilate Perrault's arguments about women's role in the creation of literary modernity.

48.   The question of the place of the fin de siècle Culture Wars in the history of misogyny in France is an important one and merits consideration. On the basis of Boileau's remarks in Satire X and related texts, it is possible to suggest that the controversy over *La Princesse de Clèves* occupied an intermediate point between two of the most dramatic societal upheavals of the seventeenth century: the Quarrel about Women and the Quarrel of the Ancients and the Moderns. The smaller controversy that surrounded Lafayette's novel also indicates the extent to which the fin de siècle Culture Wars were a continuation of the Querelle des Femmes, another epoch in misogyny's French history.

49.   Habermas contends that "in the course of the first half of the eighteenth century, in the guise of the so-called learned article, critical reasoning made its way into the daily press" (25). Once again, he postdates a phenomenon that is in fact a product of the fin de siècle. In addition, he associates this development

only with scholarly papers like *Journal des savants,* ignoring the more popular press, and *Le Mercure galant* in particular. For information on the complete range of periodicals that appeared in French at the end of the century, see Jean-Pierre Vittu.

50.   I have in mind here the teaching of literature and the practice of literary commentary and literary criticism, even though these functions were exercised at that time in places and in ways that were often very different from the ways in which they are practiced within today's university systems. For instance, the fact that the Sorbonne did not have a unit devoted to the teaching of French literature at the turn of the eighteenth century is not important to my argument, whereas I do consider significant the fact that the period witnessed the first major formulation of literary history in France, and that that phenomenon took place under Ancient control.

51.   I will return to the subject of the *code noir* in chapter 4. At the time of its promulgation, the *code noir* was justified as necessary to regulate the institution of slavery in the French colonies. The document was obsessively revised and frequently reissued until the moment when slavery was finally abolished in the French colonies in 1848. No question inspired more obsessive rewriting than the possibility of interracial marriage. It is in this light that it seems evident that, as Louis Sala-Molins has suggested, the *code noir* is a legal code designed above all to enforce racial purity—and thus that it functioned as the absolute counterdiscourse to the suggestions promoted in the Modern camp that identity should not be policed by the establishment of perfect frontiers.

52.   "Il n'y a plus qu'un sexe, et nous sommes tous femmes par l'esprit." It is difficult to date individual *pensées,* but number 1062 was written sometime around 1737.

53.   On the notion of the novel as contagious disease, see my *Tender Geographies* (157–58). On the rewriting of literary history to eliminate women writers and their accomplishments, see *Tender Geographies,* chap. 5.

CHAPTER THREE

1.   I will depart from my standard practice and leave *sensibilité* and *sensible* in French. Literal translations are inadequate, so I would constantly be including the French term in parentheses after whatever solution I chose in English.

2.   I find myself once again in the position of arguing for the existence of a phenomenon long before that phenomenon acquired its definitive designation. As we will see, however, works like Lamy's *Explication mécanique et physique de l'âme sensitive* (1678) and Gamaches's *Système du coeur ou la connaissance du coeur humain* (1704) correspond perfectly to what both the Littré and the Robert dictionaries present as *psychologie*'s original definition in French: "Psychology is the science of the soul." The naturalist Charles Bonnet is credited with having introduced the term in 1754. I also find myself once again objecting to Habermas's view of the class structure that surrounded a phenomenon's creation. "Psychology arose as a specifically bourgeois science during the eighteenth century," Habermas declares (29), whereas the science in fact shares the more complex origins of "le public."

3.   For a comprehensive overview of commentary on the emotions in antiquity, see Martha Nussbaum's *The Therapy of Desire.* Nussbaum's work makes

it clear that the early modern European philosophers who initiated the rewriting of the language of the emotions that I study here, such as Descartes, were all intimately familiar with their classical precursors.

4. Descartes's tactic—that of using the commonly accepted term, *passion,* in his title, while introducing the linguistic innovation, *émotion,* only in his text—is one evident solution to the problem of getting the original public to recognize and accept unfamiliar vocabulary. I think also of the example of J. A. Symonds, who, in 1883, may have been the first to use *homosexual.* His innovation has been overlooked because it occurs only in the body of a work whose title, *A Problem in Greek Ethics, Being an Inquiry into the Phenomenon of Sexual Inversion,* features the then standard term, "inversion."

5. These examples—as well as similar ones used to illustrate the other affective terminology I will discuss—suggest that the novel vocabulary was useful in helping identify the new types of familial ties (between parents and children, between husbands and wives) that historians of early modern family life such as Philippe Ariès and René Pillorget see as coming into being at this time.

6. In his dictionary (1680), Richelet gives as *émotion's* primary definition "disturbance, sedition." The Académie Française's 1694 dictionary says "popular uprising."

7. The year 1649 was the year that England witnessed the ultimate national crime, regicide. Since *emotion* arrived in England with the returning court, it seems likely that Descartes's treatise dictated this change in English usage. *Emotion's* unchallenged centrality in English explains the difficulty I encountered writing these pages in English. The terminology subsequently invented in French to replace *emotion*—in particular, *sensibilité* and the terms related to it—was far more transient in English, simply because it was never needed to the same extent. This terminology is even less important in American English, always farther removed from French than British usage.

8. Only Furetière includes an example of affective emotions: "A lover feels emotion at the sight of his beloved, and a brave man at the sight of his enemy." The Académie Française gives an example from *Phèdre* (1677, l. 998), in which the verb *émouvoir* is linked to sentiment: "Je pourrai de mon père émouvoir la tendresse." Since Racine is among the boldest innovators in this domain—an innovator so daring that his example was hardly ever followed—this usage is proof of how seldom *emotion* was given an affective charge. (Rousseau, describing Racine in the affective vocabulary of his day, said of his theater that "everything is emotion" [*tout est sentiment*] [180].)

9. The most recent edition of the *Robert* contends that *passion* was used as a synonym for "émotion, sentiment" from the thirteenth to the eighteenth centuries. An anonymous compilation from 1777, the two-volume *Dictionnaire des passions, des vertus et des vices,* proves that *passion's* semantic transfer had been completed more than a decade before the Revolution. In it, *passion* functions no longer as a synonym for "affection," but rather for "virtue" or "vice." The study of passions, as the editor explains in a preface, is necessary in order to "show men their duty" (ix). Descartes's first mission, that of removing "passion" from the center of the French emotional horizon, had been accomplished. Francis Hutcheson's *Essay on the Nature and the Conduct of the Passions and*

the Affections (1728) illustrates *passion*'s parallel loss of primacy in English: in the body of the text, *affection* is Hutcheson's preferred term.

10.   I stress the absence of medical connotations, because the more generally scientific connotations of some terms are obvious. For example, the first definition of *sentiment* included in all seventeenth-century dictionaries is the equivalent of the Académie Française's "the impression that objects make on the senses."

11.   In the seventeenth century, *la morale* was generally considered a branch of philosophy. The *Encyclopédie* (1751) defines psychology as "the branch of philosophy concerned with the human soul."

12.   Indeed, it may well be that *emotion* was successfully implanted in English at the same time that it was rejected in French because it was initially defined in English as a relational term. The first example given in the *OED* for *emotion* (1660) refers to "the emotions of humanity," a compassionate affective context reserved in French for the new terms preferred to *emotion*.

13.   *Emotion*'s other appearance in *Artamène*'s initial volume is on page 245. I cite the Slatkine reprint editions of Scudéry's novels, the most readily available text. In order to make a fair comparison between *Artamène* and *Clélie*, I base my calculations on only the first half of the volume of *Artamène;* its typeface is almost exactly twice as dense as that used for *Clélie*. Scudéry is quite evidently *not* among the seventeenth century's great stylists; her prose can be compared to what we would consider today journalistic prose or popular fiction. Her relaxed style should not, however, discourage readers from taking her semantic innovations seriously. I agree with Frank Baasner, who believes that Scudéry demonstrates a degree of precision in her linguistic usage quite unusual for her day.

14.   Descartes attacks popular beliefs that portray the heart as the home of the emotions because for him the soul, the origin of all affect, is housed in the brain (3:979). However, the scientific discussion with which he prefaces his presentation of the new vocabulary is devoted above all to the heart's structure and to the circulation of blood, as though he sensed that this shift of focus was inevitable.

15.   *Sentiment,* as a synonym for emotion, appears on pages 13, 38, 41, 61, 193, 202, 203, 204, 207, and 235. I discuss Scudéry's definitions of the new vocabulary before those of seventeenth-century dictionaries because many elements in dictionary definitions obviously reflect the influence of her usage.

16.   The term appears more than fifty times in the volume. *Emotion* is used no more frequently than in *Artamène* (353, 357, 359). In view of the affective explosion otherwise evident, this is the equivalent of the term's death knell.

17.   Scudéry's characters continuously strive to rationalize their feelings and thereby to control them, and for the most part they succeed in their efforts. Witness, for example, the conversation between Aronce and Horace regarding the relation between friendship and jealousy (378–81).

18.   The scene's only rival for this prominence is the princess de Clèves's avowal to her husband, around which Donneau de Visé organized the controversy in *Le Mercure galant.*

19.   Scudéry had already begun to make this move in *Artamène*'s final volume, where she speaks of trying to establish "the anatomy of the heart in love

[*coeur amoureux*]" (10:334). The anatomy was outlined by Sapho, the character thus established as Clélie's precursor. Sapho—who speaks, for example, of "les sentiments du coeur" (10:416)—already uses much of the affective vocabulary that Clélie develops. The shift from anatomy to cartography as central metaphor for her linguistic innovation reveals Scudéry's understanding of the altered balance of powers between science and psychology. *Clélie*'s initial volume, published in 1654, was composed during the final months of the French civil war, when the Bourbon monarchy was stamping out political emotions. (On Scudéry's political stance during the Fronde, see my *Tender Geographies* [46–50]). The heart attains its new status in the aftermath of political "emotion"—hence the impossibility for Scudéry of transferring *émotion* to the center of her reinvented emotions.

20. I realize the difficulty of categorizing friendship as an emotion. Since antiquity, however, treatises have done just this.

21. Even to the present day, the vocabulary of tenderness remains far more central in French than in English. And during the half-century that followed *Clélie*'s publication, it played a dominant role in affective terminology. Women writers were particularly likely to follow Scudéry's lead—see, for example, the fairy tales of Henriette de Castelnau, comtesse de Murat, and Marie-Jeanne L'Héritier.

22. Even though she neglects it in favor of *tendresse*, Scudéry nevertheless launched *sensibilité* on the road to linguistic prominence by establishing its association with the heart and with love. On several occasions, for example, characters are described as having "le coeur sensible" (69, 411, 587). Scudéry also links the adverb *sensiblement* to *heart* to create something like a synonym for "love at first sight": "he couldn't look at her without having his heart touched so *sensiblement* that . . . he became [her] prisoner" (93). Just as she does with *sentiment*, however, Scudéry forges links for *sensibilité* to emotions other than love, in particular to compassion, portraying it, in other words, as an inherently relational emotion. On one road to Tenderness, for instance, "it is necessary to pass through Sensibilité in order to realize that we have to feel even the smallest sorrows of those we love" (402).

23. The standard reference on *sensibilité*, Pierre Trahard's 1931 study, has long discouraged scholars from investigating pre-eighteenth-century material to look for the vocabulary and the ideals of literary *sensibilité*. Trahard contends that the reign of *sensibilité* truly begins only in 1730 (1:9). In his introduction, he makes a few vague references to seventeenth-century works, but only post–Culture Wars material interests him. John Spink's article is far more reliable and comprehensive. Spink focuses on early-eighteenth-century material; he does, however, cite a few late-seventeenth-century works, in particular Anne Ferrand's 1691 novel, *Histoire des amours de Cléante et de Bélise* (34). I was first alerted to the possibility that *sensibilité* had a life in French well before Trahard had led me to expect it by references to Ferrand's use of the term by Febvre and Hazard. Baasner provides by far the best overview of *sensibilité*'s early history; he alone, for example, notes the role played by Scudéry's *Clélie*. However, I do not agree with all of Baasner's conclusions about the term's meaning in the seventeenth century. None of these scholars recognizes the extent to which this affective reinvention was a fin de siècle phenomenon. It is important to remem-

ber that none of them had access to the vastly expanded resources provided by a database such as the ARTFL. Thanks to the ARTFL, a range of seventeenth-century texts has become accessible that is far broader than any scholar could have hoped to cover through traditional research procedures. Information thus made available makes possible radically new conclusions about the earliest appearances and the initial meaning of the full range of affective terminology. G. S. Rousseau concludes that "the revolution in sentiment" also took place in England in the late seventeenth century, although his assertion is based on scientific evidence alone: he contends that it took a half-century for literature to "catch up" with scientific discoveries (142).

24.   To give a better sense of the precariousness of all this usage, here are more statistics. During the same period, 1670–95, there are 19 occurrences of *sentiment* and 23 of *sensible*. All these examples are based on information gathered from the ARTFL database and are, therefore, subject to its limitations—obviously, not every text from the period is included. The sense of innovativeness is further collaborated, however, by each word's overall history during the same period. The ARTFL lists, for example, 867 appearances of *sentiment;* of these, only 19 have the now dominant meaning of "a feeling or emotion." The vast majority of the other occurrences use the word in its then dominant meaning of "an opinion." Other striking examples of clustering in an attempt to condemn the rising tide of *sensibilité* are found in Bossuet's *Traité de la concupiscence* (31, 56).

25.   It is interesting that Furetière, in my experience inevitably the seventeenth-century lexicographer most sensitive to linguistic innovation and change, when confronted with the reinvention of the emotions, is for once the least receptive to evolving usage.

26.   Richelet gives several examples that suggest that an individual is *sensible* when he feels for someone suffering because of the death of a loved one. Furetière does not go beyond the then dominant "that which makes an impression on the senses."

27.   Furetière defines it only by means of clustering: "*Tendresse: sensibilité* of the heart and the soul." *Tendre* is given an even more direct window onto the new emotionality of sharing. Furetière includes a definition that, more clearly than any other contemporary lexicographical moment, points to the psychic creativity of the vision being implanted: "A good man has a conscience that is *tender* or easily moved by compassion for his neighbor's suffering."

28.   Richelet stresses repeatedly that *sentiment* is being used in "new ways of speaking" and to designate previously unexplored feelings. (He seems to put the *tendresse* that parents feel for their children in this category.)

29.   For efficiency's sake, I will pretend that the distinction between the heart and the soul had only semantic significance. In the realm of medicine, however, this was obviously not the case. Basing his argument to a large extent on Thomas Willis's influential *Pathology of the Brain* (Latin 1667), G. S. Rousseau demonstrates convincingly the essential role played in the sentimental revolution by the vastly increased knowledge of the brain's functioning that Willis's treatise made possible (141, 145). For Rousseau, the imaginative leap that made all this happen was the beginning of the belief that the soul was housed in the brain. It is important to remember, nevertheless, that even doctors aware of

the new importance of the brain contributed to the widespread contemporary movement as a result of which the heart was enshrined as the seat of the emotions.

30. The phrase is Foucault's ("une morale de sensibilité") (*Folie* 139). I am indebted to Foucault's description of the evolution from a medicine centered on fevers to a medicine focused on nerves (see in particular 138–51). Henry de Boulainvillier's 1683 treatise, *De l'homme,* is a textbook example of the new medical speculation centered on fibers and nerves, on *sympathie* and *sensibilité* (see, in particular, 2:248–49, 257). Boulainvillier's treatise was not published in the seventeenth century, but it did circulate widely in manuscript, in France and in other European countries.

31. Though Lamy also speaks of "the soul," he in effect conflates the soul and the heart, remarking, for instance, that when we feel an emotion (*sentiment*), this feeling takes the form of "an extraordinary movement in the arteries and in the heart" (72–73). It was a commonly held theory in Lamy's day (see, for example, Blégny [3:212]) that the soul resided in the heart, so the similarity between contemporary descriptions of the heart's movements (in love and in other emotions) and Lamy's vision of the "sensitive soul" is logical. Lamy is faithful to the basic principles of semantic innovation: he consistently practices clustering, and he uses a group of new terms—in particular, *sensitif, sentiments,* and *sensible*—to help define each other. Boulainvillier's 1683 treatise testifies to the continued state of uncertainty about whether the heart or the soul should be considered the control center (2:242).

32. Boulainvillier's 1683 treatise, *De l'homme,* is typical of the contemporary medical speculation about the bodily effects of *sensibilité*: he speaks of the "intimate unions" between organs and of their mutual "attraction by means of sympathy" (2:249). For a glimpse of the influence of such theories on more popular medical speculation, see the exchange of anonymous letters on the subjects of pleasure and pain published in *Le Mercure galant.* Attractive objects, for example, are referred to as "objets sensibles" (February 1696, 40).

33. Thirty years after Lamy, Gamaches continues to use all the new affective terminology interchangeably. Curiously, the one term I would have expected to find added to Gamaches's semantic blend, *sympathie,* is missing from his *Système du coeur.* Less than a decade later, however, in his *Les Aventures de ***, ou les effets surprenants de la sympathie* (1713–14), the novelist Pierre Carlet de Marivaux established this term at the center of his version of the new emotionality. And, already in 1671, one of the founders of the new French sentimental fiction, Marie-Catherine Desjardins, known as Madame de Villedieu, had helped introduce *sympathie* as a key concept in relational affectivity (*Henriette-Sylvie* 57; note also her interesting use of *émotion* in the same passage.) *Sympathie*'s absence from a more scientifically and medically inclined discussion of the emotions such as Gamaches's is surprising both because, of all the new words proposed, it was best suited to forging the link between a science and an affectivity based on attraction, and because the beginnings of its usage in this sense are already attested in late-seventeenth-century dictionaries and in such late-seventeenth-century medical speculation as Boulainvillier's (see, for example, p. 249 on the bodily function of sympathy). The Académie Française defines *sympathie* as "the natural quality by means of which two bodies act on each other."

Furetière makes plain the term's links to both the medicine of attraction—"refers to an indisposition that happens to one part of the body through the fault of another"—as well as to the emotionality of attraction—"People of similar disposition who sympathize with each other [ont de la sympathie] live well together."

34.   My argument here is influenced by Foucault's theory of the "interior body" reimagined by each successive school of medical speculation, as well as by his view that this interior body was being reconfigured at the period that concerns me here (Folie 144). Foucault's examples, as well as those from Boulainvillier and Blégny, prove that contemporary medical texts immediately begin to borrow the vocabulary of sentiment invented by "moralists" (Folie 145–51). I use the term moralist to refer to the domain we now call "psychology" and include in this category all the very different types of writers—from novelists, to preachers, to such creators of aphorisms as La Rochefoucauld—whose joint efforts succeeded in imposing the new affective terminology.

35.   The extent to which the body was "humanized" and described as if its fluids and organs had an emotional life of their own could be remarkable. For Boulainvillier, for example, humors are "gay"; the stomach can "rejoice," or even feel "horror" (2:249, see also 259). Pain is caused by the soul's "hatred" of some guilty bodily part (2:253).

36.   The story of their public embrace is known through the account given in a letter of 3 September 1694 by none other than Abbé Du Bos, soon to become the premier French aesthetician of sensibilité (Boileau, O.c. xxxix).

37.   Perrault's critique begins on p. 30 and continues for over fifty pages. D'Aubignac's treatise is said to have been written in 1674 (Boileau, O.c. 1098 n. 1). The manuscript was found among his papers upon his death in 1677. Because of Perrault's remarks and similar statements, it is evident that it circulated widely before it was finally published in 1715 under the title Conjectures académiques, ou dissertation sur l'Iliade. The case of d'Aubignac's manuscript provides the first illustration of a phenomenon, the extensive lag between composition and publication, to which I will return on several occasions in the course of this chapter. I see this phenomenon as proof that certain ideas become of public interest only when the general intellectual context has prepared the way for their reception.

38.   Not even the publication of the final volume of Perrault's Parallèle des Anciens et des Modernes, in 1697, provoked any renewed conflict over literary matters.

39.   This does not mean, however, that fin de siècle upheaval was not present in literature itself. In fact, probably at no time prior to the present has subjectivity undergone such radical destabilization as in the last years of the seventeenth century. We will discuss in particular a story, published in Le Mercure galant in 1695 and 1696, during the period of greatest famine, "Histoire de la marquise-marquis de Banneville," which offers a sustained critique of all commonly accepted means of defining identity.

40.   To stress the continuity between the two phases, I will on occasion still use the term Culture Wars to refer to the final rounds.

41.   I stress once again that the French university at the turn of the eighteenth century had nothing like the organization of today's university systems.

Most Ancients did, however, enjoy official status of one kind or another—as professors; as critics published by the official, royal printing press. When I speak of the conflict as being aired within the Academy, I am referring, therefore, to those institutions that provided the bases from which the Ancients operated.

42.   Dacier was perhaps the most gifted and influential Hellenist of her generation. She was the daughter of one of early modern France's most noted Hellenists, Tanneguy Le Fèvre, and the wife of another respected classicist, André Dacier. Her impressive credentials as well as her connections are especially worthy of note in view of the fact that the appropriateness of Boileau's decision to appoint himself head Ancient had come under persistent challenge, even from within the ranks of the Ancients, on the grounds that he did not have sufficient knowledge of Greek.

43.   It would be interesting to speculate on why it might have been that the battle over Homer was centered almost entirely on the *Iliad*, whereas the *Odyssey* inspired virtually no hostile exchanges.

44.   French readers could have known the work in two allegedly unauthorized editions, both published outside France, in 1688 and 1693. On the composition and publication history of the *Dialogue des héros de roman,* see Adam and Escal's edition of Boileau's *Oeuvres complètes* (1089–90).

45.   The lies Boileau consistently told about every aspect of this text's history—from when it was written to why he had refused to allow it to be published—indicate a relation to the dialogue so contorted that it will probably never be convincingly explained. (See the notes to the Adam and Escal edition of Boileau's *Oeuvres complètes* for an account of some of Boileau's duplicity.) Boileau's ambivalence about the *Dialogue* is still evident in the edition in which he finally makes it officially part of his corpus. Boileau lists the texts added to his complete works for the final edition; he does not mention the *Dialogue des héros de roman.*

46.   The *privilège* for the edition is dated November 1712, which means that it was published in the early months of 1713. The final editing of Boileau's manuscript is generally considered to have been a joint effort of Valincour, best known for his attack on *La Princesse de Clèves,* and Théophraste Renaudot, one of Donneau de Visé's main rivals for control over the contemporary newspaper scene.

47.   At this point, Dacier is so far from imagining, for instance, that anyone will seek to undermine Homer's authority that she doesn't take on any of the issues that will be obsessively fought over in subsequent years. Indeed, she is so confident that everyone accepts Homer's existence that she follows her preface with a forty-five-page "Life of Homer" that rehearses all the "facts" of his life. The first edition of Dacier's translation of the *Iliad* has a *privilège* dated 27 January 1711, so its appearance would have coincided with Boileau's death in March of that year. It is not clear from Dacier's preface whether she was actually familiar with Boileau's arguments in his *Dialogue* from one of the earlier, "unauthorized" editions, or whether the terms in which she attacks the novel simply rejoin Boileau's to an uncanny degree. (When she makes similar charges three years later, she couches them in terminology so close to Boileau's as to leave no room for doubt.) Since it is quite likely that Boileau would have been aware of Dacier's enterprise, it is even possible that the knowledge that she was about to issue a major warning about the novel's societal menace prompted Boileau

finally to ready his *Dialogue* for publication just as Dacier's edition was in press. In any event, their simultaneous decision to come forward with this argument, given in particular the long lag between composition and publication in the case of Boileau's work, indicates that both sensed that the climate was right for an antinovel polemic. Dacier's status within the contemporary literary institution is confirmed by the publication of this translation, and of all her subsequent works, as the title page announces, "by Rigaud, director of the royal printing works."

48.   As Maurice Lever's bibliography proves, novels were being published in increasingly important numbers throughout the period that separates the two phases of the hostilities.

49.   Prior to the conflict, Houdar de La Motte was known for his comedies and primarily for his opera librettos. (It was surely in his honor that, in all her subsequent attacks on the novel as a force of corruption, Dacier pronounced opera as dangerous a social threat as the novel.) In 1710, just as Dacier was gearing up for her new role, Houdar de La Motte was elected to the Académie Française. Perhaps in his capacity as new head Modern—he dedicates his edition of Homer to Louis XIV with rhetoric that recalls Perrault's *Le Siècle de Louis le Grand*—he was chosen to pronounce Louis XIV's funeral eulogy there on 19 December 1715. Houdar de La Motte acknowledged that he did not know Greek and that he had simply put Dacier's prose translation into verse. He always called his edition an "imitation" of Homer and freely admitted that he had made many changes in an effort to adapt Homer to modern taste and style.

50.   D'Aubignac's editor freely admits that he was publishing the manuscript in order to capitalize on the current controversy (ii).

51.   Boivin's work might seems the reductio ad absurdum of scholarship by today's standards, but it was widely admired by his contemporaries. For instance, the highly respected scholar Bernard de Montfaucon discusses Boivin's theory at length in his *L'Antiquité expliquée* (vol. 4, chap. 3). Boivin is so obsessed by his mania to calculate the shield exactly that the last pages of his volume (281–87) are devoted to new "theories about the size of Achilles's shield" in which he justifies the figures given earlier and lists other very large ancient shields. The next "apology for Homer," by Hardouin, returns to the shield to argue that Boivin's calculations are off: it wouldn't have had to be as large as Boivin contends to hold all the scenes Homer describes. Hardouin claims to have seen just as much material covered on smaller surfaces (208–9).

52.   There is, of course, a critical difference between the death of the author and his never having existed in the first place. Nonetheless, the vehemence with which twentieth-century Ancients responded to proclamations of the author's death was foreshadowed by the intensity with which their seventeenth-century precursors criticized claims of Homer's fictional status. Since I am concerned here with commentary on the author, rather than any reality of who authors actually were at any given period, I will follow dominant practice of that commentary and identify "the author" as "he." Foucault's 1969 essay "What Is an Author?" (in which the author is always "he") is the most influential recent meditation on authorial status. Among Foucault's claims, the most intriguing for the period that concerns me here is the notion that authors began to be recognized once discourses began to be perceived as transgressive and once the

authors of works judged transgressive could be punished. (See also Chartier's discussion in the third chapter of *The Order of Books* of the role played by censorship in creating the category of the author.) In France, the period just prior to the Culture Wars, the 1650s and the 1660s, witnessed the birth of a new discourse identified only in the nineteenth century as pornographic. In the case of the first novel now recognized as pornographic, *L'Ecole des filles* (1655), the extensive legal proceedings involving the work's alleged authors have survived in their entirety. (See Lachèvre's edition.) In these documents, one can feel the interrogators groping for a sense of what it was that they were supposed to prosecute and, in the process, according a new prominence to the authors of the discourse perceived to be transgressive. For a sociological reading of the growing importance accorded authors in the seventeenth century's final decades, see Alain Viala's *La Naissance de l'écrivain*. On the diverse manifestations and ramifications of the author's death for our modernity, see Françoise Meltzer's *Hot Property*.

53.   The earliest examples of this tendency to progress from anthologies of the best works (the first impulse of French literary history) to lists of biographies appear shortly after the initial pronouncements of Homer's "death." The first case I know of illustrates this transition perfectly: beginning with the 1699 edition of a collection of "the most beautiful French letters," Pierre Richelet appends a list of biographies of the best-known contemporary authors. (In his *Dictionnaire*, Pierre Bayle responds with counterbiographies to some of Richelet's biographies, which he criticizes as based on erroneous, secondhand information.)

54.   Some of Sévigné's letters had previously been published in collections (particularly those of the correspondence of her cousin, Bussy-Rabutin), but the editions of 1725 and 1726 are the first to market Sévigné as an independent authorial commodity.

55.   Valincour, author of the critique of *La Princesse de Clèves*, was also present at the ceremony. Given the cast of characters—Ancients as well as Moderns, the novel's detractors as well as its supporters—Callières's speech can be seen as the equivalent of an official recognition of Lafayette's authorship. I am making a distinction here between public and private recognition: within some circles, Lafayette's authorship had always been an open secret.

56.   See Geneviève Mouligneau's study for details about the signs of interest in and the attempts at determining Lafayette's authorial identity—for the case of *La Princesse de Clèves* (166–68) and also that of *Zayde* (149). To readers aware that Mouligneau's volume is an attempt to prove that Lafayette wrote none of the works now attributed to her—an attempt I find unconvincing—my reference may seem ironic. However, Mouligneau's research demonstrates that the period 1694–1719, in her words, "determines the shape of modern opinion" (168).

57.   In *Des causes de la corruption du goût*, Dacier amplified this banishment of love: "Achilles cries, not because a mistress is taken away from him, for he is not in love, but because the recompense of his valor is being taken away: for he is ambitious and proud" (140).

58.   Terrasson is Boivin's obvious counterpart in the Modern camp: he was professor of Latin and Greek philosophy at the Collège de France at the time when Boivin held the chair of Greek there. A comparison of their two critical

methods contrasts perfectly Modern relativism—or, as Terrasson, a true pre-Enlightenment figure, always says, "the philosophical ethic" (iii)—with Ancient positivism. The successful implantation of the new affective language is evident in the writings of all Moderns, even in those of a philosopher such as Terrasson: the word *sentiment* is omnipresent in his defense of the emotions; he even includes a long section devoted to "*sentiments* in Homer" (2:417–40).

59.   Here and most often, Houdar de La Motte uses *sentiment*. He devotes a long section of his preface to the poem's heroes, and he specifies his view of each hero's emotional capacities. Houdar de La Motte consistently employs the full range of the new vocabulary, referring, for example, to "the place of *sensibilité* in the human heart" (xxxii).

60.   Dacier repeatedly accuses Houdar de La Motte of judging the epic according to standards developed for the novel. She dismisses, for example, his critique of Homer for having "an intelligence [that is] noble rather than refined [*délicat*]" on the grounds that "refinement" (*délicatesse*) is characteristic of "the artificial politeness of our novels" (*Corruption* 287).

61.   Throughout his discussion, Houdar de La Motte's rhetoric is loaded with the classic vocabulary of the Enlightenment—from *éclaircissement* to "reason." This is basis for all judgments made by the second category of participant. The same vocabulary is foregrounded by other second-generation Moderns. The development of the conflict confirmed, therefore, Perrault's intuition—already evident in "Le Génie"—that such debate would inevitably alter accepted definitions of intellectual activity and that those changes would prepare the way for a new episteme. Pre-Enlightenment rhetoric is nowhere more evident than in Terrasson's treatise, in which he develops a poetics entirely founded on the values of reason and progress and challenges the republic of letters to model itself on the principles that govern the natural sciences: "Philosophical enlightenment [*lumières*] must dissipate the darkness that envelops literature and culture" (xliii). Terrasson's treatise is the only work in the entire history of the Culture Wars openly to question the policies of Louis XIV's by then wildly decadent reign. (Ironically, his treatise's publication coincided almost exactly with Louis XIV's death.) He counters Dacier's explanation for "the corruption of taste" with an alternate scenario that, at first indirectly (by means of a reference to the decadence of Rome) and later more explicitly explains that corruption begins with monarchs and their policies and then, and only then, spreads to "the people": "Endless wars and the misery they bring on visibly damage culture. And in addition the moral excesses that quickly filter down from princes to the people . . . all that which puts an end to civil calm and propriety brings on the corruption and the loss of taste" (lvi). The other Modern treatise remarkable for its display of pre-Enlightenment rhetoric is Pons's *Lettre sur l'Iliade* (1714).

62.   Houdar de La Motte formulates a subtle definition of the manner in which literary controversies produce meaning: "[Positions] modify each other, and an overall meaning is created by this process, which becomes in fact the heart of the matter" (*Réflexions* 7).

63.   In addition to his treatise on Achilles' shield, for example, Jean Hardouin contributed such monuments to positivism as *Nouveau traité sur la situation du Paradis terrestre* (1730) and *Doutes proposés sur l'âge de Dante* (first published 1847).

64.   Since Batteux succeeded Terrasson in the chair of Greek and Latin philosophy at the Collège de France, his manual may be said to represent the abso-
luteness of the Ancient victory. On the development of the French educational
system in the eighteenth century, see Chartier, Compère, and Julia (in particular,
199–209). On the systematic exclusion of the novel and women writers as a
result of the Ancient takeover, see my *Tender Geographies,* chap. 5.

65.   The vision took place at Paray-le-Monial, the basilica from which Alacoque and her followers carried out their mission and still the center of the
French cult of the Sacred Heart. On the history of the modern tradition of
devotion, see Jacques Le Brun (25, 28, 36). See also Louis Cognet.

66.   Le Brun formulates this sense of Alacoque's participation in the general
cultural climate of her age in a more orthodox manner: "Divine revelation takes
shape relative to the person who receives it and to the age for which it is destined" (36).

67.   Le Brun reviews the history of devotion to the Sacred Heart to show
that it developed complexity and intensity in proportion to the increased dis-
tance from the historical figure of Christ (26). Cognet stresses that references
to the heart of Christ were rare and imprecise in the early seventeenth century
and that this imagery became increasingly more detailed as the century developed (2302–4). The years just prior to Alacoque's vision of the Sacred Heart
witnessed a veritable explosion of devotional writing centered on the heart—
human as well as divine—as the center of spiritual life in general. Note in particular Father Vincent Contenson's *Theologia mentis et cordis* (1668) and Abbé
François Querdu Le Gall's *Oratoire du coeur ou méthode très facile pour faire
oraison avec Jésus Christ* (1670). In the years following the vision at Paray-le-
Monial, such publications continued to appear (Cognet 2306), increasingly accompanied by the works of Alacoque's followers (Cognet 2307). Alacoque was
asked by her spiritual director to write the account of her experience around
1685; its first publication dates from 1733. Her works were most widely circulated during the second half of the nineteenth century, when devotion to the
Sacred Heart took on truly major and popular proportions in France. Commentators consistently note the growing importance granted the emotions in all
types of spiritual writing during the years of the Culture Wars. For example,
Jean-Louis Flandrin's comparison of the way in which a moralist (Antoine
Blanchard) described the proper examination of conscience in 1713 with the
techniques of early seventeenth-century confessors reveals above all the new role
accorded the emotions: "In the total of 153 articles which [Blanchard] devotes
to domestic relationships, he refers eighty times to sentiments, passions and
moods, and uses thirty-seven different concepts" (145).

68.   Like all the most influential contemporary medical texts, Harvey's major works, *De motu cordis* (1628) and *De circulatione* (1649), were published in
Latin, which functioned, as English does today, as a universal scientific language.
This means that, in the case of scientific discoveries, it is not necessary to factor
in the usual time lag to account for translation when trying to understand the
transmission of ideas. On the rapid spread of Harvey's discoveries to France,
see Robert Frank (110). The other crucial seventeenth-century figure in this
domain was Richard Lower, whose *Tractatus de corde* (1669)—which deals with
subjects such as blood transfusion, cardiac pathology, and hemodynamics—is

considered the first example of modern cardiology. Lower was translated into French in 1679, indicating that his treatise was expected to find a readership outside erudite circles and perhaps indicating as well that the time had come for the medical heart to circulate along with its literary counterpart. Lower's *Traité du coeur* shows that the new knowledge of the heart was intimately bound up with the nascent medicine of *sensibilité*. Lower's account of the heart's functioning relies heavily on notions of "affinity" and "attraction" between organs (see, for example, 93, 142). In addition, his treatise demonstrates how the new research on the heart contributed to a heightened awareness of the role of nerves and fibers, an awareness essential to the further development of this new medicine in the eighteenth century. A French overview of recent research in this area, Charles Malouin's *Traité des corps solides et des fluides, ou examen du mouvement du sang et celui du coeur* (1712), shows that, by the time the Culture Wars were nearing their end, consideration of "the movement of the heart" had already become actively implicated in the discussion of nerves and fibers and the process by which they become irritated. This connection established, the medicine of *sensibilité* was ready for its eighteenth-century incarnation, with a new emphasis on nervous derangements, which are seen as the result of excess sensitivity, as states of irritation caused by the excessive mobility of fibers.

69.   Perrault lists new knowledge about different aspects of the body made possible by the developing science of anatomy. All the discoveries are from the seventeenth century (5:244–45). In the *Parallèle*, in fact, Harvey's contributions are praised with greater fervor than those of, say, Galileo or Newton. One cannot overestimate the crucial new role as vulgarizers of recent scientific advances that was played by the leading Moderns of the first generation. Fontenelle—in particular in his *Entretiens sur la pluralité des mondes* (1686)—joined Perrault in his attempt at making general readers aware of the major scientific achievements that the Moderns were promoting.

70.   Cognet points out, for example, that "to [his] knowledge no seventeenth-century devotional author explicitly refers to Harvey's discoveries" (2300).

71.   Often, even discourse situated in the scientific domain reinforced the heart's metaphorical status. Thus, for example, in Blégny's review of the medical news for 1679, he discusses an autopsy performed in Beauvais on a forty-year-old man described as "unfeeling or dried out [*desséché*] in his temperament and his way of life." The doctors find that his heart was the very physical image of his emotional life, "completely shriveled and dried out" (338).

72.   Contemporary scientific research could have provided other guiding metaphors for *sensibilité*. For instance, discoveries about the brain—in particular Thomas Willis's 1667 treatise *Pathalogiae Cerebri*—could have changed its status in the popular imaginary. Willis's work was just as quickly diffused in France as that of the cardiac pathologists. The Bibliothèque Nationale has the copy of the first edition of his *Pathology of the Brain* from the library of Huet, active participant in the Culture Wars and fervent early champion of the novel. Willis's works were also published in a Latin edition in Lyons in 1676. This extensive medical speculation about the brain was never carried over, however, into other discourses. (See Rousseau for a reading of research on the brain as the necessary catalyst for the age of sensibility [140–42].) Nor, to cite but one

additional example, did contemporary research on gravity and attraction carried out in the wake of Newton's discovery (first published in 1685) perform any similar cultural work—despite the obvious metaphorical implications of theories of attraction for definitions of *sensibilité*. In seventeenth-century cultural speculation, the only medically based explanations given for affective attraction make reference to recent discoveries about nerves and fibers.

73.   Scudéry's portrayal of character is, of course, accidental, the result of a lack of technique, rather than intentional, the result of a desire to undermine literary identity. For a reading of picaresque heroes that could suggest that Scudéry's characters possess a form of interiority, see Weinstein (19–20). His reading of *La Princesse de Clèves* runs parallel to mine at times (67–71) but ultimately suggests that Lafayette's view of interiority is far less radically different from that found in earlier fiction than I maintain (73–82). The volume that can be said to play a role parallel to Scudéry's novels in the domain of religious speculation on the heart and the sentiments is Jacques Abbadie's *L'Art de se connaître soi-même* (1692). Abbadie, who refers consistently to "les sentiments du coeur" and in general provides a lexicon of relevant vocabulary, aims, in the manner of Du Bos for aesthetic theory, to make the heart the sole guide: "Those who seek to use their emotions as a means of understanding [moral ethics] have only to look into their own hearts and, with the aid of divine revelation, they will learn all the necessary principles" (9).

74.   In the first letter on Lafayette's novel that he composed for *Le Mercure galant*, Donneau de Visé praises *La Princesse de Clèves* above all because of the exquisite knowledge of emotions found in it (109). With the reception of Lafayette's novel, as the majority of the letters subsequently published by Donneau de Visé reveal, we witness the beginning of the transformation of reading into an act in the drama of *sensibilité*, a status that is fully realized only with the response to Rousseau's *Julie* (1761). Even if Lafayette's audience was not driven to tears by the affective upheaval wrought by their reading, as was the case with Rousseau's most fervent readers, they were nevertheless encouraged by the process to imagine the novel as somehow more real than other literary forms and therefore more directly applicable to their own lives. In particular, the novel inspired in them the desire to consider, in public, notions of interiority; it generated a collective exploration of some of the new affective bonds. In Valincour's attack on the novel, we witness the incursion of the values of *sensibilité* into the domain of professional literary criticism. He devotes his entire second letter to the role of feelings in the novel and begins by calling them "so natural that one can almost feel them in one's own heart" (121). Even if many of his analyses have nothing to do with what we would now think of as psychological criticism, Valincour is nevertheless trying to introduce affective values into this discourse.

75.   The conversation takes place just after they have become engaged. The entire exchange, their only recorded meeting prior to their marriage, is presented as a dissection of the princess's emotions, those she feels or does not feel, those she should or should not feel. It provides a crash course in the new affective vocabulary—featuring in particular *sentiment* and *coeur*—as well as in the symptomatology of the emotions, the exterior signs that help others decide what someone feels for them. The new husband's first thought after his marriage is that his wife "had not changed feelings along with her name" (52).

76.   In pages that give philosophical life to Lafayette's explorations, Hutcheson meditates at length on the ways in which emotions are related to "the constitution of our nature." He theorizes that certain emotions are experienced through, as it were, a separate "body which we do not call *self,* but something belonging to this *self.*" The apprenticeship of these emotions takes place in "spaces distinct from this *self*" (161).

77.   The relation between the two phenomena is undoubtedly one of mutual influence. On the one hand, aspiring writers were surely encouraged to turn to the novel and to historical fiction because of the potential for an increased readership. And the new public must certainly have been attracted, on the other hand, by the egalitarianism of this literary value: whereas great deeds were the exclusive preserve of great men, anyone could aspire to greatness as defined by the new system of value.

78.   Even though history and literature were not considered separate discourses until the end of the eighteenth century, it is nevertheless true that, during all the moments of cultural conflict I am presenting here, the distinction maintained today is already operative. In particular, during the crisis in history novelists were attacked for what was considered their attempted invasion of the historians' preserve. On the proximity between history and literature in France in the early modern period, see Lionel Gossman's *Between History and Literature,* especially "Literature and Education."

79.   For a history of the crisis in history, see Hazard, chap. 2. On the seventeenth-century critique of the inadequacies of contemporary historians, see Démoris (70–71, 78–79). Hazard demonstrates that the crisis culminated on the Ancient side in a historical positivism—in particular, in chronological history, whose practitioners tried to determine *exactly* how long the Egyptians, for example, had ruled—intimately related to the literary positivism of the second-generation Ancients, and on the Modern side in an ever increasing skepticism about traditional forms of history. This led certain Moderns to suggest, in a manner reminiscent of minority historians today, that the history of any small nation in Europe was as worthy of students' attention as that of Greece or Rome, or even, as Fontenelle did, that history in general is useless and that the urgent task is to understand the period in which we live, so that we should study the present alone (45–46).

80.   In the extensive preface to his *Histoire de France* (1713), Father Gabriel Daniel provides a textbook example of this critique of turncoat historians. He says that the controversy has been centered on the question of causes and motivations and how the historian can know them. Daniel contends that historians have no right to "feign fictional episodes" (n.p.). The adjective he uses is "romanesque," like something out of a novel, and the examples he cites of historians guilty of this practice make his attack on the new novel clear. Daniel reserves his fiercest criticism for the individual he describes as of late the most widely read historian in France, François-Eudes de Mézeray, whose *Histoire de France* (1643–51) was Lafayette's preferred source, and for Antoine Varillas, the seventeenth century's best-known practitioner of a type of fictionalized history. Varillas wrote book-length histories of the reigns of French monarchs from Louis XI to Henri III that are hard to distinguish from his novels such as *Les Anecdotes de Florence, ou histoire secrète de la maison de Médicis.* Daniel accuses Varillas

in particular of having invented details of the amorous exploits of François I that are not found in traditional historical accounts—just the type of elaboration for which contemporary historical novelists were most vehemently chastised.

81. Already in 1684, Bayle had voiced concern about the new novel, which was "poison[ing] Modern History so flagrantly" ("Catalogue" 317). Bayle thus established himself as the earliest and the most sustained critic of the kinds of historical narrative he felt were threatening traditional modes. In the case of the crisis in history once again, the chronological parallelism with events of today should be noted. In our Culture Wars, controversy over the literary canon seems to be giving way, as of the mid-1990s, to a replay of the crisis over history. In our case, Bayle's role is being played by the historian Gertrude Himmelfarb, who first denounced the "subver[sion]" of traditional historical modes by new trends, that of Annales history in particular, in her 1987 work, *The New History and the Old*. Her most recent books seem to be moving this latest controversy into full gear. Some of Himmelfarb's attacks are almost uncannily similar to late-seventeenth-century warnings against the menace of a new focus for history. Note, for example, her characterization of the work of many recent historians as an attempt to "dehistoricize history" by foregrounding daily life and small details rather than great men and great deeds (*On Looking* 17).

82. See Chamard and Rudler for documentation on Lafayette's use of contemporary historians such as Mézaray and in particular on her tendency to create the novel's historical scenes by weaving together motivations borrowed from different sources, so that her principal elaboration is the emotional context. For example, to Mézeray's account of Henri II driven by jealousy to modify his government, Lafayette adds a detailed portrayal of jealousy's effects (Chamard and Rudler 305–6).

83. Indeed, in a contemporary fairy tale by Marie-Jeanne L'Héritier, "Les Enchantements de l'éloquence" (1696), a marquis explains to his daughter that novels are much more suitable reading for young women than history because they present a vision of men and their "customs" or "everyday life [*moeurs*] as they should be," a salutary view that encourages young readers "to aspire to such perfection" (59). The desire to consider not only great men but also the "customs" or "everyday life" of the periods in which they lived was the most visible mark of the new history invented in the historical novel's wake. Since theoreticians from antiquity, notably Quintilian, treat history as a form of epic, the novel's perceived invasion of history's territory must have seemed a logical continuation of the fledgling genre's takeover of epic's role in the French tradition.

84. The latest commentator to call for a history of the emotions is François Bott, who in his weekly column in *Le Monde* recently contended that, at present, historians "are devoting as much or more attention to the emotions as battles, wars, and treatises" and asks "when will we have a history of hatred or of depression?" (2 June 1995). His question is a familiar one to readers of *mentalités* history: the founders of the Annales school—for example, Febvre (*Combats* 221, *Incroyance* 141–42) and Duby (938–39)—said just this in almost identical fashion. Indeed, for Philippe Ariès, the notion that the emotions had a history of their own was the idea upon which *mentalités* history was founded (402–3). *La Sensibilité dans l'histoire*, a collection edited by Chartier, proves the depth of the involvement of Annales historians with the history of the emotions.

85.   Le Gendre's volume, frequently reedited, is a direct precursor of the first true histories of private life, in particular Father Pierre Le Grand d'Aussy's three-volume *Histoire de la vie privée des Français depuis l'origine de la nation jusqu'à nos jours* (1782). Le Grand d'Aussy opens with a preface in which he explains that he works with all the material "excluded" by traditional historians. Thus, instead of still another history of famous men, he promises a history of "the Frenchman at work and at play, in the bosom of his family and of his children." Other contemporary works that prefigure *mentalités* history by refusing to focus exclusively on the elite and by opening up to psychological concerns include the anonymous *Dictionnaire historique des moeurs et coutumes* (1767) and André-Guillaume Constant d'Orville's *Précis d'une histoire générale de la vie privée des Français* (1779), which appears to have been the first work in which the term *private life* was used to designate this type of account.

86.   After its first edition in 1755, Velly's history was reprinted throughout the eighteenth century; in a new edition, it continued to appear well into the following century. As Chartier notes, in each of his chapters, Lafayette's historian of choice, Mézeray, discusses the manners and customs of the period, making him a precursor of the new private-life historians ("Historiography" 349).

87.   The phrase is from Henry James in *The Ambassadors* (1903). At the theater in Paris, Strether is suddenly struck by the realization of a change in Chad so complete that Chad might no longer be Chad. "You could deal with a man as himself—you couldn't deal with him as somebody else" (89–90). Witness also Conrad's Marlow in *Heart of Darkness* (1902), who, fascinated by the stationmaster's power over all around him, suggests this explanation for his "secret": "Perhaps there was nothing within him" (35).

88.   The story was first included in the periodical's February 1695 issue. An expanded version was published in the August and September 1696 issues. I cite the first version in the modern edition by Jeanne Roche-Mazon and, when necessary, refer to the second version from *Le Mercure galant.*

89.   When the first collection of Perrault's fairy tales was published (1697), the volume was attributed to his son, Pierre Darmancour. There is no evidence that anyone was ever taken in by this little inside joke.

90.   Many fairy tales feature some of the most hard-hitting references to fin de siècle decline—witness in particular Perrault's "Le Petit Poucet," which opens with an evocation of the great famine of 1695 (191). Perrault's model for the fairy tale is accepted today as the unique prototype. At the time of its creation, however, the genre was dominated by numerous women writers. Marie-Jeanne L'Héritier and Henriette de Castelnau, comtesse de Murat, invented their models for the new genre at virtually the same time as Perrault. ("Histoire de la marquise-marquis de Banneville" has been attributed to L'Héritier [Perrault, ed. Collinet 27], but no evidence has been advanced to justify the attribution.)

91.   For the evidence for this attribution, see Roche-Mazon. Perrault and Choisy knew each other from the Académie Française, to which Choisy was admitted a few months after the outbreak of the conflict between Ancients and Moderns. See Choisy's *Mémoires* for his self-presentation and to understand why commentators are always quick to point out similarities between "Histoire de la marquise-marquis de Banneville" and his work. In his *Mémoires,* Choisy refers to the story and notes that he felt "authorized" to continue his own escapades because of its

heroine's example (320). The expanded version of the story was reprinted as an independent volume, and expanded further still, in 1723, when Perrault and Donneau de Visé were long since dead, but the year before Choisy's death.

92.   Perhaps the most likely modern comparison with "Histoire de la marquise-marquis de Banneville" is the 1994 film, *Priscilla*, the send-up of road movies in which two transvestites and a transsexual cross the Australian desert and, in the process, parody sexual codes and bend all accepted ways of assigning sexual difference.

93.   Only once, in the second version, is "sexe" linked to a term that connotes permanence, "destiny" (*Le Mercure galant*, August 1696, 176).

94.   "Sex" is used a second time as a synonym for transvestism in the second version. Mariane and Bercourt are discussing cross-dressing, when she announces to him that "preachers tell us that one should neither wear disguises nor change sex," and he explains that transvestism is acceptable under certain circumstances (*Le Mercure galant*, August 1696, 67–68).

95.   In "Histoire de la marquise-marquis de Banneville," cross-dressing confirms Garber's theory by serving as "a mode of articulation . . . [that] puts into question the idea of one: of identity, . . . self-knowledge" (11). On the other hand, it does not function, as her theory would also have it, to call class into question as well as gender, to reveal that these two categories are "commutable, if not equivalent" (32). The tale is resolutely aristocratic, and there is never the slightest hint of a challenge to this form of identity established at birth. This refusal is all the more striking in view of the fact that this was the form of subversion most often practiced in the literary genres developed by Moderns in the wake of the Culture Wars. For example, Perrault's "straight" fairy tales—none more spectacularly than "Le Petit Poucet"—often suggest that, through a combination of wit and daring, individuals can rise above their condition, the seventeenth century's term for the social rank conferred at birth. In addition, the literature of *sensibilité*, as Marivaux makes clear when it reaches its apex, is fundamentally incompatible with class barriers, for the nobility of the heart proves more powerful than any title.

96.   In texts from this period, according to Laqueur's theory of the one-sex model, "sex" refers not to the modern biologically grounded view of the difference between men and women—impossible according to his presentation of premodern medical theory as considering the body to be male and female bodies simply aberrant versions of this unitary male body—but to a vision of the difference between men and women as defined in sociological and cultural terms. In such a vision, as McKeon points out, "the distinction between the biologically constructed category 'sex' and the socially constructed category 'gender' was largely unintelligible" (301). "Histoire de la marquise-marquis de Banneville" reveals, however, a use of these categories more modern than Laqueur and McKeon generally feel to have been possible in its day—perhaps because they focus on English material to make their cases. In this story, *sex* is most often used to denote a culturally defined category. In the work's opening sentence, it also refers to a biologically constructed category: "Since women have decided to become authors, . . . I don't want to be the last to show my zeal for my sex" (543).

97.   The story ends in the simultaneous triumph of biological and performative sexuality, with the announcement that the two sexually adjusted protago-

nists can soon be expected to have a child (564). Biology is, therefore, simultaneously "corrected" (544) and affirmed.

98.   Ferrand's heroine, Bélise, begins her autobiographical account by announcing, "I was born with the most *sensible* and tender heart that was ever formed by love" (7). Marivaux inaugurated his career as a novelist with what is virtually a recreation of Scudéry's model, on which he leaves his mark by vastly expanding her "anatomy of the amorous heart." In his preface, Marivaux declares that "the novel is written for the heart alone" (5) and calls this novel in particular "a work whose subject is the heart" (4).

99.   Perhaps the first perceptive assessment of Marivaux's contribution to the novel of the heart is the review of *La Vie de Marianne* published in the newspaper of his greatest rival for this literary form, Prévost's *Pour et contre*. The reviewer (not Prévost) calls Marivaux "a writer who is trying to develop the faculties of the heart as exactly as Descartes and Malebranche developed those of the mind" (Prévost 273).

100.   D'Argenson (1694–1757), a member of the first post–Culture Wars generation, wrote memoirs that were published in 1785 but were composed at the same time as Marivaux's novels.

CHAPTER FOUR

1.   See the initial chapter of Norbert Elias's *La Civilisation des moeurs* (The Civilizing Process) for his theory that "civilization" and "culture" had a radically different history in German on the one hand and in French and English on the other. In an attempt to reproduce as closely as possible the French history of the terms, I refer to the French edition of both this work and Elias's *La Société de cour* (The Court Society) and provide my own translations.

2.   In the process, Fontenelle inaugurated a major early modern tradition of cultural speculation—a tradition destined to know its finest hour in the early eighteenth century at the hands of the most significant heir of Culture Wars' debate, Montesquieu—with a complex meditation on the influence of climate on the development of civilization.

3.   Fontenelle's semantic innovation had at least a trace of precedent in Fénelon's *Traité de l'éducation des filles,* published in 1687, the year the Culture Wars were declared. Fénelon also clearly indicates "culture"'s transfer from physical to mental cultivation, though far less intricately than Fontenelle: "Many people . . . conclude from a lack of success that nature alone is responsible for forming exceptional individuals and that education is powerless; whereas one should only conclude that some individuals resemble infertile soil, upon which culture/agriculture [*la culture*] is able to do very little" (51). The near simultaneity of the two inaugural appearances of *culture* in its modern usage with the outbreak of the Culture Wars provides the surest indication of the role played by the intellectual conflict in generating still another essential modern vocabulary. The ARTFL database includes at least five other texts from the years of the Culture Wars in which *culture* is clearly used in its metaphorical, intellectual sense. Indeed, by the time Ancients and Moderns ended their hostilities, Fénelon was so confident that readers would understand the word in reference to the cultivation of the mind that, in three separate texts—the 1713 *Traité de l'existence de Dieu* (45); *Lettre à l'Académie* (39) and *Dialogues sur l'éloquence* (211),

both from 1715—he uses "culture" in reference to education and civilization on its own, without the previously obligatory reference to agriculture.

4.   It is, of course, important to remember that the initial version of Elias's study was completed in the 1930s. For his view of the history of the French language, he was, therefore, obliged to turn to the same, now outdated sources as Auerbach. In the notes to part 1 of *La Civilisation des moeurs*, Elias remarks that he relied in particular on Ferdinand Brunot's 1905 volume, *Histoire de la langue française des origines jusqu'à 1900*. In general, Elias's treatment of the French linguistic material upon which he bases his theory is perfunctory at best, in comparison with his far more detailed discussion of German sources. The earliest German examples he cites are from the 1730s, the years immediately following the Culture Wars, a period during which concepts of French origin exerted a particularly powerful influence in German intellectual debates. I want to make clear here first that *culture* had life in French prior to the German usage that is the basis for Elias's theory and second that this change to Elias's schema is no small matter. It is crucial to know when and where key terms come into existence, for that origin can inform us both about the word's initial semantic charge and about the society and the moment that felt the need to create it.

5.   Elias presents "civilization" as a French creation and Victor Riqueti, marquis de Mirabeau, as the term's inventor (in *L'Ami des hommes* from 1756). And—an occurrence unique in my experience—the ARTFL database confirms this as the term's earliest appearance in French. Elias presents "culture" as a German creation and Kant as the term's inventor (in *Ideen zu einer allgemeiner Geschichte in weltbirgerlicher Absicht* from 1775).

6.   Other, less obvious members of the semantic constellation that prepared the way for "civilization" in French include *honnête* (defined by the Académie Française as "civil, courteous, polite"); *honnêteté*, which designated, once again according to the Académie Française, "all the qualities a man can have in civil [civilized] life"; and *lettres* or *belles lettres*, used to indicate all the types of knowledge necessary for life in a "société civile," in particular grammar, eloquence, and poetry. These were the key terms used to define French civilization. When, as a result of the spread of French influence during and after the Culture Wars, France became synonymous with civilization, all civilization was subsequently defined in the same terms. See Peter France, "Polish, Police, *Polis*," on seventeenth-century usage of the terms *polir, politesse, belles lettres*, and *civilité*. On the relation between *civilité* and *politesse*, see also Chartier ("Distinction et divulgation," in *Lectures et lecteurs*).

7.   On the intimate etymological relation between the words *nation* and *race* in French in the late seventeenth century, see Merk. See Sala-Molins's study both on the development of the *code noir* and on that of the French desire to expand the colonies at the end of the seventeenth century. Linguistically, the *code noir* is perhaps most remarkable for the total absence of the civilizing vocabulary; the colonial project is presented solely in its mercantile aspects.

8.   It is interesting to note that the *OED* traces *culture*'s earliest appearance in English to 1633, with a definition, however, that crosses the dividing line neatly maintained in French by situating *culture* on the side of what in French would have been termed civilization: "The culture of good manners."

9.   Dictionaries credit Staël with having introduced *culture* into French in

De l'Allemagne (1810). It is interesting that, still in 1810 and long after Kant's example (1775), Staël obviously continued to fear that *culture* in its metaphorical sense might not be intelligible to her readers: the term occurs nine times in *De l'Allemagne,* each time with either "intellectuelle" or "d'esprit" to clarify the usage (see, for example, 15–16, 403). In *De la littérature* (1800), Staël bases important parts of her argument on "civilization" in Elias's sense of "Western national feeling" (see, for example, 163).

10.   In the late 1660s and early 1670s, it was decreed that no foreign architect would be allowed to complete the Louvre. Perrault's older brother, Claude, architect and architectural theorist, was a member of the committee chosen to oversee the project.

11.   In the *Parallèle,* Perrault uses the example of his fictive Modern, the abbé, to explain how the modern, while based on precedent, is new and not a simple imitation of traditional models. The abbé is extremely well-read and, since "his knowledge is a knowledge of reflection, digested after meditation, what he says comes sometimes from his reading, but he has made [his ideas] so much his own that they seem original" (1:3).

12.   I cite the relevant seventeenth-century documents from Alfred Franklin's study of the *collège*'s history. See also the information provided by André Cheruel (1:421–22). The sons of the elite destined to receive this education were to be chosen equally from the regions of Alsace, Pignerol, Artois, and Flanders.

13.   It is difficult to make generalizations about seventeenth-century French pedagogical practice. For example, certain religious orders such as the Oratorians used modern authors as examples of rhetorical practice far earlier than contemporary pedagogical literature would cause us to imagine. In general, however, pedagogues, like the representatives of the French state, seemed blind to the idea that, to be truly convincing, the ascendancy of French culture had to be accompanied by the rise of French as a cultural language. The only notable exception to this official blindness was Richelieu. In 1642, he had drawn up a project for a royal academy, intended to be part of Richelieu, the village the prime minister had constructed as a monument to his glory. In the volume he devoted to this proposed academy, Nicolas Legras went farther than any other French educational theorist of the classical age in proclaiming the necessity of having all instruction on French soil take place in the French language. According to Richelieu's spokesperson, only once it had developed a national linguistic politics would the French nation ever reach true greatness as an empire (16). The provinces would become truly French only when all dialects had disappeared and "linguistic conformity" had been imposed (2). Legras presents this policy of "liberating" the French from regional dialects and from "their enslavement to dead languages" as a natural extension of Richelieu's creation of the Académie Française (16, 92). Highet discusses briefly the struggle waged by some Moderns to dethrone the international language, Latin, as the dominant cultural language and to impose French in its place (644 n. 25).

14.   A number of recent studies have focused on literature's role in the formation of the nation-state. See in particular Lambropoulos's *Literature as National Institution* and Peter Uwe Hohendahl's *Building a National Literature.*

15.   Rollin's treatise was frequently reedited until the early nineteenth century.

16. Rollin develops Dacier's message concerning pedagogy's essential function to the nation and her protonationalistic rhetoric: he refers to education as "the surest source of tranquillity and happiness, not only for families, but for states and empires. In fact, what is a republic or a kingdom, if not one vast body whose vigor and health are dependent on those of the individual families that are its limbs? . . . For this reason, children must be raised . . . publicly [en public], with the same teachers and the same discipline, so that they can be inculcated early on with love of the fatherland [la patrie]" (1:418–19).

17. "When I speak of grammar, I have in mind only reading and writing, speaking French well and writing it correctly" (Fleury 171).

18. Fleury's volume was republished at regular intervals and almost as frequently as Rollin's until 1829.

19. Gedoyn's treatise appeared posthumously in 1745. It was probably written in the 1720s.

20. According to Alvin Kernan, "Charles Perrault proposed an academy in French with a belles lettres section covering grammar, eloquence, and poetry as early as 1666" (34). I have, however, been unable to find any evidence to support this claim. Professor Kernan lists no source for this idea and, in a gracious reply to my request for information, told me that he could no longer locate his reference.

21. Dominique Julia shows how the union between nationalism and education was finally achieved in France only under Napoleon (86).

22. A second contemporary document provides a view of the civilizing process compatible with Fontenelle's, a document perhaps most remarkable for the creation in it of a concept close to what is termed today "transnationalism." In 1670, Huet—the scholar who in January 1687 told Boileau that he was too ignorant to serve as head Ancient—published his "Traité de l'origine des romans." In Huet's proto-Bakhtinian portrayal, the novel is both socially and culturally subversive, a genre that actively undermines ethnic purity. Huet imagines a political entity, which he calls "our nation," a nation that, rather than enforcing the assimilation or the conversion of the foreign, would find in a multinational heritage a source of strength. For Huet, literature's civilizing mission should be to enrich French society by making it receptive to otherness—other discourses, other customs, other peoples. Huet presents a theory of what might be called the novel's transnational origin, its simultaneous rise in Spain and in Arab countries as well as in France. The novel, he suggests, is a genre that does not recognize impermeable frontiers: its practitioners travel freely and take on the nationality of the king who welcomes them, and this acceptance of otherness enriches the assimilating society.

23. Let me make clear from the outset that I am not taking a stand against the notion of a core curriculum but simply against the lack of coherence that has generally characterized such projects. I would argue that the question of a core curriculum is one of the most serious issues to be dealt with in today's university, one that should be an essential part of the reflection I call for at this chapter's close.

24. Hirsch's attempt at giving precise content to "culture" has had virtually no influence over the controversy's unfolding. Hirsch's project owes its success to the doomsday rhetoric he shares with Bloom.

25.   One of the reasons Cheney was able to take up the Ancient cause so quickly was that she, like Dacier, had the machinery of a national printing press at her disposal.

26.   See also Cheney's *American Memory* on "the Western tradition" as America's "civic glue" (7) and as the "heritage" that binds America to past civilizations (11). The principal contribution of Cheney's predecessor at the NEH, William Bennett's *To Reclaim a Legacy,* was published in 1984, before the initiation of the Culture Wars, and was not as widely cited as Cheney's publications, all of which appeared during the conflict's most intense early years.

27.   Kate Stimpson documents the acceleration in the use of *PC* by the media: "In 1988, in the media, there were 101 articles about P.C.; in 1989, there were 306 articles; in 1990, there were 656 articles; in 1991, there were 3,989 articles" (28).

28.   Herbert Lindenberger and Mary-Louise Pratt provide the best overviews of the actual content of the Stanford course and of the controversy surrounding it. On the history of Western-civilization courses in American universities, see Gilbert Allardyce.

29.   See, for example, Kernan's description of how the course allegedly functioned (4) and compare it with Lindenberger's account of what was actually involved.

30.   See, for example, Lindenberger (227) and Allardyce (695–96) on the development of Western-civilization courses in American universities with the goal of introducing Americans, not to their own heritage, but to that of European countries.

31.   On the institutionalization of literature in higher education, see Gerald Graff's study in particular. See Wallace Douglas on the history of modern-language pedagogy.

32.   Among the most recent contributions to the Culture Wars, note also *Dictatorship of Virtue: Multiculturalism and the Battle for America's Future,* in which Richard Bernstein once again blames multiculturalism for the decay of American society—while taking the rhetoric of panic to new heights—and, inevitably, proclaims the superiority of some civilizations over others.

33.   This is not to deny that excesses have been committed—in the name of multiculturalism, in the name of women's studies, and so forth. The true examples that could be cited, however, are a far cry from the revolutionary situation described by Ancient commentators. In addition, it is essential at this point to get beyond simple point-counterpoint skirmishes, to end a period of attacks, counterattacks, and self-criticism to get down to the business of pedagogical reform.

34.   The sentence is attributed to Charles Muscatine, cited by Allan Parachini in the *Los Angeles Times* (5 July 1991).

35.   The phrase about "multiple, conflicting canons" is from John Guillory's contribution to the influential 1983 issue of *Critical Inquiry* devoted to canon formation.

36.   A proliferation of analyses in the press, inspired by the conflict in the former Yugoslavia, has alerted readers to the probability that we are living the end of the period during which wars are carried out between states and their armies and the beginning of a new moment in the history of warfare during

which states will often be replaced by more informal, often tribal groupings and during which the use of ever more sophisticated technology that had come to be seen as the foundation of military encounters will be limited. (See, for example, Jacques Attali in *Le Monde*, 15 June 1995; Serge Marti in *Le Monde*, 7 July 1995; Roger Cohen in the *International Herald Tribune*, 30 May 1995.) See also John Darnton comparing the "unparalleled savagery" attained by the final phase (the twentieth century through the end of World War II) in this period of warfare to the brutality of seventeenth-century European conflicts (*New York Times*, 9 May 1995). On Vauban as the father of modern warfare, see my *Literary Fortifications*. On the self-destruction of work in our postindustrial society, see Jeremy Rifkin's *The End of Work* and Francine Aizicovici (*Le Monde des initiatives*; May 1995). Aizicovici points out that the term *work* was created in the late seventeenth century at the first glimmer of the Industrial Revolution. The first French text to feature both the term and the concept of work is *Télémaque* (1699–1717), composed by Fénelon during the same period during which he was exploiting the new word *culture*.

37.   On the changes that developing technology may have in store for newspapers, see William Glaberson in the *International Herald Tribune*, 28 July 1995. For more on this subject as well as information on the role played by these revised newspapers, the gay press in particular, in the creation of new communities of readers, see David Dunlap in the *New York Times*, 4 September 1995.

38.   A vast amount of recent work portrays the period we are entering as marking, in more ways than one, the repudiation of the so-called Cartesian revolution. The best known anti-Cartesian strain in recent thought argues that we may be witnessing the end of so-called classical man. Unlike, however, the French theorists who first made this claim—Michel Foucault, Gilles Deleuze, and Félix Guattari immediately come to mind—today's Anglo-American commentators warn of the real-life risks inherent in the promotion of the fragmented, socially constructed, "postmodern" self. In *Shattered Selves*, for example, James Glass discusses the dangers of any actual application of the celebration of multiplicity and being without limits (xix, 13). Glass deals implicitly rather than explicitly with the need for an affective revolution. For still another current anti-Cartesian trend, on an intriguing, if more superficial level, see Jeffrey Moussaieff Masson and Susan McCarthy's *When Elephants Weep: The Emotional Lives of Animals*, a study contending that animals are far more complex than the images promoted in Descartes's long-influential view, and that they are in fact capable of what we can recognize as true affective lives. (On animals and empathy, see also Natalie Angier in the *New York Times*, 9 May 1995.)

39.   The anti-Cartesian strain in recent thought likely to prove most influential is related to neurobiology and work done in this area concerning the mind's processing of the emotions and the effects of the emotions on the body's chemistry. See Damasio's work in particular and in addition the flood of recent accounts in the press about the sites of the different emotions in the brain—for example, Curt Suplee in the *International Herald Tribune*, 22 December 1994; Daniel Goldman in the *International Herald Tribune*, 30 March 1995—all of which suggest that the new vision of the brain as more site-specific in discerning emotional signals may well lead to a more finely tuned affective language.

40.   Damasio suggests, for example, that the new neurobiology can help

Western medicine undo the effects of "the amputation of the concept of humanity under which it has been operating" (255ff.). Other commentators—Roderick McGrew and Vivian Nutton, for instance—note that, at times under the influence of various types of non-Western, nontraditional practice, twentieth-century Western medicine may at least appear to be returning to some of the positions—a modified version of humoral theory, for example—commonly held in the late seventeenth century, at the time of the last major rewriting of the emotions. Both McGrew and Nutton point out ways in which humoralism could be seen as related to such currently essential concepts as endocrine function and immune reaction.

41.   See Stoll on the growing need for actual, rather than virtual exchanges. See Slouka on cyberspace as "an electronic space that mimics the forms of social life even as it confirms us in our isolation" (10). See also Jim Morrison's "Hot Modems, Cold Lives: Refugees from Cyberspace" in the *New York Times,* 30 April 1995. Morrison interviews former fanatics of "the virtual frontier" who speak of the need to see "real faces" and to hear real laughter, rather than "see[ing] the letters 'L.O.L.' [laughs out loud]." See also Steven Levy on whether "a computer game can make you cry" (*Newsweek,* 29 May 1995) and Ellen Goodman in the *International Herald Tribune,* 20 June 1995. Further proof of the current vitality of research on the emotions is the series on "The History of the Emotions" at New York University Press. See also Octavio Paz's recent revision of Denis de Rougemont's 1939 classic, *L'Amour et l'occident,* with his call for a new "affective *sensibility,*" a new emphasis on "emotion, sentiment, passion," which he terms "the heart of the soul in love" (211). See finally Herbert Muschamp on the "emerging sensibility" in strains of contemporary architecture that "signal a fundamental shift from the objectivity of the modern building toward a more subjective state of awareness" (*New York Times,* 22 September 1995).

42.   Within the university, one current movement that at the same time responds to a number of these concerns and seeks to become pedagogically creative is the newly founded discipline known as environmental studies or ecocriticism. (It is also known as green criticism, especially in Europe, where it has thus far attained some degree of visibility only in countries such as Switzerland and the Netherlands.) Ecocriticism stands for a return to the real—in this case, the actual physical universe—in reaction against postmodernism's rejection of all but "reality effects." It is also—because of its call for grief work or mourning for environmental loss and damage—playing a role in the revival of emotionalism. In addition, ecocriticism explicitly seeks to make the work of grieving creative by repoliticizing the academy—initially through a form of interdisciplinary pedagogy that attempts to go beyond what its practitioners see as the politically ineffective rhetoric of cultural studies in order to achieve a higher level of social responsibility. In this country, ecocriticism has already achieved sufficient prominence to have received an overview in the *New York Times Magazine* (by Jay Parini; 29 October 1995).

REFERENCES

Abbadie, Jacques. *L'Art de se connaître soi-même.* Rotterdam: Pierre Vander Slaart, 1692.

Académie Française. *Dictionnaire.* Paris: Coignard, 1694.

Adam, Antoine. *Histoire de la littérature française au dix-septième siècle.* 5 vols. Paris: Del Duca, 1949–56.

Allardyce, Gilbert. "The Rise and Fall of the Western Civilization Course." *American Historical Review* 87 (1982): 695–743.

Argenson, René-Louis de Voyer, marquis d'. *Les Loisirs d'un ministre, ou Essais dans le goût de Montaigne.* 1785. Paris: Baudouin Frères, 1825.

Ariès, Philippe. *Centuries of Childhood: A Social History of French Family Life.* 1960. Trans. Robert Baldick. New York: Random House, 1962.

———. "L'Histoire des mentalités." In *La Nouvelle histoire,* ed. Jacques Le Goff, Roger Chartier, and Jacques Revel, 402–23. Paris: Retz, 1978.

Aubignac, François Hédelin d'. *Conjectures académiques, ou dissertation sur l'Iliade.* Paris: Fournier, 1715.

Audiger, maître d'hôtel. *La Maison réglée.* Paris: M. Brunet, 1692.

Auerbach, Erich. "La Cour et la Ville." 1951. In *Scenes from the Drama of European Literature.* Trans. Ralph Manheim. Minneapolis: University of Minnesota Press, 1984.

Baasner, Frank. *Der Begriff "sensibilité" im 18. Jahrhundert: Aufstieg und Niedergang eines Ideals.* Heidelberg: C. Winter, 1988.

Baker, Keith Michael. "Public Opinion as Political Invention." In *Inventing the French Revolution.* Cambridge: Cambridge University Press, 1990.

Barthes, Roland. "Les Deux critiques." In *Essais critiques.* Paris: Editions du Seuil, 1964.

Batteux, Charles. *Les Beaux arts réduits à un seul principe.* Paris: Saillant, 1746.

Bayle, Pierre. "Catalogue de livres nouveaux." *Nouvelles de la République des Lettres* 8 (October 1684).

———. *Dictionnaire historique et critique.* 4 vols. Rotterdam: Reinier Leers, 1697.

193

Bellanger, Claude, et al., eds. *Histoire générale de la presse française*. Vol. 1. Paris: Presses Universitaires de France, 1969.

Bennett, William. *To Reclaim a Legacy*. Washington, D.C.: National Endowment for the Humanities, 1984.

Bernstein, Richard. *Dictatorship of Virtue: Multiculturalism and the Battle for America's Future*. New York: Alfred Knopf, 1995.

Blau, Herbert. *The Eye of Prey: Subversions of the Postmodern*. Bloomington: Indiana University Press, 1987.

Blégny, Nicolas. *Les Nouvelles découvertes sur toutes les parties de la médecine*. 3 vols. Paris: Laurent d'Hourry, 1679–81.

Bloom, Allan. *The Closing of the American Mind*. New York: Simon and Schuster, 1987.

Boileau, Nicolas. *Oeuvres*. Ed. Sylvain Menant. 2 vols. Paris: Garnier-Flammarion, 1969.

———. *Oeuvres complètes*. Ed. Antoine Adam and Françoise Escal. Paris: Gallimard, 1966.

———. *Oeuvres complètes*. Paris: Esprit Billiot, 1713.

Boivin, Jean. *Apologie d'Homère et bouclier d'Achille*. Paris: Jouenne, 1715.

Bolton, Richard, ed. *Culture Wars: Documents from the Recent Controversies in the Arts*. New York: New Press, 1992.

Bossuet, Jacques Bénigne. *Traité de la concupiscence*. 1695. Paris: Clousier, 1742.

Boswell, John. *Same-Sex Unions in Premodern Europe*. New York: Villard Books, 1994.

Boulainvillier, Henry de. "De la vie sensitive et du corps." 1683. In *Oeuvres philosophiques*. 2 vols. The Hague: Martinus Nijhoff, 1975.

Bourdaloue, Louis. "Sermons pour le carême." 1692. In *Oeuvres complètes*. 3 vols. Paris: Méquignon fils ainé, 1922.

Braudy, Leo. "Unturning the Century: The Missing Decade of the 1690s." In *Fins de Siècle: English Poetry in 1590, 1690, 1790, 1890, 1990*, ed. Elaine Scarry, 65–93. Baltimore: Johns Hopkins University Press, 1995.

[Buffier, Claude, and Anne-Thérèse de Marguenat de Courcelles, marquise de Lambert]. *Homère en arbitrage*. Paris: P. Prault, 1715.

Callières, François de. *Histoire poétique de la guerre nouvellement déclarée entre anciens et modernes*. Paris: P. Aubouin, 1688.

Chamart, H., and G. Rudler. "Les Sources historiques de *La Princesse de Clèves*." *Revue du XVIe Siècle*, no. 2 (1914): 289–321.

Chambers, Iain. *Migrancy, Culture, Identity*. London: Routledge, 1994.

Chambers, Ross. "Irony and the Canon." *Profession* (1990): 18–24.

[Charnes, Jean-Antoine de]. *Conversations sur la critique de "La Princesse de Clèves."* 1678. Tours: Université de Tours, 1973.

Chartier, Roger. *The Cultural Uses of Print in Early Modern France*. Princeton, N.J.: Princeton University Press, 1987.

———. "Historiography in the Age of Absolutism." In *A New History of French Literature*, ed. D. Hollier et al., 345–49. Cambridge: Harvard University Press, 1989.

———. *Lectures et lecteurs dans la France de l'ancien régime*. Paris: Editions du Seuil, 1987.

————. *The Order of Books*. Stanford: Stanford University Press, 1994.

————. *Les Origines culturelles de la Révolution française*. Paris: Editions du Seuil, 1991.

Chartier, Roger, ed. *La Sensibilité dans l'histoire*. Paris: Gérard Monfort, 1987.

Chartier, Roger, M.-M. Compère, and Dominique Julia. *L'Education en France au XVIIe et XVIIIe siècles*. Paris: Presses Universitaires de France, 1964.

Cheney, Lynne. *American Memory: A Report on the Humanities in the Nation's Public Schools*. Washington, D.C.: National Endowment for the Humanities, n.d.

————. *Fifty Hours: A Core Curriculum for College Students*. Washington, D.C.: National Endowment for the Humanities, 1990.

————. *Humanities in America*. Washington, D.C.: National Endowment for the Humanities, 1988.

————. *Tyrannical Machines: A Report on Educational Practices Gone Wrong and Our Best Hopes for Setting Them Right*. Washington, D.C.: National Endowment for the Humanities, 1990.

Chéruel, André. *Histoire de France sous le ministère de Mazarin*. 3 vols. Paris: Hachette, 1882.

Choisy, François-Timoléon de. *Mémoires de l'abbé de Choisy habillé en femme*. Ed. Georges Mongrédien. Paris: Mercure de France, 1966.

[Choisy, François-Timoléon de, and Charles Perrault.] "Histoire de la marquise-marquis de Banneville." *Le Mercure galant*. February 1695, 14–101; August 1696, 173–238; September 1696, 85–185.

[————.] *Histoire de la marquise-marquis de Banneville*. Paris: d'Houry, 1723.

Cognet, Louis. "Le Coeur chez les spirituels du XVIIe siècle." In *Dictionnaire de spiritualité*, vol. 2, ed. Marcel Viller et al., 2300–2307. Paris: Beauchesne, 1953.

Conrad, Joseph. *Heart of Darkness*. 1902. London: Penguin Classics, 1983.

Contenson, Father Vincent. *Theologia mentis et cordis*. Paris: L. Arnaud, 1668.

Cordemoy, Géraud de. *Histoire de France*. Paris: J.-B. Coignard, 1685–89.

Coulet, Henri. *Le Roman jusqu'à la révolution*. 2 vols. Paris: Colin, 1967.

Dacier, Anne Lefebvre. *Des Causes de la corruption du goût*. Paris: Rigaud, 1714.

————. *Homère défendu contre l'apologie du R. P. Hardouin*. Paris: Coignard, 1716.

————. *L'Iliade d'Homère traduite en français avec des remarques de Madame Dacier*. 3 vols. Paris: Rigaud, 1711.

Dagognet, François. *Une Epistémologie de l'espace concret: Néo-géographie*. Paris: Vrin, 1977.

Damasio, Antonio. *Descartes' Error: Emotion, Reason, and the Human Brain*. New York: Putnam's, 1994.

Daniel, Father Gabriel. *Histoire de France depuis l'établissement de la monarchie dans les Gaules*. 3 vols. Paris: Jean-Baptiste Delespine, 1713.

Darnton, Robert. *The Great Cat Massacre and Other Episodes in French Cultural History*. New York: Basic Books, 1984.

————. "The High Enlightenment and the Low-Life of Literature in Pre-revolutionary France." In *The Literary Underground of the Old Regime*. Cambridge: Harvard University Press, 1982.

————. "In Search of the Enlightenment: Recent Attempts to Create a Social

History of Ideas." *Journal of Modern History* 43, no. 1 (March 1971): 113–32.

Davis, Lennard. *Factual Fictions: The Origins of the English Novel.* New York: Columbia University Press, 1983.

De Grazia, Margreta. "Fin de Siècle Renaissance England." In *Fins de Siècle: English Poetry in 1590, 1690, 1790, 1890, 1990,* ed. Elaine Scarry, 37–63. Baltimore: Johns Hopkins University Press, 1995.

DeJean, Joan. *Literary Fortifications: Rousseau, Laclos, Sade.* Princeton, N.J.: Princeton University Press, 1984.

———. *Tender Geographies: Women and the Origins of the Novel in France.* New York: Columbia University Press, 1991.

Delamare, Nicolas. *Traité de la police.* 1729. 4 vols. Paris: J.-F. Herissant, 1738.

Démoris, René. *Le Roman à la première personne.* Paris: Colin, 1975.

Descartes, René. *Les Passions de l'âme.* 1649. In *Oeuvres philosophiques,* ed. Ferdinand Alquié. 3 vols. Paris: Garnier, 1973.

Desmarets de Saint-Sorlin, Jean. *Clovis, ou la France chrétienne, poème héroïque.* Paris: A. Courbé, 1657.

———. *La Comparaison de la langue et de la poésie française avec la grecque et la latine, et des poètes grecs, latins, et français.* Paris: T. Jolly, 1670.

———. *La Défense de la poésie et de la langue française addressée à M. Perrault.* Paris: Nicolas Le Gras, 1675.

———. *Lettre de Monsieur Desmarets à Monsieur l'abbé de La Chambre sur le sujet d'un discours apologétique de Monsieur l'abbé de Villeloin, pour Virgile et ses observations sur le poème de Clovis.* Paris: Sébastien Martin, 1673.

———. *Traité pour juger des poètes grecs, latins, et français.* Paris: Claude Cramoisy, 1670.

———. *Le Triomphe de Louis et de son siècle, poème lyrique dédié au roy.* Paris: Jacques Le Gras, 1674.

Dictionnaire des passions, des vertus et des vices ou recueil des meilleurs morceaux de morale pratique, tirés des auteurs anciens et moderns, étrangers et nationaux. 2 vols. Paris: Legras, 1777.

Douglas, Wallace. "Accidental Institution: On the Origin of Modern Language Study." In *Criticism in the University,* ed. Gerald Graff and Reginald Gibbons, 35–61. Evanston, Ill.: Northwestern University Press, 1985.

D'Souza, Dinesh. *The End of Racism: Principles for a Multiracial Society.* New York: Free Press, 1995.

Du Bos, Jean Baptiste. *Réflexions critiques sur la poésie et sur la peinture.* 1719. Paris: Pissot, 1770.

Duby, Georges. "Histoire des mentalités." In *L'Histoire et ses méthodes,* ed. Charles Samaran, 937–66. Paris: Gallimard, 1961.

Elias, Norbert. *La Civilisation des moeurs.* 1939. Paris: Calmann-Lévy, 1973.

———. *La Société de cour.* 1969. Paris: Calmann-Lévy, 1974.

Epstein, Joseph. "The Academic Zoo: Theory—in Practice." *Hudson Review* 44, no. 1 (spring 1991): 9–31.

Febvre, Lucien. "Comment reconstituer la vie affective d'autrefois? La sensibilité dans l'histoire." 1941. *Combats pour l'histoire.* Paris: A. Colin, 1953.

———. *Le Problème de l'incroyance au XVIe siècle.* Paris: Albin Michel, 1942.

Fénelon, François de Salignac de La Mothe. *Dialogues sur l'éloquence.* 1715. Paris: Dezobry, 1846.

———. *Lettre sur les occupations de l'Académie française, suivie des lettres de Lamotte et de Fénelon sur Homère et sur les anciens.* 1715. Ed. Ernest Depois. Paris: Dezobry, 1845.

———. *Traité de l'éducation des filles.* 1687. Paris: Delagrave, 1883.

Ferrand, Anne Bellinzani. *Histoire des amours de la jeune Bélise et de Cléante.* Paris: d'Houry, 1689.

Flandrin, Jean-Louis. *Families in Former Times.* Trans. Richard Southern. Cambridge: Cambridge University Press, 1979.

Fleury, Claude. *Traité du choix de la méthode des études.* Paris: Aubouin, 1686.

Fontenelle, Bernard Le Bovier de. *Dialogues des morts.* Paris: C. Blageart, 1683.

———. *Digression sur les anciens et les modernes.* 1688. In *Oeuvres diverses,* vol. 6. Paris: M. Brunet, 1715.

———. *Histoire du renouvellement de l'Académie des sciences.* Paris: M. Brunet, 1702.

———. *Nouveaux dialogues des morts.* 2 vols. Paris: M. Brunet, 1700.

Foucault, Michel. *Folie et déraison: Histoire de la folie à l'âge classique.* Paris: Plon, 1961.

———. "What Is an Author?" 1969. Trans. Josué Harari. In *The Foucault Reader,* ed. Paul Rabinow, 101–20. New York: Pantheon, 1984.

Fourmont, Etienne. *Examen pacifique de la querelle de Madame Dacier et de Monsieur de La Motte.* Paris: J. Rollin, 1716.

France, Peter. *Politeness and Its Discontents.* Cambridge: Cambridge University Press, 1992.

Frank, Robert. "The Image of Harvey in Commonwealth and Restauration England." In *William Harvey and His Age,* ed. Jerome Bylebyl, 103–44. Baltimore: Johns Hopkins University Press, 1979.

Franklin, Alfred. *Recherches historiques sur le collège des quatre-nations.* Paris: Auguste Aubry, 1863.

Furetière, Antoine. *Dictionnaire universel des arts et des sciences.* 1690. Ed. Alain Rey. 3 vols. Paris: Le Robert, 1978.

———. *Furetiriana.* Paris: Brunet, 1706.

Gamaches, Etienne-Simon de. *Système du coeur, ou conjectures sur la manière dont naissent les différentes affections de l'âme, principalement par rapport aux objects sensibles.* 1704. Paris: M. Brunet, 1708.

Garber, Marjorie. *Vested Interests: Cross-Dressing and Cultural Identity.* London: Routledge, 1992.

Gasté, Armand, ed. *La Querelle du "Cid," pièces et pamphlets publiés d'après les originaux.* 1898. Geneva: Slatkine Reprints, 1970.

Gedoyn, Nicolas. "De l'éducation des enfants." *Oeuvres diverses.* Paris: Buré l'aîné, 1745.

Gillot, Hubert. *La Querelle des Anciens et des Modernes en France.* Paris: Honoré Champion, 1914.

Glass, James. *Shattered Selves: Multiple Personalities in a Postmodern World.* Ithaca, N.Y.: Cornell University Press, 1993.

Gossman, Lionel. *Between History and Literature.* Cambridge: Harvard University Press, 1990.

Goubert, Pierre, and Daniel Roche. *Les Français et l'Ancien Régime*. 2 vols. Paris: Colin, 1984.

Goujet, Claude-Pierre. *Bibliothèque française, ou Histoire de la littérature française*. 18 vols. Paris: Mariette, 1740–56.

Graff, Gerald. *Professing Literature: An Institutional History*. Chicago: University of Chicago Press, 1987.

Gueret, Gabriel. *La Guerre des auteurs anciens et modernes*. Paris: Théodore Girard, 1671.

Guillory, John. *Cultural Capital: The Problem of Literary Canon Formation*. Chicago: University of Chicago Press, 1993.

———. "The Ideology of Canon Formation: T. S. Eliot and Cleanth Brooks." *Critical Inquiry* 10, no. 1 (September 1983): 173–98.

Guitton, G. *Le Père de La Chaise*. 2 vols. Paris: Beauchesne, 1959.

Habermas, Jürgen. *The Structural Transformation of the Public Sphere: An Inquiry into a Category of Bourgeois Society*. 1965. Trans. Thomas Burger. Cambridge: MIT Press, 1989.

Hallberg, Robert von. "Editor's Introduction." *Critical Inquiry* 10, no. 1 (September 1983): iii–vi.

Hardouin, Jean. *Apologie d'Homère, où l'on explique le véritable dessein de son Iliade*. Paris: Rigaud, 1716.

Hartman, Geoffrey. *Criticism in the Wilderness: The Study of Literature Today*. New Haven: Yale University Press, 1980.

Hazard, Paul. *La Crise de la conscience européenne, 1680–1715*. 1935. Paris: Fayard, 1961.

Hepp, Noémi. *Homère en France au XVIIe siècle*. Paris: Klinsieck, 1968.

Highet, Gilbert. *The Classical Tradition: Greek and Roman Influences on Western Literature*. New York: Oxford University Press, 1949.

Himmelfarb, Gertrude. *The De-Moralization of Society*. New York: Alfred Knopf, 1995.

———. *On Looking into the Abyss: Thoughts on Culture and Society*. New York: Alfred Knopf, 1994.

———. *The New History and the Old*. Cambridge: Harvard University Press, 1987.

Hirsch, E. D., Jr. *Cultural Literacy: What Every American Needs to Know*. 1987. New York: Vintage Books, 1988.

Hohendahl, Peter Uwe. *Building a National Literature: The Case of Germany, 1830–1870*. Trans. Renate Franciscono. Ithaca, N.Y.: Cornell University Press, 1989.

Houdar de La Motte, Antoine, trans. *L'Iliade avec un discours sur Homère*. Paris: Grégoire Dupuis, 1714.

———. *Réflexions sur la critique*. 3 vols. Paris: Du Puis, 1715.

Huet, Pierre-Daniel. Letter to Charles Perrault (10 October 1692). In *Dissertations sur diverses matières de religion et de philosophie*, ed. Tilladet (Voltaire), 1:477–513. The Hague: A. de Rogissart, 1720.

———. "Traité de l'origine des romans." In *Zayde*, by Marie-Madeleine Pioche de La Vergne, comtesse de Lafayette, 1–177. Paris: Claude Barbin, 1670.

Hunter, James Davidson. *Culture Wars: The Struggle to Define America*. New York: Basic Books, 1991.

Hutcheson, Francis. *An Essay on the Nature and the Conduct of the Passions and the Affections.* 1728. Ed. Paul McReynolds. Gainesville, Fla.: Scholars Facsimiles and Reprints, 1969.

Irailh, Simon-Augustin. *Querelles littéraires ou mémoires pour servir à l'histoire des révolutions dans la République des Lettres depuis Homère jusqu'à nos jours.* 3 vols. Paris: Durand, 1761.

James, Henry. *The Ambassadors.* 1903. London: Penguin Classics, 1973.

Jourdan, Adrien. *Histoire de France et l'origine de la maison royale.* Paris: Sébastien Marbre-Cramoisy, 1679.

Julia, Dominique. "La Naissance du corps professoral." *Actes de la Recherche en Sciences Sociales* 39 (September 1981): 71–86.

Jusdanis, Gregory. "Beyond National Culture?" *Boundary 2* 22, no. 1 (1995): 23–60.

Kernan, Alvin. *The Death of Literature.* New Haven: Yale University Press, 1990.

Kimball, Roger. "The Periphery vs. the Center: The MLA in Chicago." *New Criterion,* February 1991, 8–17.

La Bruyère, Jean de. *Les Caractères, ou les moeurs de ce siècle.* 1688. Ed. Robert Garapon. Paris: Garnier, 1962.

Lachèvre, Frédéric. *Le Procès du poète Théophile de Viau: Publication intégrale des pièces inédites.* Paris: H. Champion, 1909.

Lafayette, Marie-Madeleine Pioche de La Vergne, comtesse de. *La Princesse de Clèves.* 1678. Ed. Antoine Adam. Paris: Garnier-Flammarion, 1966.

Lambropoulos, Vassilis. *Literature as National Institution: Studies in the Politics of Modern Greek Criticism.* Princeton, N.J.: Princeton University Press, 1988.

———. *The Rise of Eurocentrism: Anatomy of Interpretation.* Princeton, N.J.: Princeton University Press, 1993.

Lamy, Guillaume. *Explication mécanique et physique des fonctions de l'âme sensitive, des sens, des passions, et du movement volontaire.* Paris: Lambert Roulland, 1678.

Laqueur, Thomas. *Making Sex: Body and Gender from the Greeks to Freud.* Cambridge: Harvard University Press, 1990.

Latour, Bruno. *We Have Never Been Modern.* 1991. Trans. Catherine Porter. Cambridge: Harvard University Press, 1993.

Laugaa, Maurice. *Lectures de Madame de Lafayette.* Paris: Armand Colin, 1971.

Le Bossu, Father René. *Traité du poème épique.* Paris: Michel Le Petit, 1675.

Le Brun, Jacques. "Politique et spiritualité: La dévotion au Sacré Coeur à l'époque moderne." *Concilium* 69 (1971): 25–36.

Le Gendre, Louis. *Les Moeurs et coutumes des Français dans les différents temps de la monarchie.* Paris: Collombat, 1712.

Le Grand d'Aussy, Pierre. *Histoire de la vie privée des Français depuis l'origine de la nation jusqu'à nos jours.* 3 vols. Paris: Ph.-D. Pierres, 1782.

Legras, Nicolas. *L'Académie royale de Richelieu.* N.p.: N.p., 1642.

Lever, Maurice. *La Fiction narrative en prose au XVIIème siècle.* Paris: Editions du centre national de la recherche scientifique, 1976.

Levine, Joseph. *The Battle of the Books: History and Literature in the Augustan Age.* Ithaca, N.Y.: Cornell University Press, 1991.

L'Héritier, Marie-Jeanne. "Les Enchantements de l'éloquence." In *Bigarures ingénieuses.* Paris: Guigard, 1696.

Lindenberger, Herbert. "On the Sacrality of Reading Lists: The Western Culture Debate at Stanford University." *Comparative Criticism* (fall 1989): 225–34.

[Longepierre, H.-B. de Requeleyne, baron de]. *Discours sur les anciens*. Paris: P. Ambouin, 1687.

Lower, Richard. *Traité du coeur, du mouvement et de la couleur du sang*. 1669. Paris: Estienne Michallet, 1679.

Malouin, Charles. *Traité des corps solides et des fluides ou examen du mouvement du sang, de celui du coeur, des artères et des autres vaisseaux du corps humain*. Paris: Jouenne, 1712.

Marivaux, Pierre Carlet de. *Les Aventures de ***, ou les effets surprenants de la sympathie*. 1713–14. In *Oeuvres de jeunesse*, ed. F. Deloffre. Paris: Gallimard, 1972.

Marshall, David. *The Surprising Effects of Sympathy: Marivaux, Diderot, Rousseau, and Mary Shelley*. Chicago: University of Chicago Press, 1988.

Martin, Henri-Jean, and Roger Chartier, eds. *Histoire de l'édition française*. Vol. 2. Paris: Promodis, 1984.

Masson, Jeffrey Moussaieff, and Susan McCarthy. *When Elephants Weep: The Emotional Lives of Animals*. New York: Delacorte Press, 1995.

McGrew, Roderick. "Humoralism." In *Encyclopedia of Medical History*, ed. Roderick McGrew with the collaboration of Margaret McGrew. New York: McGraw Hill, 1985.

McKeon, Michael. "Historicizing Patriarchy: The Emergence of Gender Difference in England, 1660–1760." *Eighteenth-Century Studies* 28, no. 3 (spring 1995): 295–322.

Meltzer, Françoise. *Hot Property: The Stakes and Claims of Literary Originality*. Chicago: University of Chicago Press, 1994.

Menand, Louis. "What Are Universities For? The Real Crisis on Campus Is One of Identity." *Harper's*, December 1991, 47–56.

Merk, Georges. "L'Etymologie de race: Rapports entre *generatio, ratio*, et *natio*." *Travaux de linguistique et de littérature de l'université de Strasbourg* 7, no. 1 (1969): 177–88.

Merlin, Hélène. *Public et littérature en France au XVIIe siècle*. Paris: Les Belles Lettres, 1994.

Mézeray, François Eudes de. *Abrégé chronologique, ou Extraict de l'histoire de France*. 3 vols. Paris: D. Thierry, 1668.

———. *Histoire de France depuis Faramond jusqu'à maintenant*. 6 vols. Paris: M. Guillemot, 1643–51.

Milo, Daniel S. *Trahir le temps (histoire)*. Paris: Les Belles Lettres, 1991.

Montesquieu, Charles-Louis de Secondat, baron de. *Pensées*. Ed. Louis Desgraves. Paris: Robert Laffont, 1991.

Montfaucon, Bernard de. *L'Antiquité expliquée et représentée en figures*. 5 vols. Paris: F. Delaulne, 1716.

Mouligneau, Genviève. *Madame de Lafayette, romancière?* Brussels: Université de Bruxelles, 1980.

Murat, Henriette de Castelnau, comtesse de. "Le Sauvage." In *Histoires sublimes et allégoriques*. Paris: Delaune, 1699.

Nelson, Robert J. "The Ancients and The Moderns." In *A New History of French*

Literature, ed. D. Hollier et al., 364–68. Cambridge: Harvard University Press, 1989.

Nussbaum, Martha. *The Therapy of Desire.* Princeton, N.J.: Princeton University Press, 1994.

Nutton, Vivian. "Humoralism." In *Companion Encyclopedia of the History of Medicine,* ed. W. F. Bynum and Roy Porter, 1:281–91. London: Routledge, 1993.

Ozouf, Mona. *Les Mots des femmes.* Paris: Fayard, 1995.

————. "L'Opinion publique." In *The French Revolution and the Creation of Modern Political Culture,* ed. K. Baker, 419–34. Oxford: Pergamon Press, 1992.

Paz, Octavio. *The Double Flame: Love and Eroticism.* 1993. New York: Harcourt Brace, 1995.

Perrault, Charles. *Apologie des femmes.* Paris: Veuve de Jean-Baptiste Coignard, 1694.

————. "La Belle au bois dormant." *Le Mercure galant,* February 1696, 75–117.

————. *Contes.* Ed. J.-P. Collinet. Paris: Folio-Gallimard, 1981.

————. *Les Hommes illustres qui ont paru en France pendant ce siècle.* 2 vols. Paris: Antoine Dezallier, 1696–1700.

————. *Mémoires.* Ed. Paul Bonnefon. Paris: Laurens, 1909.

————. *Parallèle des Anciens et des Modernes, en ce qui regarde les arts et les sciences.* 4 vols. Paris: Jean-Baptiste Coignard, 1688–97.

————. *Le Siècle de Louis le Grand.* Paris: Jean-Baptiste Coignard, 1687.

Pillorget, René. *La Tige et le Rameau: Familles anglaise et française XVIe–XVIIIe siècle.* Paris: Calmann-Lévy, 1979.

[Pons, Jean-François de]. *Lettre à Monsieur *** sur l'Iliade de M. de la Motte.* Paris: Laurent Seneuze, 1714.

Pratt, Mary Louise. "Humanities for the Future: Reflections on the Western Culture Debate at Stanford." *South Atlantic Quarterly* 89, no. 1 (winter 1990): 7–25.

Prévost, Antoine François, ed. Review of *La Vie de Marianne,* by Pierre Carlet de Marivaux. *Pour et contre* 9, no. 132, p. 273.

Querdun Le Gall, François. *Oratoire du coeur, ou méthode très facile pour faire oraison avec Jésus Christ dans le fond du coeur.* Paris: Laize-de-Bresche, 1670.

Racine, Jean. *Oeuvres complètes.* Ed. Pierre Clarac. Paris: Editions du Seuil, 1962.

Recueil des plus belles pièces des poètes français depuis Villon jusqu'à M. de Benserade. 5 vols. Paris: Barbin, 1692.

Reiss, Timothy. *The Meaning of Literature.* Ithaca, N.Y.: Cornell University Press, 1992.

Retz, Jean-François de Gondi, cardinal de. *Conjuration du comte de Fiesque.* 1665. In *Oeuvres.* 5 vols. Paris: Hachette, 1880.

Richelet, Pierre. *Dictionnaire.* 1680. Hildesheim and New York: Georg Olms Verlag, 1973.

————. *Les Plus belles lettres françaises sur toutes sortes de sujets, tirées des meilleurs auteurs, avec des notes.* The Hague: M. Uytserf and L. Van Dole, 1699.

Rifkin, Jeremy. *The End of Work: The Decline of the Global Labor Force and the Dawn of the Post-Market Era.* New York: Putnam's, 1995.

Rigault, Hippolyte. *Histoire de la querelle des anciens et des modernes.* Paris: Hachette, 1856.

Roche-Mazon, Jeanne. "Une Collaboration inattendue au XVIIe siècle: l'abbé de Choisy et Charles Perrault." *Mercure de France,* 1 February 1928, 513–64.

Rollin, Charles. *De la manière d'enseigner et d'étudier les belles-lettres, par rapport à l'esprit et au coeur.* 4 vols. Paris: Jacques Estienne, 1726–28.

Rosen, Stanley. *The Ancients and the Moderns: Rethinking Modernity.* New Haven: Yale University Press, 1989.

Rousseau, George S. "Nerves, Spirits, and Fibres: Towards Defining the Origins of Sensibility." In *Studies in the Eighteenth Century,* vol. 3, ed. R. F. Brissenden and J. C. Eade, 137–57. Toronto: University of Toronto Press, 1976.

Rousseau, Jean-Jacques. *Julie, ou La Nouvelle Héloïse.* 1761. Ed. Bernard Gagnebin. Paris: Gallimard, 1969.

Said, Edward. *Representations of the Intellectual.* New York: Pantheon Books, 1994.

Saint-Evremond, Charles de. "Dissertation sur la tragédie de Racine intitulée: *Alexandre le Grand.*" In *Oeuvres mêlées,* ed. Claude Giraud, 2:295–310. Paris: Techener, 1856.

Sala-Molins, Louis. *Le Code Noir, ou le calvaire de Canaan.* Paris: Presses Universitaires de France, 1987.

Scarry, Elaine. "Counting at Dusk (Why Poetry Matters When the Century Ends)." In *Fins de Siècle: English Poetry in 1590, 1690, 1790, 1890, 1990,* ed. Elaine Scarry, ix–xiii. Baltimore: Johns Hopkins University Press, 1995.

Schmitt, Carl. *Political Romanticism.* Trans. Guy Oakes. 1925. Cambridge: MIT Press, 1986.

Schwartz, Hillel. *Century's End: A Cultural History of the Fin de Siècle from the 990s through the 1990s.* New York: Doubleday, 1990.

Scudéry, Madeleine de. *Artamène, ou le grand Cyrus.* 10 vols. Paris: Augustin Courbé, 1649–53.

———. *Clélie, histoire romaine.* 10 vols. Paris: Augustin Courbé, 1654–60.

Sévigné, Marie de Rabutin-Chantal, Marquise de. *Correspondance.* Ed. Roger Duchêne. 3 vols. Paris: Gallimard, 1972.

Slouka, Mark. *War of the Worlds: Cyberspace and the High-Tech Assault on Reality.* New York: Basic Books, 1995.

Sorel, Charles. *De la perfection de l'homme, où les vrais biens sont considérés, et spécialement ceux de l'âme, avec les méthodes des sciences.* Paris: R. de Nain, 1655.

———. *La perfection de l'âme . . . en suite l'ordre et l'origine des sciences et arts . . . IVe volume et conclusion de la Science universelle.* Paris: Quinet, 1664.

Spink, John. " 'Sentiment,' 'sensible,' 'sensibilité': Les mots, les idées, d'après les 'moralistes' français et britanniques du début du dix-huitième siècle." *Zagadnienia Rodzajow Literackich* 20, no. 1 (1977): 33–47.

Staël, Germaine Necker, baronne de. *De l'Allemagne.* 1810. Ed. Comtesse Jean de Pange. Paris: Hachette, 1958–60.

———. *De la littérature considérée dans ses rapports avec les institutions sociales.* 1800. Ed. Gerard Gengembre and Jacques Goldzink. Paris: Garnier-Flammarion, 1991.

Stimpson, Catharine. *Firing Line* debate, "Resolved: Political Correctness Is a Menace and a Bore." 2 December 1993. Transcript published in *Pennsylvania Gazette,* 18 February 1994, 18–37.

Stoll, Clifford. *Silicon Snake Oil: Second Thoughts on the Information Highway.* New York: Doubleday, 1995.

Terrasson, Jean. *Addition à la dissertation critique sur l'Iliade.* Paris: Fournier, 1716.

———. *Dissertation critique sur l'Iliade.* Paris: Fournier, 1715.

Trahard, Pierre. *Les Maîtres de la sensibilité française au XVIIIe siècle (1715–1789).* 2 vols. Paris: Boivin, 1931.

[Valincour, Jean-Baptiste-Henri du Trousset de]. *Lettres à Madame la marquise *** sur le sujet de "La Princesse de Clèves."* 1678. Tours: Université de Tours, 1972.

Varillas, Antoine. *Les Anecdotes de Florence, ou histoire secrète de la maison de Médicis.* The Hague: A. Leers, 1685.

Velly, Paul-François. *Histoire de France depuis l'établissement de la monarchie jusqu'au règne de Louis XIV.* Paris: Desaint and Saillant, 1755.

Viala, Alain. *La Naissance de l'écrivain.* Paris: Editions de Minuit, 1985.

Viau, Théophile de. "Fragments d'une histoire comique." 1623. In *Oeuvres,* ed. Guido Saba. Paris: Nizet, 1978.

Vigarello, Georges. *Le Sain et le malsain: Santé et mieux-être depuis le Moyen Age.* Paris: Editions du Seuil, 1993.

Villedieu. Desjardins, Marie-Catherine known as Madame de Villedieu. *Mémoires de la vie de Henriette-Sylvie de Molière.* Ed. Micheline Cuénin. Tours: Publications de l'Université François Rabelais, 1977.

Vincent, Monique. *Donneau de Visé et "Le Mercure galant."* Paris: Aux Amateurs du livre, 1987.

———. *"Le Mercure galant* et son public féminin." *Romanistische Zeitshrift für literaturgeschichte* 3 (1979): 76–85.

Vittu, Jean-Pierre. " 'Le Peuple est fort curieux de nouvelles': L'information périodique dans la France des années 1690." *Studies on Voltaire and the Eighteenth Century* 320 (1994): 105–44.

Voltaire (François Marie Arouet). *L'Affaire Calas.* Ed. Jacques Van den Heuvel. Paris: Editions Gallimard, 1975.

———. *Le Siècle de Louis XIV.* 1756. In *Oeuvres historiques,* ed. René Pomeau. Paris: Gallimard, 1957.

Weinstein, Arnold. *Fictions of the Self, 1550–1800.* Princeton, N.J.: Princeton University Press, 1981.

Willis, Thomas. *Opera medica.* 2 vols. Lyons: J. A. Huguetan, 1676.

INDEX

Abbadie, Jacques, 181n. 73
Académie Française, 8, 35, 131, 184n.
90, 188n. 13; 1694 dictionary, xvi,
33, 87, 128–30, 153n. 12, 157n. 36,
169n. 6, 170n. 10, 173–4n. 33,
187n. 6; setting of Quarrel between
the Ancients and Moderns, 42, 47,
51, 69, 130
Adam, Antoine, 51, 162n. 25, 163n.
27, 167n. 47
Adams, Henry, 153n. 8
Aesthetics. *See* Philosophy, aesthetic
Affaire: Calas, 7, 153n. 9; Dreyfus, 7;
literary, 154n. 14, 164n. 30; use of
the term, 6–9, 44
Affection, 80, 86, 169–70n. 9
Alacoque, Marie-Madeleine, 108–9,
179nn. 65–7
Allardyce, Gilbert, 190nn. 28 and 30
Ancients: and belief in unified elite,
49–50; and French educational practice, 134–6; and history, 116–8; and
literary history, 21, 168n. 50; and
tradition, 44, 48–9; and the university, 107, 174–5n. 41; contemporary
historians, attack on, 116–8, 182n.
80; *Le Mercure galant,* attack on,
58; novel, attack on, 52–7, 105,
107, 116, 182–3n. 80, 183n. 81;
poème héroïque, attack on, 52–4;
theater, attack on, 55–6; conception
of the critic, 105–6; defined against
Moderns, 18; definition of, 5, 15,
16; origin of, 161n. 14; portrayal of
Moderns as threat to pedagogical

practice, 134–5, 137–8, 145; positions taken by in Quarrel, 44–5,
47–9, 51, 97, 176n. 51, 182n. 79.
See also Positivism
Architecture: importance of for the
Moderns, 131–2; official projects in,
132–3, 188n. 10
Argenson, René-Louis de Voyer,
Marquis d', 123, 186n. 100
Ariès, Philippe, 14, 92, 155n. 21,
169n. 5, 183n. 84
Aristocrats: and "the civilizing pro-
cess," 127; and the Enlightenment,
160n. 7; and merit, 74–5; and politeness, 127; in the Modern ranks,
131; late seventeenth century, xvi,
38, 164n. 31; role in development of
public, 64, 66
Arnauld, Antoine, 69, 94
Astronomy, importance for Moderns
of, 110
Attraction. *See* Sympathy
Aubignac, Abbé François de, 95, 97,
100, 102, 174n. 37, 176n. 50
Auerbach, Erich, xv, 32, 36, 39, 151n.
2, 160n. 5, 187n. 4
Aulnoy, Marie Catherine de Barneville,
Comtesse d', 21, 158n. 37
Author: death of, 93–4, 97, 101–3,
176n. 52, 177n. 53; definitions of,
106; importance of the concept
of, 69, 102–3, 111–2; invention of
the modern conception of, 103. *See
also* Homer, existence of; Name, author's

205

210 INDEX